INTERMEDIATE MANDARIN CHINESE

SPEAKING & LISTENING

PRACTICE BOOK

CORNELIUS C. KUBLER & YANG WANG

TUTTLE Publishing

Tokyo | Rutland, Vermont | Singapore

Published by Tuttle Publishing, an imprint of Periplus Editions (HK) Ltd.

www.tuttlepublishing.com

Copyright © 2018 Cornelius C. Kubler and Yang Wang
Front cover photo © FatCamera/istockphoto.com

ISBN 978-0-8048-5050-6
(Previously published under ISBN 978-0-8048-4019-4)

Distributed by

North America, Latin America & Europe	**Japan**	**Asia Pacific**
Tuttle Publishing	Tuttle Publishing	Berkeley Books Pte. Ltd.
364 Innovation Drive	Yaekari Building, 3rd Floor	61 Tai Seng Avenue #02-12
North Clarendon,	5-4-12 Osaki	Singapore 534167
VT 05759-9436 U.S.A.	Shinagawa-ku	Tel: (65) 6280-1330
Tel: 1 (802) 773-8930	Tokyo 141 0032	Fax: (65) 6280-6290
Fax: 1 (802) 773-6993	Tel: (81) 3 5437-0171	inquiries@periplus.com.sg
info@tuttlepublishing.com	Fax: (81) 3 5437-0755	www.periplus.com
www.tuttlepublishing.com	sales@tuttle.co.jp	
	www.tuttle.co.jp	

21 20 19 18   10 9 8 7 6 5 4 3 2 1

Printed in China   1804CM

A Note to the Learner

When it comes to learning Chinese, practice is essential, of course. This workbook offers you many options for practicing and polishing your language skills, and was designed to be used in conjunction with the book *Intermediate Mandarin Chinese Speaking & Listening*. However, it may be used to hone speaking skills no matter which book or course you're using to learn Chinese.

There are no Chinese characters to be found here because you don't need characters to learn to speak Chinese. In fact, learning the characters for everything you learn to say is an inefficient way to learn Chinese, one that significantly slows down your progress.

To help you learn to speak and understand Chinese as efficiently as possible, this workbook gives you the Chinese language portions not via characters, but instead through audio featuring native speakers (on the accompanying disc). And in the pages of this book, the Chinese is represented in Hanyu Pinyin, the official Chinese romanization system.

- If you wish to learn Chinese reading and writing, which is certainly to be recommended for most learners, you should—together with or after the spoken course—use the companion course **Intermediate Mandarin Chinese Reading & Writing**. It corresponds with *Intermediate Mandarin Chinese Speaking & Listening* and systematically introduces the highest-frequency characters (simplified and traditional) and words in context in sentences and reading passages as well as in various types of realia, to help you master reading and writing.

- For instructors and those learners with prior knowledge of Chinese characters, an *Intermediate Mandarin Chinese Speaking & Listening:* **Character Transcription** is also available free of charge from the Tuttle Publishing website (go to the *Intermediate Mandarin Chinese Speaking & Listening Practice Book* page at **www.tuttlepublishing.com** to download). It contains transcriptions into simplified and traditional characters of *Intermediate Mandarin Chinese Speaking & Listening*. Please note that the character transcription is not intended, and should not be used, as the primary vehicle for students to learn reading and writing.

- The *Intermediate Mandarin Chinese Speaking & Listening* **Instructor's Guide** contains detailed suggestions for using these materials as well as communicative exercises for use by instructors in class or by tutors during practice sessions. It is available free of charge on request from Tuttle Publishing.

附注

《进阶中文：听与说》练习册为专门练习口语的教材，因此全书内只列有汉语拼音和英文注释，不使用汉字。学习者宜与配套的光盘以及《进阶中文：听与说》一起使用。本练习册亦可作为任何中级中文课程之补充教材，以提高学习者的口语能力。此套中文教材另有《进阶中文：读与写》及《进阶中文：读与写》练习册，专供读写课使用。《进阶中文：听与说》另配有汉字版，将《进阶中文：听与说》中所有对话和补充生词的拼音版转为汉字，并分简繁体，供教师和已有汉字基础的学习者参考、使用。此套教材亦包括一张光盘的《进阶中文：教师手册》，指导教师如何使用此教材，且提供大量课堂练习，极为实用。

附注

《進階中文：聽與說》練習冊為專門練習口語的教材，因此全書內只列有漢語拼音和英文注釋，不使用漢字。學習者宜與配套的光盤以及《進階中文：聽與說》一起使用。本練習冊亦可作為任何中級中文課程之補充教材，以提高學習者的口語能力。此套中文教材另有《進階中文：讀與寫》及《進階中文：讀與寫》練習冊，專供讀寫課使用。《進階中文：聽與說》另配有漢字版，將《進階中文：聽與說》中所有對話和補充生詞的拼音版轉為漢字，並分簡繁體，供教師和已有漢字基礎的學習者參考、使用。此套教材亦包括一張光盤的《進階中文：教師手冊》，指導教師如何使用此教材，且提供大量課堂練習，極為實用。

Do you prefer single-sided pages for ease in turning in completed exercises for review & correction?

See the Disc:

Sections **5, 6,** and **7** may be printed out in single-sided format.

Contents

Every section includes practice materials for these 14 topics:

Unit 11: Getting Around Taipei

Unit 12: Shopping (I)

Unit 13: Shopping (II)

Unit 14: Eating and Drinking (I)

Unit 15: Eating and Drinking (II)

Unit 16: Eating and Drinking (III)

Unit 17: On the Telephone

Unit 18: Visiting People (I)

Unit 19: Visiting People (II)

Unit 20: Leisure Time Activities (I)

Unit 21: Leisure Time Activities (II)

Unit 22: Emergencies

Unit 23: Hong Kong and Macao

Unit 24: Singapore and Malaysia

Additional Practice Materials in Printable PDF Format: See the Disc!

How to Use These Materials

Intermediate Mandarin Chinese Speaking & Listening Practice Essentials contains extensive drills and exercises for each unit of the textbook *Intermediate Mandarin Chinese Speaking & Listening*. The purpose of this workbook is to offer learners various kinds of practice activities for both in- and out-of-class use, so as to enable learners to reinforce and "activize" their learning of the new vocabulary and grammar introduced in the textbook.

New Vocabulary and Grammar Summaries

The first section of the *Practice Book* consists of a one-page list of new vocabulary and grammar in each *Intermediate Mandarin Chinese Speaking & Listening* lesson, from Unit 11, Part 1 through Unit 24, Part 4.

The lists are divided into a section on "Vocabulary" and a section on "Grammar." In the vocabulary section, each new vocabulary item introduced in the corresponding lesson of the textbook is listed in alphabetical order of the Pinyin with English translation and indication of word class (any Additional Vocabulary is not included). In the grammar section, each new grammar pattern introduced in that part of the textbook is listed, also in alphabetical order, in most cases with one or more examples in Pinyin and English translation.

- We believe these lists of new vocabulary and grammar will be useful for all learners for review purposes. However, learners should ideally not learn new vocabulary or grammar from these lists; instead, they should always try to learn new vocabulary and grammar in the context of the Basic Conversations and Build Ups in the textbook.

- Those learners who are using the *Practice Book* to supplement other textbooks and who do not have access to the textbook for *Intermediate Mandarin Chinese Speaking & Listening*, will want to pay special attention to these lists, since the various drills and exercises in this book assume thorough familiarity with all this material.

The next two sections consist of **drills**. Don't underestimate the value of drills as enabling mechanisms that help you, the learner, to attain the ultimate goal of communicative competency. The drills are useful for improving your pronunciation, developing your fluency, and increasing your confidence in speaking Chinese. Although it's true that some of the drills in this workbook are of necessity fairly mechanical, others are more realistic and communicative, in some cases even incorporating a certain amount of cultural material.

- The drills are best done out of class in self-study mode, either in a language learning laboratory or, working with a computer or your audio player, in some other place of your choosing. If you're learning Chinese in a classroom setting, doing the drills out of class also frees up valuable time with the instructor so that you can focus on those kinds of interactive learning activities for which the instructor's guidance and active participation is essential.

- You should work with the recordings on the accompanying disc as actively as possible, speaking loudly and always thinking of the meaning of what you're hearing and saying.

- If you're learning Chinese on your own, the drills will be especially important for you and, working with the accompanying audio disc, you should try to go through each one several times. In addition, it will be to your benefit to seek out a native-speaking tutor or mentor who can work with you one or two hours a week for additional practice and to answer questions.

Substitution Drills

In the substitution drills, a model sentence is first said for you to repeat. Next, various vocabulary and grammar prompts are given that you're to substitute into the model sentence, creating a related but new sentence.

In the audio portion, after each prompt a pause is provided for you to say the new sentence with that substitution. A native speaker then provides a confirmation of the correct sentence, followed by a pause during which you should repeat the correct sentence. An English translation of each sentence is included in the workbook.

- It's most effective to do each drill at least twice: the first time with the workbook open and the second time with the workbook closed.

Transformation and Response Drills

As the name implies, these drills involve transforming one phrase or sentence into another, or responding to a question or other cue. There are also a smaller number of politeness drills, translation drills, and drills involving the conversion of Bejing-style speech to non-Beijing-style speech and vice versa.

In the audio portion, instructions for each drill are given in English before the drill. As with the substitution drills, each of the transformation and response drills is followed by a pause for your response, which is then in turn followed by confirmation of the correct response by a native speaker. A pause then allows you time to repeat the correct sentence. An English translation of each sentence or phrase is included in the workbook.

- Again, it's best to do each drill at least twice—once with the workbook open and once with the workbook closed.

- Though the transformation and response drills are in principle meant to be done by students out of class, some instructors may choose to do some of the drills in class, or some of the drills could be adapted for in-class exercises.

Role Play Exercises

The role play exercises involve conversations between two or more speakers that make use of the new vocabulary, grammar, functions, and situations introduced in the lesson.

There are one to eight role plays for each of the four parts of each unit. In many cases, the role plays are based roughly on the textbook's Basic Conversation but with some of the details changed. In other cases, the role plays focus on the the material in the Supplementary Vocabulary. Most of the role plays involve two roles (indicated by A and B), with a few involving three or four roles (A, B, C, D).

Here in the workbook, the role plays are rendered in English, but they're to be performed in Chinese. The role plays are designed to be done as one of the last activities of each lesson.

- While performing the role plays, you may glance at the English but should try to look up as much as possible when saying the Chinese.

- The role plays should be performed at a fairly rapid clip, so you may wish to practice them in advance (making a few notes is fine, but you shouldn't write out complete translations). The goal isn't laboriously translating word-for-word from English to Chinese but, rather, producing natural Chinese equivalents based on the English cues. The emphasis should be on the *performance* of the role plays. If you find that you're hesitant and choppy in performing a role play, this most likely means you haven't yet attained sufficient mastery of the material.

- If you're learning Chinese in a class, after individual students have performed a role play, the instructor will probably lead the whole class in repeating the lines of the role play one more time together.

- If you're learning Chinese on your own, then the role plays will be especially helpful in giving you practice in using the vocabulary and grammar of the lesson in new combinations. By playing all the roles in a role play exercise, you as an independent learner stand to gain extra benefits for your language skills, enhancing your fluency and becoming flexible in swiftly switching perspectives. Of course, if you're learning with a friend or have access to a native-speaking tutor, then each of you could take one role.

Listening Comprehension Exercises

The listening comprehension exercises involve conversations or monologues which are available on the accompanying disc only, since it is *listening* that we want to practice, not reading.* There are two listening passages for each lesson. To provide additional practice in listening comprehension, the passages reuse, in new contexts, the new vocabulary (including the Supplementary Vocabulary) and grammar of the current and previous lessons.

Each listening passage is followed by two to five multiple choice questions on the content of the passage. Based on the recorded passage, you should circle on your answer sheet the best response—(A), (B), or (C)—to each of the questions that follows.

- While you work on the listening comprehension exercises, feel free to listen to each passage as many times as needed.

- In a classroom setting, the listening comprehension exercises are best done as homework which students hand in the next day for the instructor to correct, grade, and return. After they have been corrected and returned to students, they can be inserted by the student into a binder for future reference.

- Independent learners will also find the listening comprehension exercises helpful for practice in comprehending new combinations of words and grammar patterns; if they have questions, they can ask a tutor or native-Chinese-speaking friend. It may also be useful to obtain the *Instructor's Guide*, since along with the scripts for the listening comprehension exercises it also includes the correct answers.

Translation Exercises

The purpose of the translation exercises is to provide you with additional practice in using the grammar patterns and important vocabulary of the unit and to serve as a check of mastery over the material. Completing the translation exercises will be helpful in reviewing for tests.

It's recommended that the instructor correct and return the translation exercises to students before the test on the corresponding unit, so that any remaining problems can be identified and addressed in a timely manner. Students should carefully study the instructor's corrections, making sure they understand why any errors occurred, and file the corrected exercises for later reference.

The translation exercises come in two different sets. The first set consists of five sentences *for each of the four Parts* or lessons of each Unit in the textbook, while the second set consists of ten sentences *for each complete Unit* of the textbook. Instructors can decide whether the students in their classes should complete both sets or only one of the two sets. Independent learners would profit from doing both sets of translation exercises and can read out their translations to a tutor or native-speaking friend for correction and comments.

- The sentences should be translated into Pinyin romanization with correct tone marks in the blank space that has been left under each sentence.

- The English in the translation exercises is in some places purposely somewhat stilted, so as to guide the student toward the correct Chinese translation.

---

* Complete scripts of the listening comprehension exercises in Chinese characters are available in the *Instructor's Guide*.

- In certain cases, additional instructions have been added in parentheses within or after the English sentence, for example, to be polite or to use or not use certain words or patterns.

- If you've forgotten the Chinese equivalent for an English word or grammar pattern, you can consult the English-Chinese Glossary, Chinese-English Glossary, or Index of Grammatical and Cultural Topics in the back of the *Intermediate Mandarin Chinese Speaking & Listening* textbook.

Abbreviations

A	Adverb	**P**	Particle
AT	Attributive	**PH**	Phrase
AV	Auxiliary Verb	**PR**	Pronoun
BF	Bound Form	**PT**	Pattern
CJ	Conjunction	**PV**	Postverb
CV	Coverb	**PW**	Place Word
EV	Equative Verb	**QW**	Question Word
EX	Expression	**RC**	Resultative Compound
I	Interjection	**RE**	Resultative Ending
IE	Idiomatic Expression	**SN**	Surname
L	Localizer	**SP**	Specifier
M	Measure	**SV**	Stative Verb
MA	Moveable Adverb	**TW**	Time Word
N	Noun	**V**	Verb
NU	Number	**VO**	Verb-Object Compound

---

* For explanations of the word classes, see the section "Word Classes of Spoken Chinese" in *Basic Mandarin Chinese Speaking & Listening*.

1. New Vocabulary and Grammar Summaries

Unit 11, Part 1: New Vocabulary and Grammar

Vocabulary

bú yàojǐn	be unimportant; "never mind" [IE]
Chóngqìng	Chongqing (city in Sichuan) [PW]
Chóngqìng Nán Lù	Chongqing South Road [PW]
dàlù	mainland [PW]
fàngxīn	be at ease, relax [VO]
Guóyǔ	Mandarin (language) [N]
jìchéngchē	taxi [N]
jiějué	solve [V]
la	(combined form of **le** and **a**) [P]
le	(indicates action continuing up to the present) [P]
màn	be slow [SV]
méi wèntí	"no problem" [IE]
ó	(indicates interest or excitement) [P]
-sǐ	to the point of death [RE]
Táiwān Yínháng	Bank of Taiwan [PW]
wèntí	question; problem [N]
xià	frighten [V]
xiàsǐ	frighten to death [RC]
yàojǐn	be important [SV]
yínháng	bank [PW]
zuò	sit in/on; take; by (car, boat, train, airplane) [CV]

Grammar

IMPERATIVES CONSISTING OF VERB + STATIVE VERB + **YÌDIǍN(R)**: **kāi màn yidian** "drive more slowly"

-LE...LE TO INDICATE TIME CONTINUING UP THROUGH PRESENT WITH TIME EXPRESSION AFTER VERB: **Tā gōngzuòle sān'ge yuè le.** "She's been working for three months."

Unit 11, Part 2: New Vocabulary and Grammar

Vocabulary

bù hǎo yìsi	be embarrassing, be embarrassed [PH]
chúzhípiào	stored-value ticket [N]
dìtiě	subway [N]
duìmiàn	across [PW]
gōngchē	public bus [N]
hǎo	very [A]
huò	or [CJ]
huòshi	or [CJ]
jiàn	see [V]
jiéyùn	mass rapid transit, MRT [N]
màiwán	finish selling, be sold out [RC]
mèng	dream [N]
Mùzhà	Muzha (suburb of Taipei) [PW]
qíguài	be strange [SV]
shèngxia	be left over [RC]
shùnbiàn	conveniently, in passing [A]
Tǒngyī	7-Eleven® (name of store) [PW]
wán	finish [V]
-wán	finish [RE]
xiǎode	know [V]
yàoburán	otherwise, or [MA]
zuòmèng	have a dream [VO]

Grammar

NEGATIVE TIME SPENT WITH TIME EXPRESSION BEFORE VERB: **Tā sān'ge yuè méi gōngzuòle.** "She hasn't been working for three months."

NUMBER OF TIMES WITHIN A PERIOD OF TIME: **Duō jiǔ yìbān?** "One (bus) every how often?", **Sānfēn zhōng yìbān.** "One (bus) every three minutes."

Unit 11, Part 3: New Vocabulary and Grammar

Vocabulary

cuòguo	miss [RC]
diàn	shop, store [N]
dòng	(for buildings) [M]
fángzi	house [N]
gàosu	tell [V]
gēn...jiǎng	tell (someone something) [PT]
gēn...shuō	tell (someone something) [PT]
gōngchǐ	meter [M]
gōngyòng	public [AT]
gōngyòng cèsuǒ	public toilet [PH]
gōngyòng diànhuà	public telephone [PH]
-guò	(indicates motion past or by) [RE]
jiājù	furniture [N]
jiājù diàn	furniture store [PH]
kàndào	see [RC]
-lái	(indicates motion toward speaker) [RE]
-lái...-qù	VERB all over the place [PT]
miào	temple, shrine [N]
shāowēi	somewhat, slightly [A]
shǒu	hand [N]
xiàngzi	lane [N]
yìhuǐr jiàn	"see you in a little while" [IE]
yóujú	post office [PW]
yòushǒu	right hand [PW]
yòushǒubiān	right-hand side [PW]
Zhōu	Zhou [SN]
zhuǎnjìnlái	turn in [RC]
zhuàn	turn, go around [V]
zhùyì	pay attention to [V/VO]
zuǒshǒu	left hand [PW]
zuǒshǒubiān	left-hand side [PW]

Grammar

GĒN...SHUŌ and **GĒN...JIǍNG**: **Qǐng nǐ gēn tā shuō.** "Please tell him.", **Qǐng nǐ gēn tā jiǎng wǒmen yǐjīng dàole.** "Please tell her that we've already arrived."

VERB-LÁI VERB-QÙ: **zǒulái zǒuqù** "walk back and forth"

ZĚMME (VERB) YĚ NEGATIVE VERB: **Tā zěmme (zhǎo) yě zhǎobudào.** "No matter how hard she searched she couldn't find it."

. . . .

Unit 11, Part 4: New Vocabulary and Grammar

Vocabulary

biānhào	serial number [N]
cóng...qǐ	starting from..., beginning from... [PT]
dà-pái-cháng-lóng	form a long line [EX]
èi	"yeah" [I]
gōngshēng	liter [M]
hǎole	"all right", "O.K." [IE]
jiāmǎn	fill up [RC]
jiàqián	price [N]
jiāyóu	add gasoline, buy gas [VO]
jiāyóuzhàn	gasoline station [PW]
kàn	think, consider [V]
mǎn	be full [SV]
-mǎn	full [RE]
mótuōchē	motorcycle [N]
qí	ride, straddle (bicycle, motorcycle, horse) [V]
qìyóu	gasoline [N]
tè	especially [A]
tèbié	especially [A]
tiáozhěng	adjust [V]
tíngchē	park a car, park [VO]
tíngchēchǎng	parking lot [PW]
tǒngyī	unite, unify [V]
yóu	oil [N]
yóujià	price of gasoline [N]
yuán	dollar (monetary unit) [M]
zhǎng	rise, go up [V]

Grammar

CÓNG...QǏ: cóng míngtiān qǐ "starting from tomorrow"

YÒU YÀO...LE: Yóujià yòu yào zhǎngle. "The price of gas is going to rise again."

Unit 12, Part 1: New Vocabulary and Grammar

Vocabulary

bīng	ice [N]
bīnggùn(r)	ice pop [N]
dú	read aloud; study [V]
dúshū	study [VO]
gēn(r)	(for long, thin things) [M]
háishi	or [CJ]
-hǎo	so that something is good [RE]
ná	hold, take [N]
náhǎo	hold well, hold firmly
nǎiyóu	cream [N]
niànshū	study [VO]
xì	department [N]
xiǎodòu	red bean [N]
yàng(r)	kind, variety [M]
zhuānyè	major, specialization [N]
zhǔxiū	major [N]
zhǔxiū	major in [V]

Grammar

A HÁISHI B IN QUESTIONS: **Nǐ yào qù Běijīng háishi Táiběi?** "Do you want to go to Beijing or to Taipei?"

A HUÒSHI B IN STATEMENTS: **Wǒ yào qù Běijīng huòshi Tiānjīn.** "I want to go to Beijing or Tianjin."

AMOUNT OF MONEY PER ITEM: **wǔmáo qián yìgēnr** "fifty cents a piece (for ice pops)"

Unit 12, Part 2: New Vocabulary and Grammar

Vocabulary

bàotíng	newspaper kiosk [PW]
bàozhǐ	newspaper [N]
běn(r)	(for books, dictionaries) [M]
běnzi	notebook [N]
bǐ	writing instrument [N]
dìtú	map [N]
fèn(r)	(for newspapers, magazines) [M]
gébì	next door [PW]
Hàn-Yīng	Chinese-English [AT]
qiānbǐ	pencil [N]
shì	city, municipality [N]
shì	try [V]
shū	book [N]
shūdiàn	book store [PW]
xiē	some [M]
yuánzhūbǐ	ball-point pen [N]
zázhì	magazine [N]
zhèixiē	these [SP+M]
zhī	(for pens, pencils) [M]
zhǐ	paper [N]
zhǒng	kind [M]
zìdiǎn	dictionary [V]

Grammar

MEASURES: **yìzhǒng yuánzhūbǐ** "a kind of ball-point pen", **zhèizhī qiānbǐ** "this pencil", **nèiběn shū** "that book", **wǔfèn bàozhǐ** "five newspapers", **něizhāng dìtú** "which map?", etc.

Unit 12, Part 3: New Vocabulary and Grammar

Vocabulary

báicài	cabbage [N]
bǎozhèng	guarantee [V]
cái	not until, just [A]
cài	vegetable [N]
càichǎng	market [N]
chūkǒu	export [N]
chūkǒu	export [V]
cuì	be crisp [SV]
duō xiè	"many thanks" [IE]
fānqié	tomato [N]
jīn	catty (500 grams) [M]
jìnkǒu	import [N]
jìnkǒu	import [V]
Lí Shān	"Pear Mountain", Li Shan [PW]
lí(r)	pear [N]
piàoliang	be pretty, look nice [SV]
qíncài	celery [N]
qīngcài	green vegetable [N]
shālā	salad [N]
shālācài	lettuce [N]
shūcài	vegetable [N]
xīnxiān	be fresh [SV]
zěmme zhèmme...	how come so... [PT]

Grammar

CÁI: Zhè shi jīntiān cái dàode. "This arrived only today (and not before then)."

ZĚMME ZHÈMME...: Fānqié zěmme zhèmme guì a? "How come tomatoes are so expensive?"

Unit 12, Part 4: New Vocabulary and Grammar

Vocabulary

bāo	wrap [V]
bāoqilai	wrap up [RC]
diǎn	count, check [V]
-jiàn	see, perceive [RE]
júzi	orange [N]
kànjian	see [RC]
lái	bring, give [V]
píngguǒ	apple [N]
pútao	grape [N]
-qǐlái	(general resultative ending) [RE]
qióng	be poor [SV]
shuǐguǒ	fruit [N]
táozi	peach [N]
tiāo	pick out, select [V]
tīngdào	hear [RC]
tīngjian	hear [RC]
xiāngjiāo	banana [N]
Yālí(r)	Ya pear [N]
yāo	weigh out [V]
yǒuqián	be rich [SV]
zǒnggòng	in all [A]

Grammar

BǏ FOLLOWED BY STATIVE VERB + **-DE DUŌ**: **Zhèizhǒng běnzi bǐ nèizhǒng běnzi piányide duō.** "This kind of notebook is much cheaper than that kind of notebook."

Unit 13, Part 1: New Vocabulary and Grammar

Vocabulary

chàbuduō	be about the same [PH]
chēng	weigh, weigh out [V]
chīsù	eat vegetarian food [VO]
féi	be fatty (of food) [SV]
fùjìn	in the vicinity, nearby [PW]
hútòng(r)	alley [N]
jī	chicken [N]
-jíle	extremely [PT]
jīròu	chicken meat [N]
miànbāo	bread [N]
miànbāo diàn	bakery [PH]
niú	cow, ox [N]
niúròu	beef [N]
qiē	cut, slice [V]
ròu	meat [N]
shípǐn	food product; groceries [N]
shípǐn diàn	grocery store [PH]
xiā	shrimp [N]
yāròu	duck meat [N]
yāzi	duck [N]
yáng	sheep [N]
yángròu	mutton [N]
yìdiǎn(r) yě bù...	not at all, not the least bit [PT]
zhū	pig [N]
zhūròu	pork [N]

Grammar

-JÍLE: **Miànbāo diàn jìnjíle.** "The bakery is extremely close."

YÌDIǍN(R) YĚ BÙ...: **Wǒ yìdiǎn(r) yě bú lèi.** "I'm not at all tired."

Unit 13, Part 2: New Vocabulary and Grammar

Vocabulary

A gēn B bǐqǐlái	comparing A and B [PT]
bíqilai	compare [RC]
chāoshì	supermarket [N]
chūkǒu(r)	exit [PW]
guìtái	counter [N]
hàn	with [CV]
huì...-de	be likely to, would, will [PT]
jiéshěng	be frugal [SV]
jiéshěng	save [V]
kāfēi	coffee [N]
mànmān lái	"take one's time" [IE]
pǔbiàn	be widespread, common [SV]
rùkǒu(r)	entrance [PW]
...shemmede	...and so on [PT]
tǔsī	white bread [N]
wèile...	in order to..., for... [PT]
xiàng	resemble, be like [V]
zhǔyì	idea, plan [N]

Grammar

A GĒN B BǏQǏLÁI: **Táiwānde chāoshì gēn Měiguode bǐqǐlái zěmmeyàng?** "How are Taiwan's supermarkets compared to America's?"

HUÌ...-DE: **Táiwānde chāoshì huì yìnián bǐ yìnián pǔbiànde.** "Taiwan's supermarkets will become more widespread each year."

...SHEMMEDE: **kāfēi, tǔsī shemmede** "coffee, white bread, and so on"

WÈILE TO EXPRESS PURPOSE: **Wèile jiéshěng shíjiān, nǐ mǎi nǐde, wǒ mǎi wǒde.** "In order to save time, you buy your things, and I'll buy my things."

YĪ + MEASURE + BǏ + YĪ + MEASURE: **yìnián bǐ yìnián guì** "more expensive year by year"

Unit 13, Part 3: New Vocabulary and Grammar

Vocabulary

A gēn B yíyàng	A is the same as B [PT]
bāng	help [V]
bù zhīdào	(I) wonder [A+V]
chuān	put on, wear (shoes, clothes) [V]
dàxiǎo	size [N]
gāogēn(r)xié	high-heeled shoes [N]
hàomǎ(r)	number [N]
shàngshì	come on the market [VO]
shuāng	pair [M]
suàn	figure, calculate [V]
wàzi	sock [N]
wánquán	completely [A]
xūyào	need [N]
yíyàng	one kind; the same [NU+M]

Grammar

A GĒN B YÍYÀNG TO INDICATE SIMILARITY: **Zhèige gēn nèige yíyàng.** "This one is the same as that one."

CONCESSIVE CLAUSES WITH **X SHI X...**: **Piàoliang shi piàoliang, dànshi yìqiān bā tài guìle.** "As for being pretty, they're pretty all right, but 1,800 is too expensive."

STATIVE VERBS FOLLOWED BY EXPRESSIONS OF QUANTITY: **dà yíhào** "be bigger by one number", "be one size bigger"

Unit 13, Part 4: New Vocabulary and Grammar

Vocabulary

bānguolai	move over [RC]
běnlái	originally [MA]
biǎo	watch (for telling time) [N]
chángkù	long pants [N]
chènshān	shirt [N]
dǎ duìzhé	give a 50% discount [PH]
dǎzhé	give a discount [VO]
dài	wear (watch, hat, jewelry) [V]
duǎn	be short (not long) [SV]
duǎnkù	short pants [N]
duìzhé	50% discount [N]
fāpiào	itemized bill; receipt [N]
gānghǎo	just, as it happens [MA]
guòlai	come over [RC]
-guòlai	(indicates movement from there to here) [RE]
guòqu	go over, pass by [RC]
-guòqu	(indicates movement from here to there) [RE]
héshì	be the right size, fit [SV]
jiǎrú	if [MA]
jiǎrú...-de huà	if... [PT]
kùzi	pants [N]
náguoqu	take over [RC]
nálai	bring here [RC]
náqu	take away [RC]
qǐng shāo hòu	"please wait briefly" [IE]
qúnzi	skirt [N]
shōu	accept [V]
shǒubiǎo	wristwatch [N]
shuākǎ	imprint a credit card [VO]
xiànjīn	cash [N]
xiǎo nánshēng	little boy [PH]
xiǎo nǚshēng	little girl [PH]
xìnyòngkǎ	credit card [N]
yīfu	clothes [N]
...yǐnèi	within... [PT]
...zhīnèi	within... [PT]

Grammar

DǍZHÉ TO EXPRESS "GIVE A DISCOUNT": **dǎ jiǔzhé** "sell at ⁹⁄₁₀ of the original price" (=10% discount), **dǎ duìzhé** "sell at half price"

JIǍRÚ...-DE HUÀ: **Jiǎrú tā bù láide huà, nǐ dǎsuan zěmme bàn?** "What do you plan to do if she doesn't come?"

TIME EXPRESSION + **YǏNÈI/ZHĪNÈI**: **sāntiān yǐnèi** "within three days"

Unit 14, Part 1: New Vocabulary and Grammar

Vocabulary

cài	dish of food [N]
càidān(r)	menu [N]
chāzi	fork [N]
dàn	egg [N]
dāozi	knife [N]
diǎn	order, choose [V]
diǎncài	order dishes of food [VO]
dòufu	tofu [N]
fànguǎn(r)	restaurant [PW]
fànwǎn	rice bowl [N]
gòu	be enough [SV]
jīdàn	chicken egg [N]
jīdàn tāng	egg soup [PH]
kuàizi	chopsticks [N]
Mápó Dòufu	Pockmarked Old Woman's Tofu [PH]
mǎyǐ	ant [N]
Mǎyǐ Shàngshù	Ants Climb Trees [PH]
ròusī(r)	meat shred [N]
sháozi	spoon [N]
shù	tree [N]
suíbiàn	"as you wish" [IE]
tāng	soup [N]
wǎn	bowl [N]
xǐ	wash [V]
xǐshǒujiān	bathroom [PW]
yòng	use [V]
yòng	using, with [CV]
Yúxiāng Ròusī	Fish Fragrant Meat Shreds [PH]
zámmen	we (you and I) [PR]

Grammar

QUESTION WORDS AS INDEFINITES: **Něige dōu xíng.** "Any one will do.", **Nǎr dōu yíyàng.** "It's the same everywhere.", **Wǒ shémme dōu chī.** "I eat everything.", **Tā shéi yě bù xǐhuan.** "She likes no one."

Unit 14, Part 2: New Vocabulary and Grammar

Vocabulary

fàng	put, place [V]
hǎo lei	"all right", "O.K." [IE]
hē	drink [V]
jíshì	urgent matter [N]
jiǔ	liquor [N]
kǔ	be bitter [SV]
là	be peppery hot [SV]
làjiāo	hot pepper [N]
lei	(sentence final particle) [P]
liǎng	ounce (50 grams) [M]
-liǎo	be able to [RE]
mántou	steamed bun [N]
mǎn	reach a certain age or time limit [V]
mǐ	rice (uncooked) [N]
mǐfàn	rice (cooked) [N]
pà	fear [V]
píjiǔ	beer [N]
píng	bottle [M]
píngzi	bottle [N]
shàngcài	bring food to a table [VO]
shòu	endure, suffer [V]
shòubuliǎo	not to be able to endure [RC]
suān	be sour [SV]
tián	be sweet [SV]
xián	be salty [SV]
zhǔshí	staple food, main food [N]

Grammar

AFTERTHOUGHTS: **Yǒu píjiǔ ma, nín zhèr?** "Do you have beer here?"

DUŌ AND **SHǍO** BEFORE VERBS TO INDICATE "MORE" AND "LESS": **Duō kàn yìdiǎnr shū.** "Read more books.", **Shǎo fàng diǎnr làjiāo.** "Put in fewer hot peppers."

Unit 14, Part 3: New Vocabulary and Grammar

Vocabulary

biāozhǔn	level [N]
cānjiā	take part in [V]
dǎsuan	plan [AV/V]
dìng	reserve, book [V]
fēn	divide, separate [V]
fēnchéng	divide into [V+PV]
gāojí	be high-class [SV]
gūji	reckon, estimate [V]
jiǔxí	banquet [N]
Xīcān	Western-style food [N]
Zhōngcān	Chinese-style food [N]
zhǔxí	chairman [N]
zhuō	(for banquets) [M]
zuòfàn	cook [VO]

Grammar

DIFFERENT WAYS TO EXPRESS ENGLISH "IF": **...-de huà, ... ; Jiǎrú ...-de huà, ... ; Rúguǒ...-de huà, ... ; Yàoshi...-de huà, ...;** etc.

USE OF THE POSTVERB **-CHÉNG**: **fēnchéng** "divide into," **huànchéng** "exchange for," **gǎichéng** "change into," **kànchéng** "see as," **qiēchéng** "slice into," **shuōchéng** "say as," **xiěchéng** "write into," **zuòchéng** "make into"

Unit 15, Part 2: New Vocabulary and Grammar

Vocabulary

cháng	taste [V]
chīdelái	can or like to eat something [RC]
chīguàn	be used to eating something [RC]
dàn	but [CJ]
gānbēi	"Cheers!", "Bottoms up" [IE]
gānbēi	drink a toast [VO]
gè-	each, every [SP]
-guàn	be used to [RE]
hēzuì	get drunk [RC]
jiànkāng	health [N]
kǎo	bake, roast [V]
kǎoyā	roast duck [N]
kèrén	guest [N]
lái	(verb substitute) [V]
tíyì	propose [V]
wèidao	taste [N]
yā zhēn'gān(r)	duck gizzard and liver [PH]
yìzhí	always, all along [A]
yuè...yuè...	the more...the more... [PT]
zàizuò	be present (at a banquet or meeting) [V]
zǎo jiù	long ago, long since [PH]
zhǔrén	host [N]
zuì	become drunk [V]
-zuì	drunk [RE]

Grammar

AFFIRMATIVE-NEGATIVE QUESTIONS WITH **-GUO** AND **MÉIYOU**: **Nǐ chīguo kǎoyā méiyou?** "Have you ever eaten roast duck?"

YUÈ...YUÈ...: **Yuè piányi yuè hǎo.** "The cheaper the better."

Unit 15, Part 3: New Vocabulary and Grammar

Vocabulary

bǎ	(moves object before verb) [CV]
báo	be thin (in dimensions) [SV]
báobǐng	pancake [N]
bǐng	pancake, biscuit [N]
chībuxià	can't eat [RC]
cōng	scallion [N]
fàngshang	put on [RC]
fēngfù	be abundant [SV]
hòu	be thick [SV]
jiā	pick up (with chopsticks) [V]
jiācài	pick up food (with chopsticks) [VO]
jiàng	thick sauce [N]
jǐn	only [A]
juǎn	roll up [V]
juánqilai	roll up [RC]
miàn	flour; pasta, noodles [N]
tiánmiànjiàng	sweet flour sauce [N]
tú	smear, daub [V]
xiān...zài...	first...then... [PT]
yǐjí	and [CJ]
zhōngjiān	in the middle [PW]

Grammar

BǍ CONSTRUCTION: **Qǐng nǐ bǎ shū fàngzai zhèr.** "Please put the books here."

XIĀN...ZÀI...: **Xiān xué Zhōngwén, zài qù Zhōngguo.** "First learn Chinese, then go to China."

Unit 15, Part 4: New Vocabulary and Grammar

Vocabulary

bié kèqi	"don't be polite" [IE]
chúle...yǐwài	besides...; except for... [PT]
chúle...zhīwài	besides...; except for... [PT]
è	be hungry [SV]
jiāng	ginger [N]
jiàngyóu	soy sauce [N]
jiǎozi	dumpling [N]
kě	be thirsty [SV]
kèqi	be polite [SV]
tiáoliào	seasoning [N]
wà	"wow" [I]
wén	smell something [V]
xiàn(r)	filling [N]
xiāngyóu	sesame oil [N]
yán	salt [N]
yuànyi	be willing to, like to [AV]
zhōumò	weekend [N]
zhǔ	boil [V]
zhǔyào	mainly [A]

Grammar

CHÚLE...ZHĪWÀI AND **CHÚLE...YǏWÀI**: **Chúle tā zhīwài, wǒ hái yǒu biéde péngyou.** "Besides her, I also have other friends.", **Chúle nǐ yǐwài, wǒ méiyou biéde péngyou.** "I don't have any friends except you."

-DE TO INDICATE EXTENT: **Wǒ mángde méi shíjiān chīfàn.** "I'm so busy that I don't have time to eat."

Unit 16, Part 1: New Vocabulary and Grammar

Vocabulary

ài	(indicates strong sentiment) [I]
biànfàn	simple meal [N]
bǔkè	make up a class [VO]
bǔxíbān	cram school [N]
cì	fish bone [N]
dùn	(for meals) [M]
fù	pay [V]
fùqián	pay money [VO]
fúwùyuán	attendant, waiter, waitress [N]
gǎi	change [V]
gǎitiān	on some other day [TW]
gāngcái	just now [TW]
-guo	(expresses completed action) [P]
hài	"hi" [I]
lǎo	be tough (of food) [SV]
mǎidān	"pay the check, "figure up the bill" [IE]
mán...de	quite [PT]
nèn	be tender [SV]
pòfèi	go to great expense [VO]
qǐngkè	treat (someone to something) [VO]
táng	(for classes) [M]
yíkuài(r)	together [A/PW]
zuòdōng	serve as host [VO]

Grammar

-GUO TO EXPRESS COMPLETED ACTION: **Nǐ chīguo fàn le ma?** "Have you eaten?"

STATIVE VERB + **LE** + **(YI)DIAN(R)** TO EXPRESS EXCESS: **Zhèige cài làle yidian.** "This dish is a little too spicy hot."

Unit 16, Part 2: New Vocabulary and Grammar

Vocabulary

bù gǎn dāng	"don't dare accept" [IE]
bù rú...	not be as good as... [PT]
gǎn	dare to [V]
gōngjìng bù rú cóng mìng	"to show respect is not as good as following orders" [EX]
hǎi	ocean, sea [N]
hǎiliàng	"ocean capacity", great capacity for drinking alcohol [N]
hé	river [N]
hú	lake [N]
huídào	come back to [V+PV]
huílai	come back [RC]
huíqu	go back [RC]
jiēfēng	give a welcome dinner [VO]
liàng qiǎn	"capacity is shallow" [IE]
qiǎn	be shallow [SV]
shēn	be deep [SV]
Shí	Shi [SN]
shítou	stone [N]
suíyì	"as you like" [IE]
tì	for [CV]
Wèi	Wei [SN]
xiān-gān-wéi-jìng	drink bottoms up before someone else to show respect [EX]
yǔliàng	rainfall [N]

Grammar

A BÙ RÚ B: **Tā Zhōngwén shuōde bù rú tā tàitai hǎo.** "He doesn't speak Chinese as well as his wife."

Unit 16, Part 3: New Vocabulary and Grammar

Vocabulary

biàndāng	box lunch [N]
bù	step, pace [M]
búyào kèqi	"don't be polite" [IE]
chīdào	succeed in eating [RC]
dàsăo	wife of oldest brother [N]
gòu	reach (by stretching) [V]
gòubuzháo	be unable to reach [RC]
gòudezháo	be able to reach [RC]
Málà Zábànr	Sesame Hot Spicy Medley [PH]
màn yòng	"take your time eating" [IE]
nèirén	one's wife (polite) [N]
shīpéi	"sorry to have to leave" [IE]
Tángcù Lĭjī	Sweet and Sour Pork [PH]
tèdì	especially [A]
wèi	for [CV]
wèir	smell, aroma [N]
xiān zŏu yíbù	"take one step first" [IE]
xiăochī	snack [N]
yùbei	prepare [V]

Grammar

APPROXIMATE NUMBERS: **liăngsānnián** "two or three years"

STATIVE VERB + **-DE** + **HĚN**: **Cài jiăndānde hěn.** "The food is very simple."

-ZHE AS PROGRESSIVE ASPECT SUFFIX MEANING "IN THE VERB-ING": **Zhèige cài wénzhe zhēn xiāng a!** "This dish of food (in the smelling of it) smells really good!"

Unit 16, Part 4: New Vocabulary and Grammar

Vocabulary

bǎo	be full, satiated [SV]
-bǎo	full, satiated [RE]
bǐbushàng	not be able to compare [RC]
cāntīng	dining room (in a house); dining hall, restaurant [PW]
chá	tea [N]
-chēng	fill to the point of bursting [RE]
chībǎo	eat one's fill [RC]
chīchēng	eat until one bursts [RC]
dài	take the place of [V]
dàikè	teach in place of someone [VO]
fēngshèng	be sumptuous [SV]
guǎnzi	restaurant [N]
guǒzhī	juice [N]
jiācháng cài	home-style cooking [PH]
kělè	cola [N]
kètīng	living room [PW]
lǎo	very [A]
ménqiánqīng	finish drinking up alcoholic beverages before leaving [EX]
qìshuǐ(r)	soda [N]
sè xiāng wèi jùquán	"color, aroma, taste all complete" [EX]
shuǐ	water [N]
suàn	consider as [V]
suīrán...	although... [PT]
xīnkǔ	endure hardship [SV]
yǐ	take [CV]
yǐ A dài B	take A to substitute for B [PT]

Grammar

SUĪRÁN...KĚSHI/DÀNSHI/HÁI SHI: **Tā suīrán hěn cōngming, dànshi bú tài yònggōng.** "Even though she's smart, she's not very hardworking."

YǏ A DÀI B: **Wǒ yǐ guǒzhī dài jiǔ.** "I'll substitute juice for wine."

Unit 17, Part 1: New Vocabulary and Grammar

Vocabulary

báibái	"bye-bye" [IE]
dìng	settle, decide [V]
duì...gǎn xìngqu	be interested in... [PT]
duì...yǒu xìngqu	be interested in... [PT]
gǎn	feel [V]
guójì	international [AT]
Guójì Jùlèbù	International Club [PW]
hài	(indicates exasperation) [I]
huài	be bad [SV]
-huài	be bad [RE]
huì	gathering, meeting [N]
jùlèbù	club [N]
kòng(r)	free time [N]
Liú	Liu [SN]
mánghuài	extremely busy [RC]
shìnèi diànhuà	local telephone call [PH]
Táng	Tang [SN]
tí	mention [V]
tíqián	move up (a time or date) [V]
xìngqu	interest [N]
yīnyuè	music [N]
yīnyuèhuì	concert [N]
yì-yán-wéi-dìng	be agreed with one word [EX]
yǒukòng(r)	have free time [VO]

Grammar

A GĒN B SHUŌ C: **Nǐ bié gēn tā shuō wǒ méi qù.** "Don't tell her I didn't go."

DUÌ...GǍN XÌNGQU/DUÌ...YǑU XÌNGQU: **Wǒ duì yīnyuè gǎn xìngqu.** "I'm interested in music.", **Nǐ duì shémme yǒu xìngqu?** "What are you interested in?"

EXTENDED USE OF **BǍ**: **Zhèijǐtiān zhēn bǎ wǒ mánghuàile.** "These last few days I've just been incredibly busy."

. . . .

Unit 17, Part 2: New Vocabulary and Grammar

Vocabulary

chuánzhēn	facsimile, fax [N]
děng...	as soon as..., once... [PT]
fēnjī	extension [N]
guà	hang, hang up [V]
jì	record [V]
jìxialai	write down, note down [RC]
kāihuì	hold or attend a meeting [VO]
kāiwán	finish holding (a meeting) [RC]
liúhuà(r)	leave a message [VO]
lǚxíng	travel [V]
lǚxíng	trip [N]
lǚxíngshè	travel agency [PW]
náshanglai	take up (to speaker) [RC]
náshangqu	take up (away from speaker) [RC]
náxiaqu	take down (away from speaker) [RC]
shànglai	come up [RC]
-shànglai	up [RE]
shàngqu	go up [RC]
-shàngqu	up [RE]
xiàlai	come down [RC]
-xiàlai	down [RE]
xiàqu	go down [RC]
-xiàqu	down [RE]
yī...jiù...	as soon as [PT]
zhànxiàn	be busy (of a telephone) [VO]
zhèng zài...	just be in the midst of... [PT]
zhuǎn	transfer [V]

Grammar

YĪ...JIÙ...: **Tā yí xiàkè jiù huíjiā.** "She goes home as soon as class is over."

ZHÈNG ZÀI...: **Wǒ zhèng zài jiǎng diànhuà ne.** "I'm speaking on the telephone right now."

Unit 17, Part 3: New Vocabulary and Grammar

Vocabulary

ānjìng	be quiet [SV]
bào	newspaper [N]
chǎo	be noisy [SV]
-chūqu	out [RE]
chúfáng	kitchen [PW]
chuānghu	window [N]
dà shēng	in a loud voice [PH]
gōngyù	apartment [N]
guǎnggào	advertisement [N]
jiān	(for rooms) [M]
kōngtiáo	air conditioning [N]
lìkè	immediately [A]
píng	(unit of area, 36 sq. ft.) [M]
-qīngchu	clear [RE]
shēngyīn	sound; voice [N]
shìde	"yes" [IE]
tīngqīngchu	hear clearly [RC]
wòshì	bedroom [PW]
xiǎo shēng	in a low voice, quietly [PH]
yùshì	bathroom [PW]
záyīn	noise, static [N]
zū	rent [V]
zūchuqu	rent out [RC]
zuìhǎo	it would be best, had better [MA]

Grammar

YǑU + QUANTITY EXPRESSION + STATIVE VERB TO INDICATE SIZE: **Yǒu duō dà?** "How large is it?", **Tā yǒu qīchǐ gāo.** "She's seven feet tall."

ZUÌHǍO: **Nǐ zuìhǎo bié wèn ta.** "You'd better not ask him."

Unit 17, Part 4: New Vocabulary and Grammar

Vocabulary

biérén	another person, others [PR]
cānzhuō	dining table [N]
cǎo	grass [N]
chuáng	bed [N]
Dèng	Deng [SN]
diàn	electricity [N]
diànfèi	electricity fee [N]
fāngbian	be convenient [SV]
fángzū	rent [N]
huā(r)	flower [N]
jiǎn	cut [V]
jiǎncǎo	mow the lawn [VO]
jiàoshì	classroom [PW]
lìngwài	in addition [MA]
qiānyuē	sign a lease [VO]
qiáng	wall [N]
shāfā	sofa, armchair [N]
shūzhuō(r)	desk [N]
shuǐdiànfèi	water and electricity fee [N]
shuǐfèi	water fee [N]
yājīn	deposit [N]
yīguì	clothes closet [N]
yìxiē	some [NU+M]
yuànzi	courtyard, yard [N]
zhòng	plant [V]

Grammar

ZHÈXIĒ "these", **NÀXIĒ** "those", **YÌXIĒ** "some": **Yǒu yìxiē jiǎndānde jiājù.** "There is some simple furniture."

Unit 18, Part 1: New Vocabulary and Grammar

Vocabulary

bófù	uncle (father's older brother) [N]
bómǔ	aunt (wife of father's older brother) [N]
dāi	stay [V]
dāibuzhù	not be able to stay [RC]
guā	scrape [V]
guā húzi	shave [PH]
húzi	beard, moustache [N]
jí	be in a hurry [SV]
liú húzi	grow a beard or moustache [PH]
máng	be busy with (something) [V]
Niú	Niu (lit. "cow") [SN]
wàigōng	grandfather (maternal) [N]
wàipó	grandmother (maternal) [N]
wàisūn	grandson (daughter's son) [N]
wàisūnnǚ(r)	granddaughter (daughter's daughter) [N]
wènhǎo	send one's regards to [RC]
wūzi	room [N]
xiǎo péngyou	child [PH]
zhè	right away [A]
-zhù	firm [RE]
zǒngshi	always [A]

Grammar

RESULTATIVE ENDING **-ZHÙ**: **dāibuzhù** "not be able to stay in one place," **zhànzhu** "stand still," **jìzhu** "remember clearly"

. . . .

Unit 18, Part 2: New Vocabulary and Grammar

Vocabulary

dàshǐ	ambassador [N]
děng huǐr	in a little while [PH]
jìrán	since [MA]
jìrán...jiù...	since... [PT]
jiē	street [N]
máfan	be troublesome [SV]
nòng	do, make [V]
nònghǎo	fix, prepare, finish [RC]
shàngjiē	go out on the street [VO]
sòng	see someone off or out [V]
tán	talk [V]
tánhuà	talk, speak [VO]
tánwán	finish talking [RC]
wǎnliú	urge someone to stay [V]
yìbiān(r)	on the one hand [PW]
yìbiān(r) A yìbiān(r) B	do B while doing A [PT]

Grammar

JÌRÁN...JIÙ...: Jìrán nǐ hái yǒu shì, wǒ jiù bù wǎnliúle. "Since you still have things to do, I won't keep you."

YÌBIĀN(R) A YÌBIĀN(R) B: Tā yìbiān chī zǎofàn, yìbiān kàn bào. "She read the newspaper while eating breakfast."

· ·

Unit 18, Part 3: New Vocabulary and Grammar

Vocabulary

bàituō	ask someone to do something [V]
bāngmáng	help [VO]
Cài	Cai [SN]
chōukòng	find time (to do something) [VO]
chōuyān	smoke [VO]
fēixīyān qū	non-smoking section [PH]
guānxi	relationship, connection [N]
kàn	call on, visit [V]
láiwǎn	come late [RC]
línshí	at the last minute [A]
pàochá	steep tea, make tea [VO]
qū	area, region [N]
shìqing	thing, matter [N]
Sòng	Song [SN]
tuō	take off (shoes, clothes) [V]
tuōxié	take off one's shoes [VO]
-wǎn	late [RE]
xī	inhale, breathe in [V]
xíguàn	custom, habit [N]
xīyān	smoke [VO]
xīyān qū	smoking section [PH]
yān	tobacco, cigarette; smoke [N]
yìdiǎn(r) xiǎo yìsi	"a little something," a gift [PH]
yìsi	intention [N]
zheige	(pause filler) [I]
zhí	be straightforward [SV]
zhí shuō	speak frankly [PH]

Grammar

DIFFERENT WAYS TO SAY "HELP": **Qǐng nín bāng wǒ xiě, hǎo bu hǎo?** "Could you please help me write it?", **Qǐng nǐ bāngzhù tā.** "Please help her.", **Qǐng nǐ bāngmáng.** "Please help.", **Qǐng nín bāng ge máng.** "Please help.", **Nǐ fàngxīn, dàjiā dōu huì bāng nǐde máng.** "Relax, everybody will help you."

Unit 18, Part 4: New Vocabulary and Grammar

Vocabulary

bàifǎng	pay a formal call on someone [V]
dáfù	answer, reply [N]
dǎrǎo	disturb [V]
dǎtīng	inquire [V]
dǎtīngdào	inquire and find out [RC]
gàocí	take leave [V]
jìnlì	do one's best [VO]
jìnliàng	to the best of one's ability [A]
...jiù shì	just..., simply... [PT]
liúbù	"don't bother to see me out" [IE]
miǎnqiǎng	do with great effort, force [V]
shànglóu	go upstairs [VO]
tūrán	suddenly [MA]
wànyī	if by chance, in case [MA]
xiàlóu	go downstairs [VO]
xiángqilai	think of [RC]
Xīnzhú	Xinzhu [PW]

Grammar

SPLIT RESULTATIVE COMPOUNDS: **Wǒ tūrán xiángqi yíjiàn shì lai.** "I suddenly thought of something.", **Tā náqi bǐ láile.** "She picked up her pen.", **Tā pǎohuí jiā qule.** "He ran back home."

Unit 19, Part 1: New Vocabulary and Grammar

Vocabulary

bìng	get sick [V]
bìng	illness, disease [N]
gōngfu	time [N]
hái bú shì...	if it isn't... [PT]
huā	spend (money, time) [V]
huāqián	spend money [VO]
kǎo	take a test [V]
kǎoshì	test [N/VO]
kǎoyūn	become dizzy from testing [RC]
pǎo	run [V]
pǎobù	run [VO]
pǎolai	run over here, come over [RC]
pǎoqu	run over there [RC]
qīmò kǎoshì	final examination [PH]
qīzhōng kǎoshì	mid-term examination [PH]
tǎng	lie down [V]
wòfáng	bedroom [PH]
yǒu yìdiǎn(r)...	be a little... [PT]
yūn	be dizzy [SV]
-yūn	dizzy [RE]
zhí dào	straight up to, until [PH]
zhuàn	earn [V]
zhuànqián	earn money [VO]

Grammar

DIFFERENT WAYS TO EXPRESS "SICK": **Tā bìngle.** "She's sick.", **Tā méiyou bìng.** "She's not sick."

DIFFERENT WORDS FOR "TIME": **Nǐ yǒu méiyou gōngfu?/Nǐ yǒu méiyou kòng(r)?/Nǐ yǒu méiyou shíjiān?** "Do you have free time?", **Nǐ shémme shíhou qù?** "What time will you go?", **Yào duō cháng shíjiān?** "How much time will it take?"

REDUPLICATION OF MEASURES AND NOUNS TO MEAN "EACH" OR "EVERY": **rénrén** "everybody", **tiāntiān** "every day", **niánnián** "every year"

YǑU (YÌ)DIǍNR + VERB: **Wǒ yǒu diǎnr yūn.** "I'm a little dizzy.", **Wǒ yǒu diǎnr è.** "I'm a bit hungry.", **Cài yǒu yìdiǎnr là.** "The food is a little spicy hot."

Unit 19, Part 2: New Vocabulary and Grammar

Vocabulary

bàogào	report [N]
bìyè lùnwén	honors thesis [PH]
chéngjī	grade (on test or in course) [N]
guānyú	about, concerning [CV]
lái diànhuà	call on the telephone [PH]
lùnwén	thesis, dissertation [N]
mámahūhū	so-so, fair, not too bad [IE]
mén	(for courses) [M]
piān	(for theses, reports, essays) [M]
xiū	study, take (courses, credits) [V]
xuǎn	choose, select [V]
xuéfēn	credit, credit hour [N]
xuéqī	semester, term [N]
xuéqī bàogào	term paper [PH]

Grammar

REDUPLICATED STATIVE VERBS AS ADVERBS: **hǎohāor(de)** "well", **mànmānr(de)** "slowly", **kuàikuār(de)** "quickly"

Unit 19, Part 3: New Vocabulary and Grammar

Vocabulary

āiya	"gosh" [I]
biāozhǔn	be standard [SV]
cíhuì	vocabulary [N]
Dīng	Ding [SN]
duì-dá-rú-liú	reply to questions fluently [EX]
fāyīn	pronunciation [N]
gàobié	bid farewell [V]
lián	even [CV]
lián...dōu...	even [PT]
liúlì	be fluent [SV]
máfan	trouble [N]
shēngchǎn	produce [V]
tiān	add [V]
xiàng	toward, to [CV]
yǔfǎ	grammar [N]
zhuǎnyǎn	blink the eyes, glance [VO]

Grammar

INVERTED SUBJECT AND VERB FOR UNSPECIFIED SUBJECTS: **Lái kèrén le.** "A guest has come.", **Sǐle bù shǎo rén.** "A lot of people died."

LIÁN...DŌU... AND **LIÁN...YĚ...**: **Lián wǒ dōu huì.** "Even I know.", **Tā lián yíkuài qián yě méiyou.** "He doesn't have even one dollar."

Unit 19, Part 4: New Vocabulary and Grammar

Vocabulary

dài A xiàng B wènhǎo	on behalf of A convey regards to B [PT]
...hòu	after... [PT]
bāoguǒ	package, parcel [N]
dài	for, on behalf of [CV]
duō kuī	be thanks to [PH]
jì	send [V]
jìgěi	send to [V+PV]
jiào-xué-yǒu-fāng	have an especially effective method in one's teaching [EX]
jiéguǒ	result [N]
jìn	carry out, fulfill [V]
jìnbù	progress [N/V]
láixìn	send a letter [VO]
liú	ask someone to stay [V]
míngxìnpiàn	picture postcard [N]
nǎrde huà	"not at all" [IE]
shīmǔ	wife of one's teacher [N]
shuō shízàide	to tell the truth [PH]
tiē	stick [V]
xìn	letter [N]
yào bú shi	if not, if it weren't for [PH]
yīng	should [AV]
yóupiào	stamp [N]
zérèn	responsibility [N]

Grammar

DÀI A XIÀNG B WÈNHǍO: Dài wǒ xiàng nǐde fùmǔ wènhǎo. "Send my regards to your parents."

YÀO BÚ SHI...: Yào bú shi nín jiào-xué-yǒu-fāng, wǒ yě bù kěnéng jìnbùde zhèmme kuài. "If it weren't for your excellent teaching, I wouldn't have been able to progress so quickly."

Unit 20, Part 1: New Vocabulary and Grammar

Vocabulary

àihào	interest, hobby [N]
bówùguǎn	museum [PW]
cānguān	visit [V]
chàng	sing [V]
chànggē(r)	sing a song [VO]
diàozi	tune, melody [N]
gāngqín	piano [N]
gē(r)	song [N]
guàibudé	no wonder [MA]
guóhuà(r)	Chinese painting [N]
hǎotīng	be nice-sounding, pretty [SV]
hēng	hum [V]
huà	paint [V]
huà(r)	painting [N]
huàhuà(r)	paint paintings [VO]
kànshū	read [VO]
shì ma	"really?" [IE]
shìhào	hobby [N]
Tiàoqí	Chinese checkers [N]
Wéiqí	Go (kind of chess) [N]
xià	play (chess or checkers) [V]
xiàqí	play chess [VO]
Xiàngqí	Chinese chess [N]
xiǎoshuō(r)	novel [N]
zhào	take (photographs) [V]
zhàoxiàng	take photographs [VO]

Grammar

GUÀIBUDÉ: **Guàibudé nǐ nèmme pàng!** "No wonder you're so fat!"

Unit 20, Part 2: New Vocabulary and Grammar

Vocabulary

bǎifēnzhī...	...percent [PT]
...diǎn...	(pattern for decimals) [PT]
fēn	part, fraction [M]
...fēnzhī...	(for fractions) [PT]
gònghéguó	republic [N]
Jīngjù	Peking opera [N]
jùchǎng	theater [PW]
méiyou yòng	not have any use [PH]
rénmín	people [N]
Rénmín Jùchǎng	People's Theater (in Beijing) [PW]
shé	snake [N]
yánjiū	study, research [N/V]
yǒuyòng	be useful [SV]
zhènghǎo(r)	just, as it happens [MA]
Zhōnghuá Mínguó	Republic of China [PW]
Zhōnghuá Rénmín Gònghéguó	People's Republic of China [PW]
zhuàn	chronicle, biography [N]

Grammar

DECIMALS: **yīdiǎnèrsì** "1.24"

FRACTIONS: **sānfēnzhī'èr** "two-thirds"

PERCENT: **bǎifēnzhīyī** "1%"

Unit 20, Part 3: New Vocabulary and Grammar

Vocabulary

bù	(measure for films) [M]
chǎng	(for a showing of a movie) [M]
dāng	serve as, work as [V]
diànyǐng(r)	movie [N]
diànyǐngyuàn	movie theater [PW]
gàn	do [V]
gāngqínjiā	pianist [N]
gùshi	story [N]
huàjiā	painter (artist) [N]
jìhua	plan [N]
jiānglái	in the future [TW]
jiǎng	tell the story of, be about [V]
jiǎng gùshi	tell a story [VO]
míng jiào	be named [PH]
niándài	decade [N]
piānzi	film, movie [N]
shàngyǎn	begin to play (of a film at a theater) [V]
shuō gùshi	tell a story [PH]
xiǎoshuōjiā	novelist [N]
yīshēng	medical doctor [N]
yínhángjiā	banker [N]
yīnyuèjiā	musician [N]
yuè	moon [N]
zhùmíng	be famous, well-known [SV]

Grammar

-JIĀ AS NOUN SUFFIX INDICATING PROFESSIONS: **yīnyuèjiā** "musician", **xiǎoshuōjiā** "novelist", **yínhángjiā** "banker"

Unit 20, Part 4: New Vocabulary and Grammar

Vocabulary

Běijīng Túshūguǎn	Beijing Library [PW]
bùfen	part, portion [M]
cónglái	all along, always [A]
cónglái méi...-guo	have never ever...before [PT]
dà bùfen	greater part, majority, most [PH]
dǎoyǎn	director [N]
diànyǐng míngxīng	movie star [PH]
gǎn	touch, move (emotionally) [V]
kāiyǎn	begin to be shown (of a film) [V]
lèi	kind, type, category [M]
lǐjiě	understand [V]
lóushàng	upstairs [PW]
lóuxià	downstairs [PW]
míngbai	understand [V]
-míngbai	understand [RE]
nèiróng	content [N]
pái	row [M]
tīngbutàimíngbai	can't understand very well [RC]
yǎnyuán	actor [N]
zhǔyào	essential, main [AT]

Grammar

CÓNGLÁI MÉI(YOU)...-GUO: Wǒ cónglái méi qùguo. "I've never ever been there before."

Unit 21, Part 1: New Vocabulary and Grammar

Vocabulary

bàngqiú	baseball [N]
bǐfang shuō	for example [PH]
bǐrú	for example [MA]
bǐrú shuō	for example [PH]
chénpǎo	jog in the morning [V]
chénggōng	succeed [V]
dǎ	play (a sport) [V]
dǎ tàijíquán	practice taiji [PH]
dǎqiú	play a ball game [VO]
dàoshi	actually, to the contrary [A]
duì	team [N]
gèzi	stature, build [N]
gōngfū	kung fu [N]
gōngyuán	park (piece of ground) [PW]
hàn	and [CJ]
lánqiú	basketball [N]
máo	feather, hair (on body), fur [N]
nǎxiē	which ones, which [QW+M]
ǒu'ěr	occasionally [MA]
pīngpāngqiú	Ping-Pong [N]
qiǎngjié	rob, loot [V]
qiú	ball [N]
shìyǒu	roommate [N]
tàijíquán	taiji [N]
wǎng	net [N]
wǎngqiú	tennis [N]
wǔshù	martial art [N]
xiàoduì	school team [N]
yóuyǒng	swim [VO]; swimming [N]
yǔmáo	feather, plumage [N]
yǔmáoqiú	badminton, shuttlecock [N]
yùndòng	sport, athletics, exercise [N]

Grammar

YǑU MÉIYOU + VERB TO INDICATE QUESTIONS: **Nǐ yǒu méiyou mǎi?** "Did you buy it?"

Unit 21, Part 2: New Vocabulary and Grammar

Vocabulary

chūnjià	spring vacation [N]
duì...lái shuō	as regards..., for..., to... [PT]
fàngjià	take a vacation [VO]
hánjià	winter vacation [N]
jià	vacation, leave [N]
jiārù	join [V]
jiàrì	holiday, day off [N]
jiāowài	countryside around a city [PW]
jiàoyù	education [N]
lǎonián	old age [N]
lǎonián rén	old people [PH]
nándào...ma	don't tell me that... [PT]
niánqīng rén	young people [PH]
pèngmiàn	meet (face-to-face) [VO]
qǐlái	get up [RC]
qǐngjià	request leave [VO]
shèhuì	society [N]
shètuán	organization, club [N]
shǔjià	summer vacation [N]
tǐyù	physical education [N]
tǐyùguǎn	gymnasium [PW]
tiàowǔ	dance [VO]
tuántǐ	group [N]
yuánlái	actually [MA]
zhěng	exact, sharp (of clock times) [BF]
zhōngnián	middle age [N]
zhōngnián rén	middle-aged people [PH]

Grammar

DUÌ...LÁI SHUŌ: **duì wǒ lái shuō** "as far as I'm concerned"

NÁNDÀO...MA: **Nándào tā lián yíkuài qián dōu méiyou ma?** "You mean he doesn't have even a dollar?"

Unit 21, Part 3: New Vocabulary and Grammar

Vocabulary

Bāxī	Brazil [PW]
bǐ	compare; to (in comparing scores) [V]
bǐsài	competition [N]
Cáo	Cao [SN]
diànshì	television [N]
diànshì jiémù	television program [PH]
diànshìtái	television station [N]
duì	pair off against; versus [V]
jiémù	program [N]
kāi	turn on (a machine, light) [V]
kàn diànshì	watch television [PH]
liánxùjù	soap opera, serial [N]
píndào	channel [N]
píng	be flat, even; tied (score) [SV]
qiáng	be strong [SV]
ruò	be weak [SV]
shìjiè	world [N]
Shìjiè Bēi	World Cup [PH]
shū	lose (i.e., not win) [V]
wǎnhuì	evening party [N]
wényì	literature and art [N]
wényì wǎnhuì	variety show [PH]
xǐjù	comedy [N]
xīnwén	news [N]
yíng	win [V]
Yīnggélán	England [PW]
yǒumíng(r)	be famous [SV]
zhànzhēng	war [N]
zúqiú	soccer [N]
zúqiúsài	soccer competition [N]

Grammar

COMPARING SPORTS SCORES WITH THE VERB **BǏ** "COMPARE": **sān bǐ yī** "three to one"

QUESTION WORDS USED IN PAIRS: **Shéi yùnqi hǎo, shéi jiù yíng.** "Whoever is lucky will win.", **Nǐ chī shémme, wǒ jiù chī shémme.** "I'll eat whatever you eat.", **Nǐ dào nǎr qù, wǒ jiù dào nǎr qù.** "I'll go wherever you go."

Unit 21, Part 4: New Vocabulary and Grammar

Vocabulary

bānyùn	transport [V]
bú dào Cháng Chéng fēi hǎohàn	"if you don't go to the Great Wall you're not a brave man" [EX]
búduànde	continuously [A]
cáiliào(r)	material [N]
dàodǐ(r)	after all, really [MA]
dēng	climb [V]
dēngshang	climb onto [RC]
gōnglǐ	kilometer [M]
gòu...-de	quite... , rather... [PT]
hǎohàn	brave man [N]
jiàn	build [V]
kào	depend on [V]
kě bu shì	"that's for sure" [IE]
kuān	be wide [SV]
kuòjiàn	expand [V]
lìdài	successive dynasties [N]
Méi	Mei [SN]
míng-bù-xū-chuán	have a well deserved reputation [EX]
Míngcháo	Ming Dynasty [TW]
réngōng	human labor [N]
shídài	period [N]
suàndeshang	can be regarded as [RC]
suànshang	include, count [RC]
xiū	build [V]
xiūqilai	in the constructing of something [RC]
yīnglǐ	mile [M]
Zhànguó Shídài	Warring States Period [TW]
zhōngyú	finally [A]

Grammar

GÒU + STATIVE VERB + **-DE**: **Zhèjǐtiān kě zhēn gòu lěngde.** "These last few days sure have been pretty cold."

Unit 22, Part 1: New Vocabulary and Grammar

Vocabulary

biànhuà	change [N]
bú dà	not very much [PH]
dàifu	doctor [N]
ěxin	be nauseous, feel like vomiting [SV]
fāshāo	have a fever [VO]
fèi	lung [N]
fèiyán	pneumonia [N]
gǎnmào	catch cold [V]
húnshēn	entire body [N]
jìn(r)	energy [N]
kànbìng	see a doctor [VO]
nào	suffer (from an illness) [V]
nàobuhǎo	suffer from an illness and not get better [RC]
qìwēn	temperature [N]
shēngbìng	become sick [VO]
téng	be painful, hurt [SV]
tóu	head [N]
tù	spit, throw up [V]
yěxǔ	perhaps, maybe [MA]
yīyuàn	hospital [PW]
yòngbuzháo	not need to [RC]
zǎowǎn	morning and evening [MA]
zháoliáng	catch cold [VO]
zhuǎnchéng	turn into [V+PV]

Grammar

YǑU (YÌ)DIǍNR + VERB: **Wǒ yǒu diǎnr fāshāo.** "I have a bit of fever."

Unit 22, Part 2: New Vocabulary and Grammar

Vocabulary

bèi	(indicates passive) [CV]
diào	fall, drop [V]
-diào	away [RE]
fēi...bù kě	must [PT]
gǎnkuài	quickly [A]
Guóyǔ Zhōngxīn	Mandarin Center [PW]
-huílai	come back [RE]
-huíqu	go back [RE]
hùzhào	passport [N]
jí	be worried, anxious [SV]
jǐngchájú	police station [PW]
mà	scold, curse [V]
nèixiē	those [SP+M]
pǎodào	run to [RC]
pǎodiào	run away [RC]
pǎohuíqu	run back [RC]
píbāo	purse [N]
piàn	trick, deceive [V]
qiánbāo	wallet [N]
Shīdà	National Taiwan Normal University [PW]
tōu	steal [V]
xiǎotōu	thief [N]
zěmme huí shì(r)	"what's the matter?" [IE]
zhǎohuílai	find and get back [RC]
zhèngjiàn	identification paper [N]
zhuā	catch [V]
zhuāzhù	catch hold of [RC]

Grammar

FĒI...BÙ KĚ: **Nǐ fēi qù bù kě.** "You must go."

PASSIVE: **Tā bèi lǎoshī màle.** "He was scolded by the teacher."

Unit 22, Part 3: New Vocabulary and Grammar

Vocabulary

bèi	time(s) [M]
cuò	error, mistake [N]
diào	lose [V]
diū	lose [V]
guójiā	country [N]
huán	give back [V]
huángěi	give back to [V+PV]
jiǎn	pick up [V]
jiǎnchá	inspect, examine [V]
jiǎndào	pick up [RC]
jiè	borrow; lend [V]
jièshūzhēng	library card [N]
jiùmìng	"help!" [IE]
méi cuò	"that's right" [IE]
méi shémme	"you're welcome" [IE]
qiānmíng	sign one's name [VO]
Rénmínbì	RMB (PRC currency) [N]
shīhuǒ	fire breaks out [VO]
Táibì	NT (Taiwan currency) [N]
tèzhēng	special characteristic [N]
xuéshēngzhèng	student I.D. [N]
Yè	Ye [SN]
yīnggāide	"something one ought to do" [IE]
yòngwán	finish using [RC]

Grammar

BÈI TO EXPRESS "TIMES": **Tāde fángzi bǐ wǒde dà yíbèi.** "Her house is twice as big as mine."

JIÈ AS "BORROW" AND "LEND": **Wǒ néng bu néng gēn nǐ jiè yidianr qián?** "Could I borrow some money from you?", **Jīntiān shi xīngqītiān, suóyi túshūguǎn bú jiè shū.** "Today is Sunday, so the library doesn't lend books."

. . . .

Unit 23, Part 2: New Vocabulary and Grammar

Vocabulary

bǎ A jiào(zuo) B	call A B [PT]	**màopái**	counterfeit, fake, imitation [AT]
bǎihuò gōngsī	department store [PH]	**měishí**	fine foods, delicacy [N]
bǎocún	preserve, keep, maintain [V]	**měishí tiāntáng**	food heaven [PH]
bàokān	newspapers and periodicals [N]	**miǎnde...**	so as to avoid..., lest... [PT]
bǐjiào	compare [V]	**miǎnshuì**	be exempt from tax or duty [VO]
chāshāobāo	steamed white flour bun [N]	**miǎnshuìgǎng**	duty free port [N]
chǎnpǐn	product [N]	**páimíng**	be ranked, rank [VO]
chuántǒng	be traditional [SV]	**rónghé**	mix together, merge, fuse [V]
dàobǎn	pirate (a book, film, etc.) [V]	**shāngdiàn**	shop, store [N]
diǎnxin	snack, pastry, dim sum [N]	**shāngpǐn**	goods, merchandise [N]
diànzǐ chǎnpǐn	electronic product, electronics [PH]	**shāomài**	small steamed dumpling [N]
dùzi	belly, abdomen, stomach [N]	**shífēn**	very, extremely [A]
fādá	be developed [SV]	**tèsè**	characteristic [N]
fāngmiàn	aspect, area, side [N]	**tiāntáng**	paradise, heaven [N]
fēngshuǐ	feng shui, geomancy [N]	**xiājiǎo**	shrimp dumpling [N]
gòuwù	buy things, shop [V]	**xiàngjī**	camera [N]
gòuwùzhě	one who buys things, shopper [N]	**yǐ...wéi zhǔ**	take...as the main thing [PT]
gǔshì	stock market, stock exchange [N]	**yìbān**	general, ordinary [AT]
		yìbān	generally, ordinarily [A]
guānshuì	customs duty [N]	**yǐnchá**	drink tea and eat dim sum [VO]
guāng	only, just [A]		
jiǎngjià	bargain, haggle [VO]	**yínhángyè**	banking industry, banking [N]
jiāohuì	connect up, meet, intersect [V]	**yíqiè**	everything, all [N]
jiàozuo	call; be called, be known as [V]	**zhēng**	levy, collect (taxes or duty) [V]
jīnróng	finance [N]	**zhēnzhèng**	real, true, genuine [AT]
jiǔlóu	restaurant [PW]	**...zhīyī**	one of... [PT]
lùtiān shìchǎng	open-air market [PH]	**zhòngyào**	be important [SV]

Grammar

BǍ A JIÀO(ZUO) B: Dàjiā bǎ Xiānggǎng jiàozuo "měishí tiāntáng". "Everybody calls Hong Kong 'food heaven.'"

MIǍNDE...: Yào xiǎoxīn miǎnde bèi piàn! "You have to be careful lest you get cheated!"

PÁIMÍNG: Xiānggǎng gǔshì zài shìjièshang páimíng dìwǔ. "The Hong Kong stock exchange is ranked number five in the world."

YǏ...WÉI ZHǓ: Tīngshuō Xiānggǎng yíqiè yǐ jīngjì wéi zhǔ. "I've heard that in Hong Kong everything takes the economy as the most important component."

...ZHĪYĪ: Xiānggǎng shi shìjièshang zhòngyàode jīnróng hé màoyì zhōngxīn zhīyī. "Hong Kong is one of the important financial and trade centers in the world."

Unit 23, Part 3: New Vocabulary and Grammar

Vocabulary

A gēn B yǒuguān	A is related to B [PT]
dāngshí	at that time, then [TW]
fántǐzì	traditional Chinese character [N]
gōnglì	public [AT]
gōnglì xuéxiào	public school [PH]
guānfāng	official [AT]
guānfāng yǔyán	official language [PH]
jiǎntǐzì	simplified Chinese character [N]
jiāoxué	teach [V]
jiàoyù shuǐpíng	educational level [PH]
jīběn	basic, fundamental [AT]
jīběnshang	basically [MA]
kěnéng	possibility [N]
mǔyǔ	native language [N]
mǔyǔ jiàoyù	education in one's native language [PH]
qiāng	accent, intonation [N]
shíxíng	put into practice, implement [V]
shòukè	give classes, offer instruction [VO]
shuǐpíng	level, standard [N]
...yǐshàng	more than... [PT]
...yǐxià	less than..., below... [PT]
yìbān lái shuō	generally speaking, in general [PH]
yìnshuā	print [V]
zhèngcè	policy [N]
zhōu	week [M]
zìcóng...yǐhòu	since (a certain point in time) [PT]
zuò shēngyì	engage in business, do business [PH]

Grammar

A GĒN B YǑUGUĀN: **Zhè gēn tāmende jiàoyù shuǐpíng yǒuguān.** "This has to do with their educational level."

...YǏSHÀNG AND **...YǏXIÀ**: **bǎifēnzhījiǔshiwǔ yǐshàngde rén** "more than 95% of the people", **língdù yǐxià** "below zero (degrees)"

ZHŌU: **zhōuyī** "Monday," **zhōu'èr** "Tuesday," **zhōusān** "Wednesday," **zhōusì** "Thursday," **zhōuwǔ** "Friday," **zhōuliù** "Saturday," **zhōurì** "Sunday," **běnzhōu** "this week," **shàngyìzhōu** "last week," **xiàyìzhōu** "next week," **měizhōu** "every week"

ZÌCÓNG...YǏHÒU: **Xiānggǎng zìcóng 1997 nián huíguī Zhōngguo yǐhòu** "since Hong Kong's return to China in 1997"

. . . .

Unit 23, Part 4: New Vocabulary and Grammar

Vocabulary

bùguǎn...	no matter..., regardless... [PT]	**lǚyóuyè**	the tourism industry [N]
dàzhì	generally, roughly, for the most part [A]	**mìdù**	density [N]
		míngcài	famous dish, famous food [N]
dàntǎ	egg tart [N]	**niánlíng**	age [N]
Dàngzǎi	Taipa (name of island in Macao) [PW]	**niánlíng xiànzhì**	age limit [PH]
dìguózhǔyìzhě	imperialist [N]	**pǐncháng**	taste, sample [V]
dìlǐ	geography [N]	**píngjūn**	average, mean [AT]
Dōngnányà	Southeast Asia [PW]	**píngjūn shòumìng**	average life expectancy [PH]
dǔbó	gamble [V]	**Pú'ào**	Portuguese-Macanese [AT]
dǔbóyè	the gambling industry [N]		
dǔchǎng	casino [PW]	**Pútáoyá**	Portugal [PW]
dúchuàng	create as something unique [V]	**qīngsōng**	be relaxed, easy [SV]
		rénkǒu mìdù	population density [PH]
ér	and, yet, but [CJ]	**rì**	day of the month (formal style) [M]
Fēizhōu	Africa [PW]		
gālí	curry [N]	**róuhé**	mix together [V]
gāojū	be high (in rank), occupy (a high position) [V]	**ròuguì**	cinnamon [N]
		rùchǎng	enter; be admitted [VO]
ha ha	(sound of laughter) [I]	**shòumìng**	life span, life [N]
héfǎ	be legal [SV]	**wéichí**	maintain [V]
hòubànqī	latter half [TW]	**wèiyú**	be located at, be situated at [V+PV]
huí-wèi-wú-qióng	"savor the aftertaste a long time" [EX]		
		xīyǐn	attract [V]
jì...zhīhòu	follow... [PT]	**xiànzhì**	limit, restriction [N]
jiào	make, cause [V]	**xiànzhuàng**	present conditions, status quo [N]
jiǔwén	have heard of for a long time [IE]		
		xiāngliào	spice [N]
jūmín	resident, inhabitant [N]	**yēzhī**	coconut juice [N]
kǒu	mouth; opening [N]	**yōujiǔ**	be very old, be age-old [SV]
láiyuán	source, origin [N]		
lǎo zǎo	very early, for a long time now [PH]	**yǒuqù**	be interesting, funny, amusing [SV]
lídǎo	offshore island [N]	**zài...zhèngcè xià**	under the policy of... [PT]
lìng	another [SP]	**zhèngfǔ**	government [N]
Lùhuán	Coloane (name of island in Macao) [PW]	**zhèngshì**	formally, officially [A]
		zhíde	be worth, deserve [V]
lǚyóu	tour [V]	**Zhūjiāng**	Pearl River [PW]

Grammar

BÙGUǍN...: **Bùguǎn shi dìlǐ, lìshǐ háishi wénhuà, wǒ shémme dōu xiǎng zhīdao.** "No matter whether it's geography, history, or culture, I want to know everything."

CAUSATIVE VERB **JIÀO**: **Jiào rén huí-wèi-wú-qióng.** "It makes people savor the aftertaste for a long time."

Unit 24, Part 1: New Vocabulary and Grammar

Vocabulary

chuànglì	found, create, establish [V]
cǐdì	this place, here [PW]
dàiyǒu	carry, bear [V]
dà-tóng-xiǎo-yì	be largely the same [EX]
fāngyán	dialect [N]
gòngxiàn	contribution [N]
gōngzuò yǔyán	working language [PH]
Huárén	Chinese person, Chinese [N]
Huáyǔ	Chinese (language) [N]
jiāngjìn	be close to, nearly be, almost be [V]
jù wǒ suǒzhī	according to what I know [PH]
Mǎláiyǔ	Malay (language) [N]
péizhí	cultivate (plants or human talent) [V]
qíyú	other, the remaining, the rest [AT]
quánqiú	the whole world, the entire globe [N]
rèdài	the tropics [N]
shòudào	receive [V]
shòudào...yǐngxiǎng	be influenced by... [PT]
suǒyǒu	all, every [AT]
Tǎnmǐ'ěryǔ	Tamil (language) [N]
xiàngjiāo	rubber [N]
xiàngjiāo shù	rubber tree [PH]
Xīnjiāpō Zhíwùyuán	Singapore Botanic Gardens [PW]
yīndiào	accent, intonation, tone [N]
yǐngxiǎng	influence [N]
zhèngshì	be formal [SV]
zhìshǎo	at least [A]
zhíwù	plants, vegetation [N]
zhíwùyuán	botanic garden [PW]

Grammar

SHÒU(DÀO)...YǏNGXIǍNG: **Yǒu yíbùfen cíhuì shòudàole běndì qítā sānzhǒng yǔyánde yǐngxiǎng.**
"There's a part of the vocabulary that has been influenced by the other three local languages."

Unit 24, Part 2: New Vocabulary and Grammar

Vocabulary

bǎohù	protect [V]
bú shì ma	"isn't it?", "isn't that so?" [IE]
cánrěn	be cruel [SV]
chángjiàn	be commonly seen, common [SV]
dà xióngmāo	giant panda [PH]
dàhòunián	year after next [TW]
dàole...dìbù	reach the point that/where... [PT]
dàzìrán	nature [N]
dìbù	point, situation, condition [N]
duànnǎi	wean [VO]
duì	(used for pairs) [M]
guǎnlǐ	manage, administer, control [V]
hóng xīngxing	orangutan [PH]
hóuzi	monkey [N]
huánjìng	environment, surroundings [N]
jiāng	will, would (formal style) [AV]
juézhǒng	become extinct, die out [V]
kěxī	be a shame, be a pity, regrettable [SV]
lǎohǔ	tiger [N]
lóngzi	cage [N]
miànlín	face, be faced with [V]
mùqián	at present, currently [TW]
pòhuài	destroy, damage [V]
qiān	sign [V]
qǐdào...zuòyong	have a...function or effect [PT]
shīzi	lion [N]
xiàng	(for documents, clauses, items) [M]
xiāngdāng	quite, rather, pretty [A]
xiàngzhēng	symbol, emblem [N]
xiédìng	agreement [N]
Yìnní	Indonesia [PW]
yóuyú...	because of..., due to... [PT]
zèngsòng	present as a gift [V]
zhìshāng	intelligence, IQ [N]
zìrán	be natural [SV]
zìrán huánjìng	natural environment [PH]
zuòyong	function, effect [N]

Grammar

DÀOLE...DÌBÙ: Hóng xīngxing dàole miànlín juézhǒngde dìbù. "Orangutans have reached the point where they're facing extinction."

QǏ(DÀO)...ZUÒYONG: Dòngwùyuán kéyi qǐdào xiāngdāng dàde jiàoyù zuòyong. "Zoos can have a pretty big educational function."

YÓUYÚ: yóuyú zìrán huánjìng bèi pòhuài "due to destruction of the natural environment"

Unit 24, Part 3: New Vocabulary and Grammar

Vocabulary

Bīngchéng	Penang [PW]
dà duōshù	the great majority [PH]
děng	and so on, et cetera [BF]
dúlì	be independent [SV]
duōmínzú	multi-ethnic [AT]
duōshù	majority [N]
duōyuán	diverse [AT]
Huáshè	Chinese community [N]
Huáwén	Chinese language [N]
jìlǜ	discipline [N]
kē	school subject, branch of study [N]
kūzào	be dull, dry, uninteresting [SV]
Mǎlái	Malay [AT]
méijièyǔ	language or medium of instruction [N]
nánnǚ tóngxiào	coeducation [PH]
nǚxiào	girls' school [N]
quēshǎo	lack, be short of [V]
shùxué	mathematics [N]
suǒ	(for schools, hospitals, houses) [M]
wúqù	be uninteresting, dull [SV]
yímín	immigrant, migrant [N]
yuánzhùmín	native people [N]
yǔwén	language and literature [N]
zànzhù	support, sponsor [V]

Grammar

DĚNG AND **DĚNGDĚNG**: **shùxué, dìlǐ, lìshǐ děng** "math, geography, history and so on"

· ·

Unit 24, Part 4: New Vocabulary and Grammar

Vocabulary

ānzhuāng	install [V]
bǎoxiūqī	warranty period [N]
bǐjìběn diànnǎo	notebook computer [PH]
cāozuò	operate, manipulate [V]
cāozuò xìtǒng	operating system [PH]
dìnggòu	order [V]
duōméitǐ	multimedia [N]
fēnqī fùkuǎn	pay by installments [PH]
fùkuǎn	pay a sum of money, pay [VO]
gōngnéng	function, feature [N]
Línjí	Ringgit (Malaysian currency) [M]
nìngyuàn	would rather, prefer to [AV]
qiángdà	be powerful [SV]
ruǎnjiàn	software [N]
shàngwǎng	go online, get on the Internet [VO]
wúxiàn	wireless, Wi-Fi [AT]
xínghào	model, model number [N]
xīnxíng	new type of, new model of [AT]
xìtǒng	system [N]
yìngyòng	apply [V]
yìngyòng ruǎnjiàn	software application, app [PH]
yúlè	entertainment, recreation [N]
zànshí	temporarily, for the time being [A]
zhìzào	manufacture [V]
zhuāng	install [V]

Grammar

NÌNGYUÀN...YĚ BÙ...: Wǒ nìngyuàn zǒulù yě bú zuò nǐde chē! "I'd rather walk than go in your car!"

2. Substitution Drills

Unit 11, Part 1: Substitution Drills

Listen to the audio; after each prompt, say the new sentence using that substitution. Do each drill at least twice: first with the book open, then with the book closed. Each drill starts with a model sentence for you to repeat.

1. Nǐde	Guóyǔ	shi zài náli xuéde?	Where did you learn your Mandarin?
	Hànyǔ		Where did you learn your Chinese?
	Zhōngguo huà		Where did you learn your spoken Chinese?
	Běijīng huà		Where did you learn your Beijing Mandarin?
	Pǔtōnghuà		Where did you learn your Mandarin?
	Zhōngwén		Where did you learn your Chinese?
	Guóyǔ		Where did you learn your Mandarin?

2. Wǒde Zhōngwén shi zài	dàlù	xuéde.	I learned my Chinese in mainland China.
	Táiwān		I learned my Chinese in Taiwan.
	Zhōngguo		I learned my Chinese in China.
	Měiguo		I learned my Chinese in America.
	gāozhōng		I learned my Chinese in high school.
	zhōngxué		I learned my Chinese in middle school.
	dàxué		I learned my Chinese in college.
	dàlù		I learned my Chinese in mainland China.

3. Nǐ lái	Táiwān	duō jiǔ le?	How long have you been in Taiwan?
	Táiběi		How long have you been in Taipei?
	Zhōngguo		How long have you been in China?
	Běijīng		How long have you been in Beijing?
	Měiguo		How long have you been in the U.S.?
	wǒmende gōngsī		How long have you been at our company?
	zhèr		How long have you been here?
	zhèli		How long have you been here?
	Táiwān		How long have you been in Taiwan?

4. Tā láile	sān'ge duō yuè	le.	She has been here for more than three months.
	yíge duō yuè		She has been here for more than a month.
	yíge duō xīngqī		She has been here for more than a week.
	sìge duō xīngqī		She has been here for more than four weeks.
	sìge duō zhōngtóu		She has been here for more than four hours.
	sān'ge duō zhōngtóu		She has been here for more than three hours.
	sān'ge duō yuè		She has been here for more than three months.

5. Wǒ děngle	yíge xiǎoshí	le.	I've been waiting for an hour.
	wǔshífēn zhōng		I've been waiting for 50 minutes.
	sāntiān		I've been waiting for three days.
	liùge yuè		I've been waiting for six months.

	jǐnián	I've been waiting for several years.
	liǎngge xīngqī	I've been waiting for two weeks.
	yíge xiǎoshí	I've been waiting for an hour.

6. **Wǒ xué Zhōngwén xuéle**	**wǔge yuè**	le.	I've been studying Chinese for five months.
	shíge xīngqī		I've been studying Chinese for ten weeks.
	èrshínián		I've been studying Chinese for twenty years.
	jiǔge xīngqī		I've been studying Chinese for nine weeks.
	qīnián		I've been studying Chinese for seven years.
	wǔge yuè		I've been studying Chinese for five months.

7. **Kě bu kéyi**	**kāi**	**màn yidian?**	Could you please drive a bit slower?
	zǒu		Could you please walk a bit slower?
	shuō		Could you please talk a bit slower?
	zuò		Could you please do it a bit slower?
	chī		Could you please eat a bit slower?
	xiě		Could you please write a bit slower?
	kāi		Could you please drive a bit slower?

8. **Xiānsheng, qǐng nǐ shuō**	**màn**	**yidianr.**	Sir, please say it a little slower.
	kuài		Sir, please say it a little faster.
	qīngchu		Sir, please say it a little clearer.
	màn		Sir, please say it a little slower.

9. **Méi wèntí,**	**fàngxīn la**	.	No problem, don't worry about it.
	wǒ yídìng qù		No problem, I'll definitely go.
	yídìng kéyi		No problem, it can definitely be done.
	mǎshàng jiù lái		No problem, I'll come immediately.
	mǎshàng jiù hǎo		No problem, it will be all right very soon.
	fàngxīn la		No problem, don't worry about it.

10. **Bú yàojǐn,**	**míngtiān qù yě kéyi**	. Never mind, we can go tomorrow, too.
	nǐ yàoshi méiyou qián, wǒ kéyi gěi nǐ	Never mind, if you don't have money, I can give you some.
	wǎn yidianr yě kéyi	Never mind, if it's a little late, that's O.K., too.
	zhè bù néng zháojí	Never mind, one mustn't get excited about this.
	wǒ bú pà	Never mind, I'm not afraid of it.
	míngtiān qù yě kéyi	Never mind, we can go tomorrow, too.

11. **Wǒde wèntí**	**tāmen yǐjīng gěi wǒ jiějuéle**	. They have already solved my problem for me.
	nǐ bú shi bù zhīdào	It isn't as if you don't know about my problem.
	yě biànchéng nǐde wèntí le	My problem has also become your problem.
	bú shi nǐ yíge rén néng jiějuéde	My problem isn't one that can be solved by you alone.
	yǐjīng bú shi xiǎo wèntí le	My problem is no longer a small problem.
	tāmen yǐjīng gěi wǒ jiějuéle	They have already solved my problem for me.

Unit 11, Part 2: Substitution Drills

Listen to the audio; after each prompt, say the new sentence using that substitution. Do each drill at least twice: first with the book open, then with the book closed. Each drill starts with a model sentence for you to repeat.

1. **Qǐng wèn, dào**

Mùzhà qù yào zuò jǐhào?	Excuse me, what number bus should I take to go to Muzha?
Táizhōng	Excuse me, what number bus should I take to go to Taizhong?
Táinán	Excuse me, what number bus should I take to go to Tainan?
Gāoxióng	Excuse me, what number bus should I take to go to Gaoxiong?
Táidōng	Excuse me, what number bus should I take to go to Taidong?
Huālián	Excuse me, what number bus should I take to go to Hualian?
Táiběi	Excuse me, what number bus should I take to go to Taipei?
Mùzhà	Excuse me, what number bus should I take to go to Muzha?

2. **Wǒ hǎo jiǔ méi**

zuò gōngchē	le.	I haven't taken a bus for a long time.
chī táng		I haven't eaten candy for a long time.
lái		I haven't come for a long time.
xuéxí		I haven't studied for a long time.
shuìjiào		I haven't slept for a long time.
jiāoshū		I haven't taught for a long time.
xiūxi		I haven't rested for a long time.
zuò gōngchē		I haven't taken a bus for a long time.

3. **Tā liǎngtiān méi**

shuìjiào	le.	She hasn't slept for two days.
chīfàn		She hasn't eaten for two days.
shuōhuà		She hasn't spoken for two days.
dǎ diànhuà		She hasn't called for two days.
qù túshūguǎn		She hasn't gone to the library for two days.
huíjiā		She hasn't come home for two days.
shuìjiào		She hasn't slept for two days.

4. **Wǒ bù xiǎode**

yào zuò jǐhào gōngchē	.	I don't know what number bus to take.
nǐ yào wǒ zuò shémme		I don't know what you want me to do.
nǐ jiào shémme míngzi		I don't know what your name is.
nǐ yào shémme		I don't know what you want.
shi shéi zài jiào wǒ		I don't know who it is that's calling me.
yào zuò jǐhào gōngchē		I don't know what number bus to take.

5. **Yàoburán, nǐ yě kéyi**

dào duìmiàn qù wènwen kàn .	Otherwise, you can also go across the street and ask.
zuò huǒchē	Otherwise, you can also take the train.

dào Zhōngguo qù xué		Otherwise, you can also go to China to learn it.
qù wèn jiāotōngjǐng		Otherwise, you can also go ask a traffic policeman.
dǎdī qù		Otherwise, you can also take a taxi to go there.
dào duìmiàn qù wènwen kàn		Otherwise, you can also go across the street and ask.

---

6. Èr-sān-liù   huòshi   èr-sān-qī   dōu kéyi.   236 or 237 would both be fine.

Zhèige	nèige	This one or that one would both be fine.
Jīntiān	míngtiān	Today or tomorrow would both be fine.
Xiànzài	xiàge xīngqī	Now or next week would both be fine.
Jīnnián	míngnián	This year or next year would both be fine.
Èr-sān-liù	èr-sān-qī	236 or 237 would both be fine.

---

7. Hǎoxiàng   wǔfēn zhōng   yìbān.   Apparently there's a bus every 5 minutes.

yíkè zhōng	Apparently there's a bus every 15 minutes.
èrshífēn zhōng	Apparently there's a bus every 20 minutes.
bàn'ge xiǎoshí	Apparently there's a bus every half hour.
yíge zhōngtóu	Apparently there's a bus every hour.
sānkè zhōng	Apparently there's a bus every 45 minutes.
wǔfēn zhōng	Apparently there's a bus every 5 minutes.

---

8. Wǒ píngcháng   yíge yuè   qù liǎngcì.   I usually go twice a month.

yíge xīngqī	I usually go twice a week.
yíge xiǎoshí	I usually go twice an hour.
yíge zhōngtóu	I usually go twice an hour.
shífēn zhōng	I usually go twice every 10 minutes.
yìtiān	I usually go twice a day.
yìnián	I usually go twice a year.
yíge yuè	I usually go twice a month.

---

9. Lǎoshī, wǒmen yǐjīng   mài   wánle.   Teacher, we've already finished selling them.

zuò	Teacher, we've already finished doing it.
chī	Teacher, we've already finished eating.
kàn	Teacher, we've already finished watching.
xiě	Teacher, we've already finished writing.
shuō	Teacher, we've already finished talking about it.
wèn	Teacher, we've already finished asking.
mài	Teacher, we've already finished selling them.

---

10. Wǒ zuótiān yèli zuòle yíge hěn   qíguài   de mèng.   Last night I had a very strange dream.

kěpà	Last night I had a very scary dream.
kěxiào	Last night I had a very funny dream.
yǒu yìsi	Last night I had a very interesting dream.
cháng	Last night I had a very long dream.
qíguài	Last night I had a very strange dream.

Unit 11, Part 3: Substitution Drills

Listen to the audio; after each prompt, say the new sentence using that substitution. Do each drill at least twice: first with the book open, then with the book closed. Each drill starts with a model sentence for you to repeat.

1. **Wǒ gēn nǐ shuō,**

wǒ zěmme zhǎo yě zhǎobudào .	Listen, no matter how hard I looked, I couldn't find it.
míngtiān yídìng huì xiàyǔ	Listen, it will definitely rain tomorrow.
yóujú jiù zài zuǒshǒubiān	Listen, the post office is on the left-hand side.
shítángde fàn bú tài hǎochī	Listen, the food in the cafeteria isn't very tasty.
Jiāzhōude qìhou hěn shūfu	Listen, the climate in California is very comfortable.
zhèrde tiānqi bǐjiào cháoshī	Listen, the weather here is relatively humid.
wǒ zěmme zhǎo yě zhǎobudào	Listen, no matter how hard I looked, I couldn't find it.

2. **Tā**

zhuàn	lái	**zhuàn**	qù.	She drove all over the place.
shuō		**shuō**		She talked about it over and over.
zhǎo		**zhǎo**		She looked for it here and there.
bān		**bān**		She moved all over the place.
zǒu		**zǒu**		She walked back and forth.
xiǎng		**xiǎng**		She thought about it over and over.
zhuàn		**zhuàn**		She drove all over the place.

3. **Tā zěmme**

zhǎo	yě	**zhǎobudào**	.	No matter how hard he searched, he couldn't find it.
xué		**xuébuhuì**		No matter how hard he studied, he couldn't learn it.
zuò		**zuòbuhǎo**		No matter how he did it, he couldn't do it well.
shuō		**shuōbuduì**		No matter how he said it, he couldn't say it correctly.
wèn		**wènbuqīngchu**		No matter how he asked, he couldn't ask clearly.
zhǎng		**zhǎngbugāo**		No matter how he grows, he can't grow tall.
zhǎo		**zhǎobudào**		No matter how hard he searched, he couldn't find it.

4. **Wǒ zài nǐ shuōde**

xiǎo miào	ménkǒu.	I'm at the entrance to the little temple you mentioned.
xiǎo diàn		I'm at the entrance to the little store you mentioned.
jiājù diàn		I'm at the entrance to the furniture store you mentioned.
túshūguǎn		I'm at the entrance to the library you mentioned.
yóujú		I'm at the entrance to the post office you mentioned.
sùshè		I'm at the entrance to the dormitory you mentioned.
gōngsī		I'm at the entrance to the company you mentioned.
xiǎo miào		I'm at the entrance to the little temple you mentioned.

5. Wǒ gàosu nǐ,

nǐ jìxù wàng yóujú nèibiān zǒu .	Let me tell you, you continue walking towards the post office.
diàn bú tài dà, búyào cuòguo	Let me tell you, the store is not too big, don't miss it.
nǐ huì kàndào yìjiā jiājù diàn	Let me tell you, you'll see a furniture store.
tā bú huì gěi nǐ dǎ diànhuà le	Let me tell you, she won't call you.
fángzi jiù zài yòushǒubiān	Let me tell you, the house is on the right-hand side.
nǐ jìxù wàng yóujú nèibian zǒu	Let me tell you, you continue walking towards the post office.

6. **Zuǒshǒubiān dì'èrdòng** jiù shi wǒmen jiā.   The second building on the left-hand side is our home.

Zuǒshǒubiān dìsāndòng	The third building on the left-hand side is our home.
Yòushǒubiān dìyīdòng	The first building on the right-hand side is our home.
Yòushǒubiān dì'èrdòng	The second building on the right-hand side is our home.
Zuǒshǒubiān dì'èrdòng	The second building on the left-hand side is our home.

Unit 11, Part 4: Substitution Drills

Listen to the audio; after each prompt, say the new sentence using that substitution. Do each drill at least twice: first with the book open, then with the book closed. Each drill starts with a model sentence for you to repeat.

1. Tā yào jiā	èrshígōngshēng	.	She wants to add 20 liters.
	shígōngshēng	.	She wants to add 10 liters.
	sānshígōngshēng	.	She wants to add 30 liters.
	sìshígōngshēng	.	She wants to add 40 liters.
	mǎn	.	She wants to fill it up.
	duōshǎo	?	How much does she want to add?
	èrshígōngshēng	.	She wants to add 20 liters.

2. Wǒ kàn hái shi	jiāmǎn	hǎole.	The way I see it, why not just fill it up.
	màiwán		The way I see it, why not just sell them all.
	zhuǎnjìnlái		The way I see it, why not just turn in here.
	děng yixiar		The way I see it, why not just wait a litte bit.
	chī Zhōngguo cài		The way I see it, why not just eat Chinese food.
	jiāmǎn		The way I see it, why not just fill it up.

3. Cóng	líng	kāishǐ .	Starting from zero.
	shí	.	Starting from ten.
	xiànzài	.	Starting from now.
	jīntiān	.	Starting from today.
	míngtiān	.	Starting from tomorrow.
	wǔhào	.	Starting from the 5th.
	shíyuè	.	Starting from October.
	shémme shíhou	?	Starting from when?
	líng	.	Starting from zero.

4. Qìyóu	de jiàqián yòu yào zhǎngle.	The price of gasoline is going to rise again.
Mótuōchē		The price of motorcycles is going to rise again.
Chēpiào		The price of bus tickets is going to rise again.
Jiājù		The price of furniture is going to rise again.
Zhōngfàn		The price of lunch is going to rise again.
Píxié		The price of leather shoes is going to rise again.
Qìyóu		The price of gasoline is going to rise again.

5. Tā yòu yào	lái	le.	She's going to come again.
	zǒu		She's going to leave again.
	qù túshūguǎn		She's going to go to the library again.
	shuì		She's going to sleep again.
	wèn		She's going to ask again.
	mǎi fángzi		She's going to buy a house again.
	lái		She's going to come again.

6. Cóng	**míngtiān**	qǐ, wǒ měitiān bādiǎn qǐchuáng.	Starting from tomorrow, I'm getting up every day at 8:00.
	jīntiān		Starting from today, I'm getting up every day at 8:00.
	bāhào		Starting from the 8th, I'm getting up every day at 8:00.
	xiànzài		Starting from now, I'm getting up every day at 8:00.
	xiàge yuè		Starting from next month, I'm getting up every day at 8:00.
	xiàge xīngqī		Starting from next week, I'm getting up every day at 8:00.
	míngtiān		Starting from tomorrow, I'm getting up every day at 8:00.

7. Jīntiān	**jiāyóude chē**	tèbié duō.	There are especially many cars filling up today.
	mǎi jiājùde rén		There are especially many people buying furniture today.
	qùde rén		There are especially many people going today.
	láide rén		There are especially many people coming today.
	qí mótuōchēde rén		There are especially many people riding motorcycles today.
	xuéde dōngxi		I learned especially much today.
	jiāyóude chē		There are especially many cars filling up today.

8. Zhèli màide jiājù tèbié	**guì**	.	The furniture sold here is especially expensive.
	piányi		The furniture sold here is especially cheap.
	hǎo		The furniture sold here is especially good.
	jiù		The furniture sold here is especially old.
	xīn		The furniture sold here is especially new.
	guì		The furniture sold here is especially expensive.

9. Nèige rén tè	**hǎo**	.	That person is especially good.
	bèn		That person is especially stupid.
	huài		That person is especially bad.
	lǎn		That person is especially lazy.
	zāng		That person is especially dirty.
	màn		That person is especially slow.
	máng		That person is especially busy.
	hǎo		That person is especially good.

Unit 12, Part 1: Substitution Drills

Listen to the audio; after each prompt, say the new sentence using that substitution. Do each drill at least twice: first with the book open, then with the book closed. Each drill starts with a model sentence for you to repeat.

1. **Bīnggùnr,**	**wǔmáo**	qián yìgēnr!	Ice pops, 50 cents each.
	yìmáo		Ice pops, 10 cents each.
	liǎngmáo		Ice pops, 20 cents each.
	sānmáo		Ice pops, 30 cents each.
	yíkuài		Ice pops, a dollar each.
	liǎngkuài		Ice pops, two dollars each.
	wǔmáo		Ice pops, 50 cents each.

2. **Nǎiyóude**	háishi	**xiǎodòude** ?	Cream ones or red bean ones?
Wǔmáo qiánde		**yíkuài qiánde**	The 50 cent one or the dollar one?
Zhèige		**nèige**	This one or that one?
Dàde		**xiǎode**	The big one or the small one?
Nǐde		**tāde**	Yours or hers?
Jīntiān		**míngtiān**	Today or tomorrow?
Zhèr		**nàr**	Here or there?
Zuǒshǒubiān		**yòushǒubiān**	Left side or right side?
Nǎiyóude		**xiǎodòude**	Cream ones or red bean ones?

3. **Zhǎo nín**	**sìkuài**	. Nín náhǎo!	Here's four yuan in change. Hold it carefully!
	shíkuài		Here's ten yuan in change. Hold it carefully!
	èrshíkuài		Here's twenty yuan in change. Hold it carefully!
	yìmáo		Here's 10 cents in change. Hold it carefully!
	wǔmáo		Here's 50 cents in change. Hold it carefully!
	yíkuài		Here's one yuan in change. Hold it carefully!
	sìkuài		Here's four yuan in change. Hold it carefully!

4. **Tāde zhuānyè shi**	**Xībānyáyǔ** .	His major is Spanish.
	màoyi	His major is trade.
	dōngfāng yǔyán	His major is Oriental languages.
	diànnǎo	His major is computer science.
	Hànyǔ	His major is Chinese.
	Rìyǔ	His major is Japanese.
	wàiguoyǔ	His major is foreign languages.
	Xībānyáyǔ	His major is Spanish.

5. Wǒ hái méi juédìng **wǒde zhuānyè shi shémme**   . I haven't yet decided what my major will be.

zhǔxiū shémme   I haven't yet decided what to major in.

shàng něiwèi lǎoshīde kè   I haven't yet decided which teacher's class to take.

qù dàlù háishi qù Táiwān   I haven't yet decided whether to go to the mainland or to go to Taiwan.

xīngqītiān zuò shémme   I haven't yet decided what to do on Sunday.

wǒ yào shémme yàngde diànnǎo   I haven't yet decided what kind of computer I want.

wǒde zhuānyè shi shémme   I haven't yet decided what my major will be.

Unit 12, Part 2: Substitution Drills

Listen to the audio; after each prompt, say the new sentence using that substitution. Do each drill at least twice: first with the book open, then with the book closed. Each drill starts with a model sentence for you to repeat.

1. Wǒ xiǎng shìshi zhèizhǒng	**yuánzhūbǐ** , xíng ma?	Could I try out this type of ball-point pen?
	bǐ	Could I try out this type of pen?
	qiānbǐ	Could I try out this type of pencil?
	yǐzi	Could I try out this type of chair?
	táng	Could I try this type of candy?
	bēizi	Could I try out this type of cup?
	yuánzhūbǐ	Could I try out this type of ball-point pen?

2. **Zhèi**	zhǒng yuánzhūbǐ	.	This type of ball-point pen.
Nèi		.	That type of ball-point pen.
Jǐ		?	How many types of ball-point pens?
Yì		.	One type of ball-point pen.
Liǎng		.	Two types of ball-point pens.
Měi		.	Every type of ball-point pen.
Něi		?	Which type of ball-point pen?
Zhèi		.	This type of ball-point pen.

3. Nín yào	**hóng**	de háishi	**hēi**	de?	Do you want the red one or the black one?
	lán		**lǜ**		Do you want the blue one or the green one?
	hēi		**zǐ**		Do you want the black one or the purple one?
	dà		**xiǎo**		Do you want the big one or the small one?
	guì		**piányi**		Do you want the expensive one or the cheap one?
	wǒ		**tā**		Do you want mine or hers?
	hóng		**hēi**		Do you want the red one or the black one?

4. **Yuánzhūbǐ**	duōshǎo qián yì/yí	**zhī**	?	How much for a ball-point pen?
Zhǐ		**zhāng**		How much for a sheet of paper?
Běnzi		**ge**		How much for a notebook?
Zázhì		**fèn**		How much for a magazine?
Zhuōzi		**zhāng**		How much for a table?
Qìchē		**liàng**		How much for a car?
Xiǎo gǒu		**zhī**		How much for a little dog?
Fángzi		**dòng**		How much for a house?
Qìyóu		**gōngshēng**		How much for a liter of gasoline?
Yuánzhūbǐ		**zhī**		How much for a ball-point pen?

5. Yǒu	piányi	diǎnrde ma?	Do you have any cheaper ones?
	guì		Do you have any more expensive ones?
	hǎo		Do you have any better ones?
	dà		Do you have any bigger ones?
	zhòng		Do you have any heavier ones?
	hǎokàn		Do you have any better-looking ones?
	kuài		Do you have any faster ones?
	piányi		Do you have any cheaper ones?

6. Zhèige bǐ nèige	piányi	yidianr.	This one is a little cheaper than that one.
	chà		This one is a little worse than that one.
	lǎo		This one is a little older than that one.
	xiǎo		This one is a little smaller than that one.
	qīng		This one is a little lighter than that one.
	màn		This one is a little slower than that one.
	cháng		This one is a little longer than that one.
	piányi		This one is a little cheaper than that one.

7. Qiānbǐ	, nín gěi wǒ liǎng	zhī	Give me two pencils.
Zìdiǎn		běn	Give me two dictionaries.
Bàozhǐ		fèn	Give me two newspapers.
Diànnǎo		tái	Give me two computers.
Yú		tiáo	Give me two fish.
Dìtú		zhāng	Give me two maps.
Yǐzi		bǎ	Give me two chairs.
Bīnggùnr		gēnr	Give me two ice pops.
Yuánzhūbǐ		zhī	Give me two ball-point pens.
Qiānbǐ		zhī	Give me two pencils.

8. Nín hái	yào	diǎnr shémme ma?	Do you want anything else?
	mǎi		Do you want to buy anything else?
	chī		Do you want to eat anything else?
	jiā		Do you want to add anything else?
	dài		Do you want to bring anything else?
	bān		Do you want to move anything else?
	yào		Do you want anything else?

9. Shémme	dōu kéyi.	Anything will do.
Shéi		Anyone will do.
Nǎr		Anywhere will do.
Jǐge		Any number will do.
Zěmmeyàng		Any way will do.
Duōshǎo		However much will do.
Shémme		Anything will do.

10. Yìběn	Hàn-Yīng	zìdiǎn.	A Chinese-English dictionary.
	Yīng-Hàn		An English-Chinese dictionary.
	Hàn-Rì		A Chinese-Japanese dictionary.
	Rì-Hàn		A Japanese-Chinese dictionary.
	Hàn-Fǎ		A Chinese-French dictionary.
	Fǎ-Hàn		A French-Chinese dictionary.
	Hàn-Dé		A Chinese-German dictionary.
	Dé-Hàn		A German-Chinese dictionary.
	Hàn-Yīng		A Chinese-English dictionary.

11. Yìzhāng	Běijīng shì	dìtú.	A map of the city of Beijing.
	Tiānjīn shì		A map of the city of Tianjin.
	zuì xīnde		One of the newest maps.
	hěn lǎode		A very old map.
	xīn mǎide		A newly purchased map.
	Zhōngguo		A map of China.
	Jiāzhōu		A map of California.
	Běijīng shì		A map of the city of Beijing.

12. Tā yào	zhèi	xiē dōngxi	.	She wants these things.
	nèi		.	She wants those things.
	yì		.	She wants some things.
	něi		?	Which things does she want?
	zhèi		.	She wants these things.

Unit 12, Part 3: Substitution Drills

Listen to the audio; after each prompt, say the new sentence using that substitution. Do each drill at least twice: first with the book open, then with the book closed. Each drill starts with a model sentence for you to repeat.

1. Lǎobǎn,	fānqié	zěmme mài?	How much are tomatoes?
	báicài		How much is cabbage?
	lír		How much are pears?
	qīngcài		How much are green vegetables?
	qíncài		How much is celery?
	shālācài		How much is lettuce?
	fānqié		How much are tomatoes?

2. Bànjīn	èrshiwǔkuài.	25 yuan for half a catty.
Yìjīn		25 yuan per catty.
Liǎngjīn		25 yuan for two catties.
Yìgōngshēng		25 yuan per liter.
Yìgōngchǐ		25 yuan per meter.
Yìgōnglǐ		25 yuan per kilometer.
Bàngōnglǐ		25 yuan for half a kilometer.
Bànjīn		25 yuan for half a catty.

3. Zěmme zhèmme	guì	a?	How come it's so expensive?
	chà		How come it's so bad?
	hǎochī		How come it's so tasty?
	zāng		How come it's so dirty?
	luàn		How come it's so messy?
	zhòng		How come it's so heavy?
	xiǎo		How come it's so small?
	guì		How come it's so expensive?

4. Nàr zěmme nèmme	lěng	a?	How come it's so cold there?
	rè		How come it's so hot there?
	cháoshī		How come it's so humid there?
	gānzào		How come it's so dry there?
	bù shūfu		How come it's so uncomfortable there?
	nuǎnhuo		How come it's so warm there?
	lěng		How come it's so cold there?

5. Zhè shi jīntiān cái	dào	de.	These arrived only today.
	lái		These came only today.
	mǎi		These were bought only today.
	zuò		These were made only today.
	jiā		These were added only today.
	dào		These arrived only today.

6. Lǎo Zhāng míngtiān cái | **lái** | . | Old Zhang won't be coming until tomorrow.

	zǒu		Old Zhang won't be leaving until tomorrow.
	qù		Old Zhang won't be going until tomorrow.
	huíguó		Old Zhang won't be returning to his country until tomorrow.
	zuò huǒchē qù		Old Zhang won't be taking the train to go there until tomorrow.
	lái zhǎo nǐ		Old Zhang won't come looking for you until tomorrow.
	dào		Old Zhang won't get here until tomorrow.
	lái		Old Zhang won't be coming until tomorrow.

7. Yào bu yao

mǎi diǎnr shālācài huòshi qíncài	?	Want to buy some lettuce or celery?
qù Zhōngguo huòshi Rìběn		Want to go to China or Japan?
yìdiǎnr fānqié huòshi báicài		Want some tomatoes or cabbage?
yìzhī qiānbǐ huòshi yuánzhūbǐ		Want a pencil or pen?
huí Měiguo huòshi Jiā'nádà		Want to return to the U.S. or Canada?
mǎi diǎnr shālācài huòshi qíncài		Want to buy some lettuce or celery?

8. Zhèixiē dōu shi cóng

Měiguo	jìnkǒude.	These were all imported from the U.S.
Zhōngguo		These were all imported from China.
Táiwān		These were all imported from Taiwan.
Hánguo		These were all imported from Korea.
Rìběn		These were all imported from Japan.
Fǎguo		These were all imported from France.
Déguo		These were all imported from Germany.
Jiā'nádà		These were all imported from Canada.
Měiguo		These were all imported from the U.S.

9. Wǒ bǎozhèng zhèixiē shūcài

hěn xīnxiān	.	I guarantee these vegetables are fresh.
shi cóng Měiguo jìnkǒude		I guarantee these vegetables were imported from the U.S.
hěn hǎochī		I guarantee these vegetables are tasty.
zuì piányile		I guarantee these vegetables are the cheapest.
tè hǎo		I guarantee these vegetables are especially good.
hěn cuì		I guarantee these vegetables are crisp.
hěn xīnxiān		I guarantee these vegetables are fresh.

10. Zhèizhǒng bǐ nèizhǒng	xīnxiān	.	This type is fresher than that type.
	piàoliang		This type is prettier than that type.
	cuì		This type is crisper than that type.
	màn		This type is slower than that type.
	dī		This type is lower than that type.
	héshì		This type is more appropriate than that type.
	shūfu		This type is more comfortable than that type.
	zhǔn		This type is more accurate than that type.
	xīnxiān		This type is fresher than that type.

11. Yòu piàoliang yòu	cuì	.	Both nice-looking and crisp.
	hǎochī		Both nice-looking and tasty.
	dà		Both nice-looking and big.
	xīnxiān		Both nice-looking and fresh.
	piányi		Both nice-looking and cheap.
	cuì		Both nice-looking and crisp.

12. Jīntiān jiù mǎi	fānqié	ba.	I suppose I'll only buy tomatoes today.
	báicài		I suppose I'll only buy cabbage today.
	lí		I suppose I'll only buy pears today.
	qíncài		I suppose I'll only buy celery today.
	shālācài		I suppose I'll only buy lettuce today.
	qīngcài		I suppose I'll only buy green vegetables today.
	qiānbǐ		I suppose I'll only buy pencils today.
	yuánzhūbǐ		I suppose I'll only buy ball-point pens today.
	bīnggùnr		I suppose I'll only buy ice pops today.
	fānqié		I suppose I'll only buy tomatoes today.

Unit 12, Part 4: Substitution Drills

Listen to the audio; after each prompt, say the new sentence using that substitution. Do each drill at least twice: first with the book open, then with the book closed. Each drill starts with a model sentence for you to repeat.

1. Qǐng nín gěi tiāo	xīnxiān	yidianr de.	Please pick out fresher ones.
	piàoliang		Please pick out prettier ones.
	cuì		Please pick out crisper ones.
	hóng		Please pick out redder ones.
	dà		Please pick out bigger ones.
	xiǎo		Please pick out smaller ones.
	hǎokàn		Please pick out nicer-looking ones.
	xīnxiān		Please pick out fresher ones.

2. Wǒ yào	yíkuài wǔ	yìjīnde.	I want the 1.50 per catty ones.
	liǎngkuài		I want the two yuan per catty ones.
	sānmáo		I want the 30 cents per catty ones.
	liùkuài bàn		I want the 6.50 per catty ones.
	shíkuài		I want the ten yuan per catty ones.
	qīmáo		I want the 70 cents per catty ones.
	yíkuài wǔ		I want the 1.50 per catty ones.

3. Yíkuài wǔde	bǐ	yíkuàide	dàde duō.	The 1.50 ones are much bigger than the 1.00 ones.
Zhèige		nèige		This one is much bigger than that one.
Zhèixiē		nèixiē		These are much bigger than those.
Nǐde		wǒde		Yours are much bigger than mine.
Zhèrde		nàrde		The ones here are much bigger than the ones there.
Zhōngguo		Rìběn		China is much bigger than Japan.
Yíkuài wǔde		yíkuàide		The 1.50 ones are much bigger than the 1.00 ones.

4. Zhèizhǒng bǐ nèizhǒng	dà	de duō.	This type is much bigger than that type.
	xīnxiān		This type is much fresher than that type.
	hǎo		This type is much better than that type.
	cuì		This type is much crisper than that type.
	kuài		This type is much faster than that type.
	guì		This type is much more expensive than that type.
	xiǎo		This type is much smaller than that type.
	zhòng		This type is much heavier than that type.
	dà		This type is much bigger than that type.

5. Mǎi diǎnr	**xiāngjiāo**	**zěmmeyàng?**	How about buying some bananas?
	júzi		How about buying some oranges?
	lí		How about buying some pears?
	píngguǒ		How about buying some apples?
	pútao		How about buying some grapes?
	táozi		How about buying some peaches?
	Yālír		How about buying some Ya pears?
	xiāngjiāo		How about buying some bananas?

6. **Píngguǒ**	**duōshǎo qián yìjīn?**	How much are apples per catty?
Xiāngjiāo		How much are bananas per catty?
Júzi		How much are oranges per catty?
Lí		How much are pears per catty?
Pútao		How much are grapes per catty?
Táozi		How much are peaches per catty?
Yālír		How much are Ya pears per catty?
Píngguǒ		How much are apples per catty?

7. Nín gěi wǒ lái	**liǎngjīn**	**ba.**	Why don't you give me two catties.
	yìjīn		Why don't you give me one catty.
	bànjīn		Why don't you give me half a catty.
	yìdiǎnr		Why don't you give me a little.
	sān'ge		Why don't you give me three.
	jǐge		Why don't you give me several.
	liǎngjīn		Why don't you give me two catties.

For the remaining pages of Substitution Drills (**Unit 13**, **Part 1** through **Unit 24**, **Part 4**) please refer to the disc.

3. Transformation and Response Drills
Unit 11, Part 1: Transformation and Response Drills

1. Answer the questions using the cues provided.

Nǐ xué Zhōngwén xuéle jǐnián le? (liǎngnián)
"How long have you been studying Chinese?"

Wǒ xuéle liǎngnián le.
"I've been studying it for two years."

Nǐ niàn yánjiūshēng niànle duō cháng shíjiān le? (yìnián bàn)
"How long have you been studying in graduate school?"

Wǒ niànle yìnián bàn le.
"I've been studying for a year and half."

Nǐ zài zhèr děngle duō jiǔ le? (bàn'ge zhōngtóu)
"How long have you been waiting here?"

Wǒ děngle bàn'ge zhōngtóu le.
"I've been waiting for half an hour."

Zhèli dǔchē dǔle jǐge xiǎoshí le? (yíge xiǎoshí)
"How long has it been clogged up with cars here?"

Zhèli dǔle yíge xiǎoshí le.
"It's been clogged up with cars here for an hour."

Nǐ dàgē zuò mǎimai zuòle duō cháng shíjiān le? (shíwǔnián)
"How long has your brother been in business?"

Tā zuò mǎimai zuòle shíwǔnián le.
"He's been in business for fifteen years."

Nǐ lái Jiùjīnshān duō jiǔ le? (sān'ge yuè)
"How long have you been in San Francisco?"

Wǒ láile sān'ge yuè le.
"I've been here for three months."

2. You will hear a series of complaints. Using the pattern VERB + STATIVE VERB + **yidian**, transform each complaint into an imperative sentence that tells someone what they should do.

Nǐ kāide tài kuàile.
"You drive too fast."

Kāi màn yidian.
"Drive slower."

Nǐ zǒulù zǒude tài mànle.
"You walk too slowly."

Zǒu kuài yidian.
"Walk faster."

Nǐ màide tài guìle.
"You're selling them at too high a price."

Mài piányi yidian.
"Sell them cheaper."

Nǐ xiěde tài luànle.
"You write too messily."

Xiě zhěngqí yidian.
"Write neater."

Nǐ jiǎngde tài bù qīngchule.
"You speak too unclearly."

Jiǎng qīngchu yidian.
"Speak more clearly."

Shàngcì nǐ láide tài wǎnle.
"Last time you came too late."

Xiàcì lái zǎo yidian.
"Next time come earlier."

· ·
Unit 11, Part 2: Transformation and Response Drills

1. The speaker will state that somebody has been doing something for a certain period of time. You should respond that you haven't done the same thing for just as long as the other person has been doing it.

Tā qùle hǎo jiǔ le.

"She's been there for a long time."

Wǒ hǎo jiǔ méi qù le.

"I haven't been there for a long time."

Xiǎo Wáng chīle hěn jiǔ le.

"Little Wang has been eating for a long time."

Wǒ hěn jiǔ méi chī le.

"I haven't eaten for a long time."

Lǎo Lǐ huíjiā bànnián le.

"Old Li has been back home for half a year."

Wǒ bànnián méi huíjiā le.

"I haven't been back home for half a year."

Tā shuìle liǎngtiān le.

"He's been sleeping for two days."

Wǒ liǎngtiān méi shuìle.

"I haven't slept for two days."

Tā kāichē kāile yìnián le.

"She's been driving for a year."

Wǒ yìnián méi kāichē le.

"I haven't driven for a year."

2. Reply that, during each period of time, you perform the action mentioned four times or for four hours.

Nǐ yìtiān jiāo jǐge zhōngtóu?

"How many hours do you teach per day?"

Wǒ yìtiān jiāo sìge zhōngtóu.

"I teach four hours per day."

Nǐ yíge xīngqī qù jǐcì?

"How many times do you go in a week?"

Wǒ yíge xīngqī qù sìcì.

"I go four times a week."

Nǐ yíge yuè zuò jǐcì gōngchē?

"How many times do you take the bus in a month?"

Wǒ yíge yuè zuò sìcì gōngchē.

"I take the bus four times a month."

Nǐ yìtiān shuì jǐge xiǎoshí?

"How many hours do you sleep per day?"

Wǒ yìtiān shuì sìge xiǎoshí.

"I sleep four hours a day."

Nǐ yíge wǎnshang zuò jǐcì mèng?

"How many dreams do you have per night?"

Wǒ yíge wǎnshang zuò sìcì mèng.

"I have four dreams per night."

Nǐ yìtiān zuò jǐcì jiéyùn?

"How many times do you take the MRT per day?"

Wǒ yìtiān zuò sìcì jiéyùn.

"I take the MRT four times per day."

3. Respond to the questions you hear. In each case, use the adverb **yǐjīng** and resultative ending **-wán** to indicate that you have already finished performing the action of the verb in the question.

Nǐ chīle ma?

"Have you eaten?"

Wǒ yǐjīng chīwánle.

"I've already finished eating."

Nǐ zuòle ma?

"Have you done it?"

Wǒ yǐjīng zuòwánle.

"I've already finished doing it."

Nǐ jiāole ma?

"Have you taught it?"

Nǐ xiěle ma?

"Have you written it?"

Nǐ shuōle ma?

"Have you said it?"

Nǐ kànle ma?

"Have you read it?"

Wǒ yǐjīng jiāowánle.

"I've already finished teaching it."

Wǒ yǐjīng xiěwánle.

"I've already finished writing it."

Wǒ yǐjīng shuōwánle.

"I've already finished saying it."

Wǒ yǐjīng kànwánle.

"I've already finished reading it."

. . . .

Unit 11, Part 3: Transformation and Response Drills

1. Change the basic form of the verb to the VERB-**lái** VERB-**qù** pattern.

zhǎo	**zhǎo lái zhǎo qù**
"look for"	"look here and look there"
zǒu	**zǒu lái zǒu qù**
"walk"	"walk here and there"
bān	**bān lái bān qù**
"move"	"move here and there"
pǎo	**pǎo lái pǎo qù**
"run"	"run to and fro"
xiǎng	**xiǎng lái xiǎng qù**
"think"	"rack your brains"
kàn	**kàn lái kàn qù**
"look"	"look all over"
zhuàn	**zhuàn lái zhuàn qù**
"turn"	"turn back and forth"

2. Transform the sentences you hear with the verb **gàosu** to sentences using the pattern **gēn...shuō**.

Tā gàosu wǒ le.	**Tā gēn wǒ shuōle.**
"He told me."	"He told me."
Nǐ bié gàosu tā!	**Nǐ bié gēn tā shuō!**
"Don't tell her!"	"Don't tell her!"
Nǐmen gàosu wǒmen ba.	**Nǐmen gēn wǒmen shuō ba.**
"Why don't you tell us."	"Why don't you tell us."
Wǒ yǐjīng gàosu Xiǎo Wángde nǚpéngyou le.	**Wǒ yǐjīng gēn Xiǎo Wángde nǚpéngyou shuōle.**
"I already told Little Wang's girlfriend."	"I already told Little Wang's girlfriend."
Jiějie yǐjīng gàosu mèimei le.	**Jiějie yǐjīng gēn mèimei shuōle.**
"Older sister already told younger sister."	"Older sister already told younger sister."
Lín Lǎoshī yǐjīng gàosu Zhāng Lǎoshī le.	**Lín Lǎoshī yǐjīng gēn Zhāng Lǎoshī shuōle.**
"Teacher Lin already told Teacher Zhang."	"Teacher Lin already told Teacher Zhang."
Wáng Xiānsheng yǐjīng gàosu Gāo Xiáojie le.	**Wáng Xiānsheng yǐjīng gēn Gāo Xiáojie shuōle.**
"Mr. Wang already told Miss Gao."	"Mr. Wang already told Miss Gao."

3. Transform **gēn...jiǎng** to **gàosu**.

Wǒ gēn nǐ jiǎng, bú shi wǒ zuòde!

"I tell you, it wasn't me who did it!"

Wǒ gàosu nǐ, bú shi wǒ zuòde!

"I tell you, it wasn't me who did it!"

Tā gēn wǒ jiǎng nǐ shi tāde nánpéngyou.

"She told me you're her boyfriend."

Tā gàosu wǒ nǐ shi tāde nánpéngyou.

"She told me you're her boyfriend."

Wǒ gēn nǐmen jiǎng, jīntiān shi xīngqīsān!

"I tell you, today is Wednesday!"

Wǒ gàosu nǐmen, jīntiān shi xīngqīsān!

"I tell you, today is Wednesday!"

Tāmen yǒu méiyou gēn nǐ jiǎng wǒ yào qù Fǎguo liúxué?

"Did they tell you that I'm going to study abroad in France?"

Tāmen yǒu méiyou gàosu nǐ wǒ yào qù Fǎguo liúxué?

"Did they tell you that I'm going to study abroad in France?"

Wǒ gēn tāmen jiǎng jīntiān shi wǒde shēngrì.

"I told them today is my birthday."

Wǒ gàosu tāmen jīntiān shi wǒde shēngrì.

"I told them today is my birthday."

Lín Xiáojie gēn wǒ jiǎng Xiǎo Zhāng yào bānjiāle.

"Ms. Lin told me that Little Zhang is going to move."

Lín Xiáojie gàosu wǒ Xiǎo Zhāng yào bānjiāle.

"Ms. Lin told me that Little Zhang is going to move."

4. Your classmate comments that the two of you are unable to do something. In your response, express strong agreement, using the pattern **zěmme yě** + NEGATIVE VERB for emphasis.

Wǒmen xuébuhuì.

"We can't learn it."

Duì, wǒmen zěmme yě xuébuhuì!

"Yes, we can't learn it no matter what!"

Wǒmen zhǎobudào.

"We can't find it."

Duì, wǒmen zěmme yě zhǎobudào!

"Yes, we can't find it no matter what!"

Wǒmen mǎibuzháo.

"We can't get (buy) one."

Duì, wǒmen zěmme yě mǎibuzháo!

"Yes, we can't get (buy) one no matter what!"

Wǒmen shuìbuzháo.

"We can't fall asleep."

Duì, wǒmen zěmme yě shuìbuzháo!

"Yes, we can't fall asleep no matter what!"

Dōngxi wǒmen màibuwán.

"We can't finish selling the stuff."

Duì, dōngxī wǒmen zěmme yě màibuwán!

"Yes, we can't finish selling the stuff no matter what!"

Wǒmen zuòbuwán.

"We can't finish doing it."

Duì, wǒmen zěmme yě zuòbuwán!

"Yes, we can't finish doing it no matter what!"

Unit 11, Part 4: Transformation and Response Drills

1. In the sentences you hear, transform the pattern **cóng...kāishǐ** to the pattern **cóng...qǐ**.

Cóng míngtiān kāishǐ, wǒmen zǎoshang bādiǎn shàngkè.

"Starting tomorrow, we'll have class at 8:00 A.M."

Cóng míngtiān qǐ, wǒmen zǎoshang bādiǎn shàngkè.

"Starting from tomorrow, we'll have class at 8:00 A.M."

Wǒ juédìng cóng xià xīngqīyī kāishǐ, wǒ yào nǔlì xuéxí Zhōngwén.

"I've decided that, starting from next Monday, I'll study Chinese diligently."

Wǒ juédìng cóng xià xīngqīyī qǐ, wǒ yào nǔlì xuéxí Zhōngwén.

"I've decided that, starting from next Monday, I'll study Chinese diligently."

Jiéyùn cóng jīntiān kāishǐ piàojià yòu tiáozhěngle.

"Starting today, ticket prices for the MRT have been adjusted again."

Jiéyùn cóng jīntiān qǐ piàojià yòu tiáozhěngle.

"Starting today, ticket prices for the MRT have been adjusted again."

Yóujià cóng hòutiān kāishǐ yòu yào zhǎngle.

"The price of gas is going up again starting the day after tomorrow."

Yóujià cóng hòutiān qǐ yòu yào zhǎngle.

"The price of gas is going up again starting the day after tomorrow."

Tāmen cóng zhèige xīngqīwǔ kāishǐ zuò mǎimai.

"They'll be in business as of this Friday."

Tāmén cóng zhèige xīngqīwǔ qǐ zuò mǎimai.

"They'll be in business as of this Friday."

2. Respond to the questions you hear. In your responses, use the pattern **M, wǒ kàn hái shi...hǎole** to indicate that, on reflection, you do want to perform the action being considered after all.

Nǐ zhēnde bú yào jiāmǎn ma?

"You really don't want to fill it up?"

M, wǒ kàn hái shi jiāmǎn hǎole.

"Hmm, I think it's better to fill it up after all."

Nǐ zhēnde bú yào zài shítáng chīfàn ma?

"You really don't want to eat at the cafeteria?"

M, wǒ kàn hái shi zài shítáng chīfàn hǎole.

"Hmm, I think it's better to eat at the cafeteria after all."

Nǐ jīntiān zhēnde bú yào táokè ma?

"You really don't want to skip class today?"

M, wǒ kàn jīntiān hái shi táokè hǎole.

"Hmm, I think it's better to skip class today after all."

Nǐ zhēnde bú yào zuò jìchéngchē ma?

"You really don't want to take a taxi?"

M, wǒ kàn hái shi zuò jìchéngchē hǎole.

"Hmm, I think it's better to take a taxi after all."

Nǐ zhēnde bú yào gàosu tā ma?

"You really don't want to tell her?"

M, wǒ kàn hái shi gàosu tā hǎole.

"Hmm, I think it's better to tell her after all."

3. Respond affirmatively to the questions you hear, using the pattern **yòu yào...le** to indicate that something will happen again.

Yóujià yào zhǎng ma?

"Is the price of gas going to increase?"

Duì, yóujià yòu yào zhǎngle.

"Yes, the price of gas is going to increase again."

Lǎo Bái yào lái ma?

"Is Old Bai coming?"

Yào xiàxuě ma?

"Is it going to snow?"

Tāmen yào táokè ma?

"Are they going to skip class?"

Nǐ bàba māma yào lái ma?

"Are your father and mother going to come?"

Tā yào qù mǎi mótuōchē ma?

"Is he going to go buy a motorcycle?"

Duì, Lǎo Bái yòu yào láile.

"Yes, Old Bai is going to come again."

Duì, yòu yào xiàxuě le.

"Yes, it's going to snow again."

Duì, tāmen yòu yào táokèle.

"Yes, they're going to skip class again."

Duì, tāmen yòu yào láile.

"Yes, they're going to come again."

Duì, tā yòu yào qù mǎi mótuōchē le.

"Yes, he's going to go buy a motorcycle again."

Unit 12, Part 1: Transformation and Response Drills

1. Transform the simple choice-type questions to questions with **háishi** "or."

   Nánde, nǔde?
   "Boy or girl?"

   Nánde háishi nǔde?
   "Boy or girl?"

   Zhèr hǎo, nàr hǎo?
   "Is it better here or there?"

   Zhèr hǎo háishi nàr hǎo?
   "Is it better here or there?"

   Nǐ yào zhèige, yào nèige?
   "Do you want this one or do you want that one?"

   Nǐ yào zhèige háishi nèige?
   "Do you want this one or that one?"

   Nǐde zhǔxiū shi Yīngwén, Zhōngwén?
   "Is your major English or Chinese?"

   Nǐde zhǔxīu shi Yīngwén háishi Zhōngwén?
   "Is your major English or Chinese?"

   Zhèitiáo lù, nèitiáo lù?
   "This road or that road?"

   Zhèitiáo lù háishi nèitiáo lù?
   "This road or that road?"

2. Answer the questions using the cues provided.

   Nǐde zhuānyè shi shémme? (Yīngwén)
   "What is your major?"

   Wǒde zhuānyè shi Yīngwén.
   "My major is English."

   Nǐde zhuānyè shi shémme? (shùxué)
   "What is your major?"

   Wǒde zhuānyè shi shùxué.
   "My major is math."

   Nǐde zhuānyè shi shémme? (rénlèixué)
   "What is your major?"

   Wǒde zhuānyè shi rénlèixué.
   "My major is anthropology."

   Nǐ tóngwūde zhuānyè shi shémme? (yìshu)
   "What is your roommate's major?"

   Wǒ tóngwūde zhuānyè shi yìshu.
   "My roommate's major is art."

   Tāmende zhuānyè shi shémme? (tiānwén)
   "What is their major?"

   Tāmende zhuānyè shi tiānwén.
   "Their major is astronomy."

   Xiǎo Wángde zhuānyè shi shémme? (dìlǐ)
   "What is Little Wang's major?"

   Xiǎo Wángde zhuānyè shi dìlǐ.
   "Little Wang's major is geography."

   Xiǎo Míngde zhuānyè shi shémme? (lìshǐ)
   "What is Little Ming's major?"

   Xiǎo Míngde zhuānyè shi lìshǐ.
   "Little Ming's major is history."

3. Answer the questions using the cues provided.

   Nǐ jiějie zài dàxué zhǔxiū shémme? (shēngwù)
   "What did your older sister major in in college?"

   Wǒ jiějie zài dàxué zhǔxiū shēngwù.
   "My older sister majored in biology in college."

   Nǐ dìdi yǐqián zài dàxuéde shíhou zhǔxiū shémme? (fǎlǜ)
   "What did your younger brother major in when he was in college?"

   Wǒ dìdi yǐqián zài dàxuéde shíhou zhǔxiū fǎlǜ.
   "My younger brother majored in law when he was in college."

Nǐ yǐhòu yào zài dàxué zhǔxiū shémme? (wǔdǎo)

"What do you want to major in in the future when you go to college?"

Wǒ yǐhòu yào zài dàxué zhǔxiū wǔdǎo.

"I want to major in dance in the future when I go to college."

Tāmende nǚ'ér zài dàxué zhǔxiū shémme? (guójì guānxi)

"What is their daughter majoring at in college?"

Tāmende nǚ'ér zài dàxué zhǔxiū guójì guānxi.

"Their daughter's majoring in international relations in college."

Tā zài dàxué zhǔxiū shémme? (wénxué)

"What is his major in college?"

Tā zài dàxué zhǔxiū wénxué.

"He's majoring in literature in college."

Tā mèimei zài dàxué zhǔxiū shémme? (Yàzhōu Yánjiū)

"What is her little sister majoring in in college?"

Tā mèimei zài dàxué zhǔxiū Yàzhōu Yánjiū.

"Her little sister is majoring in Asian Studies in college."

Xiǎo Lǐ zài dàxué zhǔxiū shémme? (jīngjì)

"What is Little Li majoring in in college?"

Xiǎo Lǐ zài dàxué zhǔxiū jīngjì.

"Little Li is majoring in economics in college."

Unit 12, Part 2: Transformation and Response Drills

1. Tell the woman that you want two of each item she asks about. Be sure to use the correct measure.

Nǐ yào yuánzhūbǐ ma?
"Do you want ballpoint pens?"

Yào, wǒ yào liǎngzhī.
"Yes, I want two."

Nǐ yào zìdiǎn ma?
"Do you want dictionaries?"

Yào, wǒ yào liǎngběn.
"Yes, I want two."

Nǐ yào dìtú ma?
"Do you want maps?"

Yào, wǒ yào liǎngzhāng.
"Yes, I want two."

Nǐ yào xiǎo gǒu ma?
"Do you want puppies?"

Yào, wǒ yào liǎngzhī.
"Yes, I want two."

Nǐ yào běnzi ma?
"Do you want notebooks?"

Yào, wǒ yào liǎngge.
"Yes, I want two."

Nǐ yào qiānbǐ ma?
"Do you want pencils?"

Yào, wǒ yào liǎngzhī.
"Yes, I want two."

Nǐ yào zhuōzi ma?
"Do you want tables?"

Yào, wǒ yào liǎngzhāng.
"Yes, I want two."

Nǐ yào bàozhǐ ma?
"Do you want newspapers?"

Yào, wǒ yào liǎngfèn.
"Yes, I want two."

Nǐ yào zhǐ ma?
"Do you want paper?"

Yào, wǒ yào liǎngzhāng.
"Yes, I want two pieces."

Nǐ yào bīnggùnr ma?
"Do you want ice pops?"

Yào, wǒ yào liǎnggēnr.
"Yes, I want two."

2. Your interlocutor will say that something is too (some stative verb, for example, **duǎn** "be short"). Using question particle **ma**, you should ask if there are any that are more (the antonym of the stative verb your interlocutor used).

Zhèige tài duǎnle.
"This is too short."

Yǒu cháng yìdiǎnrde ma?
"Are there longer ones?"

Zhèige tài xiǎole.
"This is too small."

Yǒu dà yìdiǎnrde ma?
"Are there bigger ones?"

Zhèige tài zhòngle.
"This is too heavy."

Yǒu qīng yìdiǎnrde ma?
"Are there lighter ones?"

Zhèige tài guìle.
"This is too expensive."

Yǒu piányi yìdiǎnrde ma?
"Are there cheaper ones?"

Zhèige wèntí tài nánle.

"This question is too hard."

Zhèizhī māo tài pàng le.

"This cat is too fat."

Yǒu róngyi yìdiǎnrde ma?

"Are there easier ones?"

Yǒu shòu yìdiǎnrde ma?

"Are there skinnier ones?"

3. Answer the woman's questions with **Duì**, ... and then use the pattern STATIVE VERB + **yìdiǎn** to comment that "this kind" is a little more (whatever the stative verb is).

Zhèizhǒng bǐjiào piányi ma?

"Is this kind cheaper?"

Zhèizhǒng bǐjiào hǎochī ma?

"Is this kind better tasting?"

Zhèizhǒng bǐjiào hǎo ma?

"Is this kind better?"

Zhèizhǒng bǐjiào hǎokàn ma?

"Does this kind look better?"

Zhèizhǒng bǐjiào máfan ma?

"Is this kind more troublesome?"

Zhèizhǒng bǐjiào qīngchu ma?

"Is this kind clearer?"

Duì, zhèizhǒng piányi yìdiǎn.

"Yes, this kind is a little cheaper."

Duì, zhèizhǒng hǎochī yìdiǎn.

"Yes, this kind is a little better tasting."

Duì, zhèizhǒng hǎo yìdiǎn.

"Yes, this kind is a little better."

Duì, zhèizhǒng hǎokàn yìdiǎn.

"Yes, this kind looks a little better."

Duì, zhèizhǒng máfan yìdiǎn.

"Yes, this kind is a little more troublesome."

Duì, zhèizhǒng qīngchu yìdiǎn.

"Yes, this kind is a little clearer."

4. Your poorly informed interlocutor is asking about bilingual dictionaries. The order of languages should actually be the opposite of what she mentions. For example, the first dictionary is not an "English-Chinese" dictionary but a "Chinese-English" dictionary; continue in a similar manner with the other language combinations mentioned.

Zhè shi Yīng-Hàn zìdiǎn ma?

"Is this an English-Chinese dictionary?"

Zhè shi Rì-Hàn zìdiǎn ma?

"Is this a Japanese-Chinese dictionary?"

Zhè shi Fǎ-Hàn zìdiǎn ma?

"Is this a French-Chinese dictionary?"

Zhè shi Dé-Hàn zìdiǎn ma?

"Is this a German-Chinese dictionary?"

Zhè shi É-Hàn zìdiǎn ma?

"Is this a Russian-Chinese dictionary?"

Bú shi, zhè shi Hàn-Yīng zìdiǎn.

"No, it's a Chinese-English dictionary."

Bú shi, zhè shi Hàn-Rì zìdiǎn.

"No, it's a Chinese-Japanese dictionary."

Bú shi, zhè shi Hàn-Fǎ zìdiǎn.

"No, it's a Chinese-French dictionary."

Bú shi, zhè shi Hàn-Dé zìdiǎn.

"No, it's a Chinese-German dictionary."

Bú shi, zhè shi Hàn-É zìdiǎn.

"No, it's a Chinese-Russian dictionary."

Unit 12, Part 3: Transformation and Response Drills

1. Reply to the woman with the pattern **Zěmme zhèmme...** followed by the stative verb in her comment.

Zhèrde fānqié bǐjiào guì, yìjīn wǔshíkuài.

"The tomatoes here are comparatively expensive.
One catty is fifty dollars."

Zěmme zhèmme guì a?

"How come they're so expensive?"

Zhēn màn, wǒmen yǐjīng děngle bàntiān le.

"It's really slow. We've already been waiting for a long time."

Zěmme zhèmme màn a?

"How come it's so slow?"

Hǎo kuài, wǒmen yǐjīng dàole.

"It's very fast. We're already there."

Zěmme zhèmme kuài a?

"How come it's so fast?"

Zhèige qíncài shi jīntiān gāng dàode, hěn xīnxiān ba?

"This celery just arrived today. It's fresh, huh?"

Zěmme zhèmme xīnxiān a?

"How come it's so fresh?"

**Zhèijiàn xíngli bǐjiào zhòng yidian,
yīnwei lǐmiàn yǒu hěn duō dōngxi.**

"This piece of luggage is relatively heavy,
because there are many things in it."

Zěmme zhèmme zhòng a?

"How come it's so heavy?"

Jīnnián xiàtiān tèbié rè.

"This summer is especially hot."

Zěmme zhèmme rè a?

"How come it's so hot?"

2. Your interlocutor will make a series of comments using the adverb **cái** to stress that she didn't do, or won't do, something until a certain time. You are to use the cue provided plus the adverb **jiù** to boast that you did, or will do, the same thing earlier than she.

Wǒ shi jīntiān cái dàode. (zuótiān)

"I didn't arrive until today."

Wǒ zuótiān jiù dàole!

"I arrived yesterday!"

Wǒ qùnián cái kāishǐ xué Zhōngwén. (qiánnián)

"I didn't start learning Chinese until last year."

Wǒ qiánnián jiù kāishǐ xuéle!

"I started the year before!"

Wǒ wǔyuè cái néng qù. (sìyuè)

"I can't go until May."

Wǒ sìyuè jiù néng qù!

"I can go in April!"

Wǒ sìsuì cái kāishǐ shàng yòuzhìyuán. (sānsuì)

"I didn't start going to kindergarten until I was four."

Wǒ sānsuì jiù shàng yòuzhìyuán le!

"I went to kindergarten when I was three!"

Wǒ xià xīngqī cái néng zuòwán. (zhèi xīngqī)

"I can't finish it until next week."

Wǒ zhèi xīngqī jiù néng zuòwán!

"I can finish it this week!"

Wǒ hòunián cái yào jiéhūn. (míngnián)

"I'm not getting married until the year after next."

Wǒ míngnián jiù yào jiéhūn le!

"I'm getting married next year!"

Unit 12, Part 4: Transformation and Response Drills

1. Use the A **bǐ** B STATIVE VERB **-de duō** pattern to comment that the first item is much more (STATIVE VERB) than the second item.

Tā bǐ nǐ qióng ma?
"Is he poorer than you?"

Tā bǐ wǒ qióngde duō.
"He is much poorer than me."

Zhèige bǐ nèige hǎo ma?
"Is this better than that?"

Zhèige bǐ nèige hǎode duō.
"This is much better than that."

Xiǎo māo bǐ xiǎo gǒu kě'ài ma?
"Are kittens cuter than puppies?"

Xiǎo māo bǐ xiǎo gǒu kě'àide duō.
"Kittens are much cuter than puppies."

Xiǎo Wáng bǐ Xiǎo Zhèng dà ma?
"Is Little Wang older than Little Zheng?"

Xiǎo Wáng bǐ Xiǎo Zhèng dàde duō.
"Little Wang is much older than Little Zheng."

Xiǎo Wáng bǐ Xiǎo Lǐ cōngming ma?
"Is Little Wang smarter than Little Li?"

Xiǎo Wáng bǐ Xiǎo Lǐ cōngmingde duō.
"Little Wang is much smarter than Little Li."

Zhāng Xiáojie bǐ Lín Xiáojie piàoliang ma?
"Is Ms. Zhang prettier than Ms. Lin?"

Zhāng Xiáojie bǐ Lín Xiáojie piàoliangde duō.
"Ms. Zhang is much prettier than Ms. Lin."

. . . .

Unit 13, Part 1: Transformation and Response Drills

1. Answer each question affirmatively, using the stative verb from the question plus **-jíle**.

Nǐ zuìjìn máng bu máng?
"Have you been busy recently?"

Wǒ zuìjìn mángjíle.
"I've been extremely busy recently."

Zhèrde shān hǎo bu hǎokàn?
"Are the mountains here pretty?"

Zhèrde shān hǎokànjíle.
"The mountains here are extremely pretty."

Zhèixie jīròu xīn bu xīnxiān?
"Is this chicken meat fresh?"

Zhèixie jīròu xīnxiānjíle.
"This chicken meat is extremely fresh."

Zhèrde miànbāo hǎo bu hǎochī?
"Is the bread here good to eat?"

Zhèrde miànbāo hǎochījíle.
"The bread here is extremely delicious."

Nǐmen dúshū dúde lèi bu lèi?
"Are you guys tired from studying?"

Wǒmen dúshū dúde lèijíle.
"We're extremely tired from studying."

Wáng Xiānshengde tàitai piàoliang ma?
"Is Mr. Wang's wife pretty?"

Wáng Xiānshengde tàitai piàoliangjíle.
"Mr. Wang's wife is extremely pretty."

2. Use **Qíshí** "Actually" plus **yìdiǎnr yě bù** or **yìdiǎnr yě méi** to respond to the questions you hear.

Nǐ lèile ba?
"I guess you must be tired?"

Qíshí, wǒ yìdiǎnr yě bú lèi.
"Actually, I'm not tired at all."

Zhèige yángròu hǎochī ba?
"This mutton is tasty, right?"

Qíshí, zhèige yángròu yìdiǎnr yě bù hǎochī.
"Actually, this mutton is not tasty at all."

Zhèige niúròu hěn guì ba?
"This beef must be expensive, right?"

Qíshí, zhèige niúròu yìdiǎnr yě bú guì.
"Actually, this beef is not expensive at all."

Tā shuōle hěn duō huà ba?
"He said a lot, right?"

Qíshí, tā yìdiǎnr yě méi shuō.
"Actually, he didn't say anything at all."

Zhèige zhūròu tài féile ba?
"This pork is too fatty, right?"

Qíshí, zhèige zhūròu yìdiǎnr yě bù féi.
"Actually, this pork is not fatty at all."

Nǐ mǎile hěn duō shuǐguǒ ba?
"I suppose you bought a lot of fruits?"

Qíshí, wǒ yìdiǎnr yě méi mǎi.
"Actually, I didn't buy any at all."

Unit 13, Part 2: Transformation and Response Drills

1. You and **Xiǎo Lǐ** "Little Li" are good buddies. The woman on the audio disc will ask if you do something alone. Respond **Bù, wǒ hé Xiǎo Lǐ yìqǐ...** to indicate that you and Little Li do whatever is being asked about together.

Nǐ yíge rén chīfàn ma?
"Do you eat alone?"

Bù, wǒ hé Xiǎo Lǐ yìqǐ chīfàn.
"No, I eat together with Little Li."

Nǐ yíge rén dúshū ma?
"Do you study alone?"

Bù, wǒ hé Xiǎo Lǐ yìqǐ dúshū.
"No, I study together with Little Li."

Nǐ yíge rén zhù ma?
"Do you live alone?"

Bù, wǒ hé Xiǎo Lǐ yìqǐ zhù.
"No, I live together with Little Li."

Nǐ yíge rén lái ma?
"Are you coming by yourself?"

Bù, wǒ hé Xiǎo Lǐ yìqǐ lái.
"No, I'm coming together with Little Li."

Nǐ yíge rén qù ma?
"Are you going by yourself?"

Bù, wǒ hé Xiǎo Lǐ yìqǐ qù.
"No, I'm going together with Little Li."

Nǐ yíge rén huíjiā ma?
"Are you going home alone?"

Bù, wǒ hé Xiǎo Lǐ yìqǐ huíjiā.
"No, I'm going home together with Little Li."

2. Add **...shemmede** to each of the sentences you hear.

Wǒ yào mǎi diǎn tǔsī, kāfēi.
"I want to buy some white bread and coffee."

Wǒ yào mǎi diǎn tǔsī, kāfēi shemmede.
"I want to buy some white bread, coffee, and so on."

Tā bù néng chī yú, xiā.
"She can't eat fish or shrimp."

Tā bù néng chī yú, xiā shemmede.
"She can't eat fish, shrimp, and so forth."

Tā mài zìdiǎn, bàozhǐ.
"He sells dictionaries and newspapaers."

Tā mài zìdiǎn, bàozhǐ shemmede.
"He sells dictionaries, newspapers, and stuff."

Tāmen mài jīròu, yāròu.
"They sell chicken meat and duck meat."

Tāmen mài jīròu, yāròu shemmede.
"They sell chicken meat, duck meat, et cetera."

Tāmen jiāo Zhōngwén, Rìwén.
"They teach Chinese and Japanese."

Tāmen jiāo Zhōngwén, Rìwén shemmede.
"They teach Chinese, Japanese, and so forth."

Wǒ qù shìchǎng mǎi diǎnr pútao, Yālír.
"I'm going to the market to buy some grapes and Ya pears."

Wǒ qù shìchǎng mǎi diǎnr pútao, Yālír shemmede.
"I'm going to the market to buy some grapes, Ya pears, and so on."

3. Use **wèile** "in order to" to combine the two short sentences into one longer sentence.

Tā yào xué Zhōngwén. Tā bāndao Běijīng qùle.

"He wants to learn Chinese. He moved to Beijing."

Tā wèile xué Zhōngwén, bāndao Běijīng qùle.

"He moved to Beijing in order to learn Chinese."

Tā yào chī xiāngjiāo. Tā qùle shìchǎng yítàng.

"She wanted to eat bananas. She made a trip to the market."

Tā wèile chī xiāngjiāo, qùle shìchǎng yítàng.

"She made a trip to the market so she could eat bananas."

Wǒ yào jiéshěng shíjiān. Wǒ zhǐhǎo jiào jìchéngchē.

"I wanted to save time. I had no choice but to call a cab."

Wǒ wèile jiéshěng shíjiān, zhǐhǎo jiào jìchéngchē.

"In order to save time, I had no choice but to call a cab."

Wǒ xūyào mǎi yìběn zìdiǎn. Wǒ děi qù shūdiàn yítàng.

"I need to buy a dictionary. I must make a trip to the bookstore."

Wǒ wèile mǎi yìběn zìdiǎn děi qù shūdiàn yítàng.

"I must make a trip to the bookstore in order to buy a dictionary."

Wǒ gēge yào hē kāfēi. Tā dào Tǒngyī qùle.

"My brother wanted to drink coffee. He went to 7-Eleven."

Wǒ gēge wèile hē kāfēi dào Tǒngyī qùle.

"My brother went to 7-Eleven to drink coffee."

Wǒ yào zhǎo wǒ zuì xǐhuan hēde kāfēi. Wǒ wènle hǎojǐjiā kāfēi diàn.

"I wanted to find the coffee I liked to drink most. I asked quite a few coffee shops."

Wǒ wèile zhǎo wǒ zuì xǐhuan hēde kāfēi, wènle hǎojǐjiā kāfēi diàn.

"In order to find the coffee I liked to drink most, I asked quite a few coffee shops."

4. Add **huì...de** "be likely to" or "will" to each of the sentences that you hear.

Tā bù lái.

"He's not coming."

Tā bú huì láide.

"He's not likely to come."

Wǒ bú gàosu ta.

"I won't tell him."

Wǒ bú huì gàosu tāde.

"I won't tell him."

Wǒ huānyíng tāmen.

"I welcome them."

Wǒ huì huānyíng tāmende.

"I'll welcome them."

Tā mài piányi yìdiǎn.

"He sells them cheaper."

Tā huì mài piányi yìdiǎnde.

"He'll sell them cheaper."

Tāmen bú pà wǒ.

"They're not scared of me."

Tāmen bú huì pà wǒde.

"They're not going to be scared of me."

Wǒmen qù Fǎguo.

"We're going to France."

Wǒmen huì qù Fǎguode.

"We'll go to France."

Unit 13, Part 3: Transformation and Response Drills

1. The speaker will tell you that she doesn't have time to do something on a certain day. Using the polite expression **Nèmme, bù zhīdào...** "Then, I wonder if...," ask her if she would have time on the following day.

Duìbuqǐ, wǒ xīngqīsān méiyou kòng.
"Sorry, I don't have time on Wednesday."

Nèmme, bù zhīdào nǐ xīngqīsì yǒu méiyou kòng?
"Then, I wonder if you would have time on Thursday?"

Duìbuqǐ, wǒ lǐbàiyī méiyou kòng.
"Sorry, I don't have time on Monday."

Nèmme, bù zhīdào nǐ lǐbài'èr yǒu méiyou kòng?
"Then, I wonder if you'd have time on Tuesday?"

Duìbuqǐ, wǒ xīngqī'èr méiyou kòng.
"Sorry, I don't have time on Tuesday."

Nèmme, bù zhīdào nǐ xīngqīsān yǒu méiyou kòng?
"Then, might you have time on Wednesday?"

Duìbuqǐ, wǒ lǐbàisì méiyou kòng.
"Sorry, I don't have time on Thursday."

Nèmme, bù zhīdào nǐ lǐbàiwǔ yǒu méiyou kòng?
"Then, might you have time on Friday?"

Duìbuqǐ, wǒ xīngqīwǔ méiyou kòng.
"Sorry, I don't have time on Friday."

Nèmme, bù zhīdào nǐ xīngqīliù yǒu méiyou kòng?
"Then, I wonder if you'd have time on Saturday?"

Duìbuqǐ, wǒ lǐbàiliù méiyou kòng.
"Sorry, I don't have time on Saturday."

Nèmme, bù zhīdào nǐ lǐbàitiān yǒu méiyou kòng?
"Then, I wonder if you'd have time on Sunday?"

Duìbuqǐ, wǒ xīngqīrì méiyou kòng.
"Sorry, I don't have time on Sunday."

Nèmme, bù zhīdào nǐ xīngqīyī yǒu méiyou kòng?
"Then, I wonder if you'd have time on Monday?"

2. You're determined to do what you want to do, so don't let yourself get talked out of anything! Use a concessive clause with **X shi X, dànshi...** to express that, despite the problem the speaker mentions, you still want to go.

Nǐ bú shi hěn lèi ma?
"Aren't you tired?"

Wǒ lèi shi lèi, dànshi wǒ hái shi xiǎng qù.
"I'm tired, all right, but I still want to go."

Nǐ bú shi hěn máng ma?
"Aren't you busy?"

Wǒ máng shi máng, dànshi wǒ hái shi xiǎng qù.
"I'm busy, to be sure, but I still want to go."

Nǐ bú shi shuō nǐ hěn qióng ma?
"Didn't you say you were poor?"

Wǒ qióng shi qióng, dànshi wǒ hái shi xiǎng qù.
"I'm poor, all right, but I still want to go."

Nèige dìfang bú shi hěn yuǎn ma?

"Isn't that place far away?"

Nèige dìfang yuǎn shi yuǎn, dànshi wǒ hái shi xiǎng qù.
"That place is far away, all right, but I still want to go."

Dào nàr qù bú shi hěn guì ma?
"Isn't it expensive to go there?"

Guì shi guì, dànshi wǒ hái shi xiǎng qù.
"It's expensive, to be sure, but I still want to go."

3. Use the cue provided to answer the question.

Zhèizhǒng guì jǐkuài? (shíkuài)

"How much more expensive is this kind?"

Zhèizhǒng guì shíkuài.

"This kind is more expensive by ten dollars."

Nèizhǒng piányi duōshǎo? (wǔmáo)

"How much cheaper is that kind?"

Nèizhǒng piányi wǔmáo.

"That kind is fifty cents cheaper."

Zuò huǒchē kuài jǐge zhōngtóu? (liǎngge zhōngtóu)

"How much faster is it by train?"

Zuò huǒchē kuài liǎngge zhōngtóu.

"It's two hours faster by train."

Nǐ bàba bǐ nǐ māma dà jǐsuì? (sānsuì)

"How much older is your father than your mother?"

Wǒ bàba bǐ wǒ māma dà sānsuì.

"My father is three years older than my mother."

Zhèishuāng xiézi dà jǐ hào? (liǎnghào)

"How many sizes bigger is this pair of shoes?"

Zhèishuāng xiézi dà liǎnghào.

"This pair of shoes is two sizes bigger."

Unit 13, Part 4: Transformation and Response Drills

1. Use the pattern **Jiǎrú...de huà** to tell your Chinese friend that if things are as she says, then you'd like to invite her to your home to eat pizza.

Wǒ yǒu shíjiān.

"I have time."

Jiǎrú nǐ yǒu shíjiānde huà, wǒ xiǎng qǐng nǐ dào wǒ jiā lái chī "pizza".

"If you have time, I'd like to invite you to my house to eat pizza."

Wǒ míngtiān xiàwǔ yǒukòng.

"I have time tomorrow afternoon."

Jiǎrú nǐ míngtiān xiàwǔ yǒukòngde huà, wǒ xiǎng qǐng nǐ dào wǒ jiā lái chī "pizza".

"If you have time tomorrow afternoon, I'd like to invite you to my house to eat pizza."

Wǒ hòutiān bú yòng shàngbān.

"I don't have to work the day after tomorrow."

Jiǎrú nǐ hòutiān bú yòng shàngbānde huà, wǒ xiǎng qǐng nǐ dào wǒ jiā lái chī "pizza".

"If you don't have to work the day after tomorrow, I'd like to invite you to my house to eat pizza."

Wǒ wǎnshang méiyou shì.

"I have nothing to do tonight."

Jiǎrú nǐ wǎnshang méiyǒu shìde huà, wǒ xiǎng qǐng nǐ dào wǒ jiā lái chī "pizza".

"If you have nothing to do tonight, I'd like to invite you to my house to eat pizza."

Wǒ xǐhuan Yìdàlì cài.

"I like Italian food."

Jiǎrú nǐ xǐhuan Yìdàlì càide huà, wǒ xiǎng qǐng nǐ dào wǒ jiā lái chī "pizza".

"If you like Italian food, I'd like to invite you to my house to eat pizza."

2. Respond with **Ò, tāmen dǎ...zhé** to indicate how large of a discount "they" are giving.

Běnlái yìbǎikuài, xiànzài bāshíkuài.
"It was 100 dollars; now it's 80 dollars."

Ò, tāmen dǎ bāzhé!
"Oh, it's 20 percent off!"

Běnlái yìbǎikuài, xiànzài liùshíkuài.
"It was 100 dollars; now it's 60 dollars."

Ò, tāmen dǎ liùzhé!
"Oh, it's 40 percent off!"

Běnlái yìbǎikuài, xiànzài wǔshíkuài.
"It was 100 dollars; now it's 50 dollars."

Ò, tāmen dǎ duìzhé!
"Oh, it's half off!"

Běnlái yìbǎikuài, xiànzài jiǔshíkuài.
"It was 100 dollars; now it's 90 dollars."

Ò, tāmen dǎ jiǔzhé!
"Oh, it's 10 percent off!"

Běnlái yìqiānkuài, xiànzài wǔbǎikuài.
"It was 1,000 dollars; now it's 500 dollars."

Ò, tāmen dǎ duìzhé!
"Oh, it's half off!"

Běnlái yìqiānkuài, xiànzài sìbǎikuài.
"It was 1,000 dollars; now it's 400 dollars."

Ò, tāmen dǎ sìzhé!
"Oh, it's 60 percent off!"

Běnlái yìqiānkuài, xiànzài qībǎikuài.
"It was 1,000 dollars; now it's 700 dollars."

Ò, tāmen dǎ qīzhé!
"Oh, it's 30 percent off!"

Unit 14, Part 1: Transformation and Response Drills

1. You're not a very particular person. Use a question word in an indefinite sense followed by **dōu** to respond that "any" item, place, time, person, etc. would do.

Shémme lǐwù hǎo?

"What kind of present would be good?"

Shémme lǐwù dōu hǎo.

"Any present would be good."

Něijiā fànguǎnr héshì?

"Which restaurant would be appropriate?"

Něijiā fànguǎnr dōu héshì.

"Any restaurant would be appropriate."

Jǐsuì kéyi jìnqu?

"How old do you have to be to go in?"

Jǐsuì dōu kéyi jìnqu.

"You can go in at any age."

Náli hǎo wán?

"Where is a good place to have fun?"

Náli dōu hǎo wán.

"Any place would be good for having fun."

Něizhǒng hǎochī?

"Which kind tastes better?"

Něizhǒng dōu hǎochī.

"Any kind tastes good."

Jǐge cài cái gòu?

"How many dishes do we need to be enough?"

Jǐge cài dōu gòu.

"Any number of dishes would be enough."

Shémme yàngde dāozi hǎo qiē?

"What kind of knife is good for cutting?"

Shémme yàngde dāozi dōu hǎo qiē.

"Any kind of knife is good for cutting."

Shéi huì zhīdao?

"Who would know?"

Shéi dōu huì zhīdao.

"Anyone would know."

2. Reply that there are not enough of the items mentioned and ask the speaker to give you one more.

Dāozi gòu bu gòu?

"Are there enough knifes?"

Bú gòu. Qǐng nín zài gěi wǒ yìbǎ.

"No, not enough. Please give me another one."

Shū gòu bu gòu?

"Are there enough books?"

Bú gòu. Qǐng nín zài gěi wǒ yìběn.

"No, not enough. Please give me another one."

Kuàizi gòu bu gòu?

"Are there enough chopsticks?"

Bú gòu. Qǐng nín zài gěi wǒ yìshuāng.

"No, not enough. Please give me another pair."

Yú gòu bu gòu?

"Are there enough fish?"

Bú gòu. Qǐng nín zài gěi wǒ yìtiáo.

"No, not enough. Please give me another one."

Tāng gòu bu gòu?

"Is there enough soup?"

Bú gòu. Qǐng nín zài gěi wǒ yìwǎn.

"No, not enough. Please give me another bowl."

Jīdàn gòu bu gòu?

"Are there enough eggs?"

Bú gòu. Qǐng nín zài gěi wǒ yíge.

"No, not enough. Please give me another one."

Yuánzhūbǐ gòu bu gòu?

"Are there enough ball-point pens?"

Bú gòu. Qǐng nín zài gěi wǒ yìzhī.

"No, not enough. Please give me another one."

Unit 14, Part 2: Transformation and Response Drills

1. In each case, tell the woman speaking to ask Old Wang to do more of the action described.

Lǎo Wáng chīle yìdiǎnr fàn.
"Old Wang ate a little food."

Qǐng tā duō chī yìdiǎnr.
"Ask him to eat some more."

Lǎo Wáng hēle yìdiǎnr jiǔ.
"Old Wang drank a little liquor."

Qǐng tā duō hē yìdiǎnr.
"Ask him to drink some more."

Lǎo Wáng xuéle yìdiǎnr Yīngwén.
"Old Wang studied a little English."

Qǐng tā duō xué yìdiǎnr.
"Ask him to study some more."

Lǎo Wáng diǎnle yìdiǎnr cài.
"Old Wang ordered a little food."

Qǐng tā duō diǎn yìdiǎnr.
"Ask him to order some more."

Lǎo Wáng zuòle yìhuǐr.
"Old Wang sat for a while."

Qǐng tā duō zuò yìhuǐr.
"Ask him to sit for a while longer."

Lǎo Wáng zhùle jǐtiān.
"Old Wang stayed for a few days."

Qǐng tā duō zhù jǐtiān.
"Ask him to stay for a few days longer."

2. Tell your interlocutor to do less of the action described in the future. Use **yǐhòu** for "in the future."

Wǒ zuótiān wǎnshang hēle hěn duō jiǔ.
"I drank a lot last night."

Yǐhòu qǐng nǐ shǎo hē yìdiǎnr.
"In the future, please drink a bit less."

Wǒ zuótiān wǎnshang chīle hěn duō cài.
"I ate a lot of food last night."

Yǐhòu qǐng nǐ shǎo chī yìdiǎnr.
"In the future, please eat a bit less."

Wǒ zuótiān wǎnshang shuōle hěn duō huà.
"I talked a lot last night."

Yǐhòu qǐng nǐ shǎo shuō yìdiǎnr.
"In the future, please talk a bit less."

Wǒ zuótiān wǎnshang zuòle hěn duō cài.
"I made a lot of dishes last night."

Yǐhòu qǐng nǐ shǎo zuò yìdiǎnr.
"In the future, please don't make so many."

Wǒ zuótiān wǎnshang sòngle hěn duō lǐwù.
"I gave a lot of presents last night."

Yǐhòu qǐng nǐ shǎo sòng yìdiǎnr.
"In the future, please don't give so many."

3. Transform the Beijing-style sentences you hear containing afterthoughts to the normal Mandarin word order.

Yǒu píjiǔ ma, nín zhèr?
"Do you have beer here?"

Nín zhèr yǒu píjiǔ ma?
"Do you have beer here?"

Màn zǒu, nín!
"You take it easy!"

Nín màn zǒu!
"You take it easy!"

Hěn hǎokàn, nèibianrde shān.
"Very beautiful, the mountains over there."

Nèibianrde shān hěn hǎokàn
"The mountains over there are very pretty."

Hǎo qíguài, zhèixiē rén.
"Very strange, these people."

Zhèixiē rén hǎo qíguài.
"These people are very strange."

Zhēn kǔ, zhèizhǒng kāfēi!
"Really bitter, this kind of coffee!"

Zhèizhǒng kāfēi zhēn kǔ!
"This kind of coffee is really bitter!"

Zhēn piàoliang, nèige nǚháir.
"Very pretty, that girl."

Nèige nǚháir zhēn piàoliang.
"That girl is very pretty."

Unit 14, Part 3: Transformation and Response Drills

1. You're in charge of the arrangements for a large banquet. Your interlocutor will tell you how many people she thinks will be attending. Based on the principle of 10 people per table, you should state how many tables that number of people should be divided into. Use the post verb construction **fēnchéng** "divide into."

Wǒ gūjì yǒu wǔshíge rén cānjiā.
"I reckon there'll be 50 people attending."

Wǒ kàn fēnchéng wǔzhuō ba.
"The way I see it, why don't we divide them into five tables."

Wǒ gūjì yǒu èrshíge rén cānjiā.
"I reckon there'll be 20 people attending."

Wǒ kàn fēnchéng liǎngzhuō ba.
"The way I see it, why don't we divide them into two tables."

Wǒ gūjì yǒu sìshíge rén cānjiā.
"I reckon there'll be 40 people attending."

Wǒ kàn fēnchéng sìzhuō ba.
"The way I see it, why don't we divide them into four tables."

Wǒ gūjì yǒu liùshíge rén cānjiā.
"I reckon there'll be 60 people attending."

Wǒ kàn fēnchéng liùzhuō ba.
"The way I see it, why don't we divide them into six tables."

Wǒ gūjì yǒu sānshíge rén cānjiā.
"I reckon there'll be 30 people attending."

Wǒ kàn fēnchéng sānzhuō ba.
"The way I see it, why don't we divide them into three tables."

Wǒ gūjì yǒu qīshíge rén cānjiā.
"I reckon there'll be 70 people attending."

Wǒ kàn fēnchéng qīzhuō ba.
"The way I see it, why don't we divide them into seven tables."

2. The woman on the audio disc will say a number of conditional ("If...") sentences containing **jiǎrú**, **rúguǒ**, or **yàoshi**. You are to add **-de huà** to each of these conditional sentences.

Rúguǒ xiàyǔ, wǒ jiù bú qù.
"If it rains, I'm not going."

Rúguǒ xiàyǔde huà, wǒ jiù bú qù.
"If it rains, I'm not going."

Yàoshi nǐ fàng làjiāo, wǒ chībuliǎo.
"If you put on hot sauce, I can't eat it."

Yàoshi nǐ fàng làjiāode huà, wǒ chībuliǎo.
"If you put on hot sauce, I can't eat it."

Rúguǒ wǒmen diǎn liǎngge cài, wǒ pà bú gòu chī.
"If we order two dishes, I'm afraid it's not enough to eat."

Rúguǒ wǒmen diǎn liǎngge càide huà, wǒ pà bú gòu chī.
"If we order two dishes, I'm afraid it's not enough to eat."

Jiǎrú yǒu sānshíge rén cānjiā, wǒmen jiù fēnchéng sānzhuō.
"If 30 people attend, we'll divide them into three tables."

Jiǎrú yǒu sānshíge rén cānjiāde huà, wǒmen jiù fēnchéng sānzhuō.
"If 30 people attend, we'll divide them into three tables."

Rúguǒ nǐ xiǎng dìng gāojí yìdiǎnrde jiǔxí, wǒmen yě yǒu yìbǎiyuánde.
"If you want to make reservations for a higher-class banquet, we also have 100 yuan ones."

Rúguǒ nǐ xiǎng dìng gāojí yìdiǎnrde jiǔxíde huà, wǒmen yě yǒu yìbǎiyuánde.
"If you want to make reservations for a higher-class banquet, we also have 100 yuan ones."

Yàoshi nǐde péngyou shi Měiguo rén, wǒmen yīnggāi dìng xīcānde jiǔxí.
"If your friend is American, we should make reservations for a banquet with Western food."

Yàoshi nǐde péngyou shi Měiguo rénde huà, wǒmen yīnggāi dìng xīcānde jiǔxí.
"If your friend is American, we should make reservations for a banquet with Western food."

Unit 14, Part 4: Transformation and Response Drills

1. Since you're an "eager beaver," use the coverb **yóu** "by, from" followed by **ba** at the end of the sentence to volunteer to do whatever is asked of you.

Zhèixiē cài yóu shéi lái pèi ne?
"Who is going to arrange these dishes?"

Yóu wǒ lái pèi ba!
"Let me arrange them!"

Zhèige wèntí yóu shéi lái jiějué ne?
"Who is going to solve this problem?"

Yóu wǒ lái jiějué ba!
"Let me solve it!"

Zhèijiàn shìr yóu shéi lái juédìng ne?
"Who is going to decide this matter?"

Yóu wǒ lái juédìng ba!
"Let me decide it!"

Jīntiān yóu shéi lái kāichē ne?
"Who is going to drive today?"

Yóu wǒ lái kāi ba!
"Let me drive!"

Chēpiào yóu shéi lái mǎi ne?
"Who is going to go buy the bus tickets?"

Yóu wǒ lái mǎi ba!
"Let me buy them!"

Zhèijiā gōngchǎng yóu shéi lái guǎn ne?
"Who is going to run this factory?"

Yóu wǒ lái guǎn ba!
"Let me run it!"

2. Using the pattern **tóng...liánxì**, respond that you'll definitely contact the person mentioned.

Zhè shi Xiǎo Héde míngpiàn.
"This is Little He's name card."

Hǎo, wǒ yídìng tóng tā liánxì.
"O.K., I'll definitely contact him."

Zhè shi Lǐ Xiānsheng, Lǐ Tàitaide diànhuà.
"This is Mr. and Mrs. Li's phone number."

Hǎo, wǒ yídìng tóng tāmen liánxì.
"O.K., I'll definitely get in touch with them."

Qǐng nǐ xiàbān hòu dǎ diànhuà gěi wǒ.
"Please give me a call when you get off work."

Hǎo, wǒ xiàbān hòu yídìng tóng nǐ liánxì.
"O.K., I'll definitely contact you when I get off work."

Qǐng nǐ míngtiān qù zhǎo Lín Xiáojie.
"Please go look for Ms. Lin tomorrow."

Hǎo, wǒ míngtiān yídìng tóng tā liánxì.
"O.K., I'll definitely get in touch with her tomorrow."

Qǐng nǐ juédìng hòu gēn wǒmen shuō yíxià.
"Please tell us after you you decide."

Hǎo, wǒ juédìng hòu yídìng tóng nǐmen liánxì.
"O.K., I'll definitely get in touch with you after I decide."

Unit 15, Part 1: Transformation and Response Drills

1. Respond to the questions you hear by adding **yǐlái** "the past few..." and state that during the period of time mentioned, you have been studying Chinese.

Zhèijǐge xīngqī nǐ zài zuò shémme?

"What have you been doing the last few weeks?"

Zhèijǐge xīngqī yǐlái wǒ zài xué Zhōngwén.

"The past few weeks I've been studying Chinese."

Zhèijǐnián nǐ zài zuò shémme?

"What have you been doing the last few years?"

Zhèijǐnián yǐlái wǒ zài xué Zhōngwén.

"The past few years I've been studying Chinese."

Zhèijǐtiān nǐ zài zuò shémme?

"What have you been doing the last few days?"

Zhèijǐtiān yǐlái wǒ zài xué Zhōngwén.

"The past few days I've been studying Chinese."

Zhèijǐge yuè nǐ zài zuò shémme?

"What have you been doing the last few months?"

Zhèijǐge yuè yǐlái wǒ zài xué Zhōngwén.

"The past few months I've been studying Chinese."

Zhèijǐge lǐbài nǐ zài zuò shémme?

"What have you been doing the last few weeks?"

Zhèijǐge lǐbài yǐlái wǒ zài xué Zhōngwén.

"The past few weeks I've been studying Chinese."

2. Use the adverbial marker **-de** to connect the adverbial expression to the verb.

jiǎndān, shuō jǐjù huà

"be simple, say a couple of sentences"

jiǎndānde shuō jǐjù huà

"simply say a few words"

nǔlì, qù zuò

"be diligent, go do something"

nǔlìde qù zuò

"diligently go do something"

hěn kuài, qù zhǎo

"be very quick, go find"

hěn kuàide qù zhǎo

"very quickly go find"

dàshēng, jiǎnghuà

"in a loud voice, speak"

dàshēngde jiǎnghuà

"speak loudly"

xiǎoshēng, tánhuà

"in a low voice, talk"

xiǎoshēngde tánhuà

"talk quietly"

gāoxìng, chīfàn

"be happy, eat"

gāoxìngde chīfàn

"eat happily"

xiǎoxīn, kāichē

"be careful, drive"

xiǎoxīnde kāichē

"drive carefully"

Unit 15, Part 2: Transformation and Response Drills

1. Your interlocutor will make a statement. Agree by starting out with **Duì, ...** , and then transform her statement into a comment containing the pattern **yuè...yuè....**

Yàoshi jìn yìdiǎn, jiù hǎole.

"If it were a little closer, that would be good."

Duì, yuè jìn yuè hǎo.

"Yes, the closer, the better."

Rúguǒ piányi yìdiǎn, jiù hǎole.

"If it were a little cheaper, that would be good."

Duì, yuè piányi yuè hǎo.

"Yes, the cheaper, the better."

Tā chīde hěn duō, xiànzài pàngle.

"He eats a lot; now he's gotten fat."

Duì, tā yuè chī yuè pàng.

"Yes, the more he eats, the fatter he gets."

Jiǎndānde shuō jǐjù huà jiù hǎole.

"To simply say a few words will be fine."

Duì, yuè jiǎndān yuè hǎo.

"Yes, the simpler, the better."

Niúròu kǎojiǔle, wèidao jiù bù hǎo.

"Beef will taste bad if roasted for a long time."

Duì, niúròu yuè kǎo wèidao yuè bù hǎo.

"Yes, the longer beef is roasted, the worse the taste."

Lǎo Gāo bǐ niánqīngde shíhou hái hǎokàn.

"Old Gao looks even better than when he was young."

Duì, Lǎo Gāo yuè lǎo yuè hǎokàn.

"Yes, the older Old Gao gets, the better he looks."

2. Transform the sentences you hear into sentences with **zǎo jiù** "a long time ago."

Wǒ yǐjīng láile hěn jiǔ le.

"I've already been here for a long time."

Wǒ zǎo jiù láile.

"I came a long time ago."

Wǒ yǐjīng zhīdao hěn cháng shíjiān le.

"I have already known for a long time."

Wǒ zǎo jiù zhīdaole.

"I knew a long time ago."

Tā yǐjīng jiéhūn èrshínián le.

"He has been married for twenty years."

Tā zǎo jiù jiéhūn le.

"He got married a long time ago."

Xiǎo Wáng yǐjīng shàng dàxué sìniánjí le.

"Little Wang is already a senior in college."

Xiǎo Wáng zǎo jiù shàng dàxué le.

"Little Wang started college a long time ago."

Kèrén yǐjīng láile sān'ge xiǎoshí le.

"The guests have been present for three hours."

Kèrén zǎo jiù láile.

"The guests came quite a while ago."

3. Transform the sentences spoken by the woman, which contain the Southern Chinese–style pattern **yǒu méiyou** + VERB + **-guo**, to sentences containing the Northern Chinese–style pattern VERB + **-guo** + **méiyou.**

Nǐ yǒu méiyou qùguo?

"Have you ever gone there?"

Nǐ qùguo méiyou?

"Have you ever gone there?"

Tā yǒu méiyou chīguo kǎoyā?

"Has she ever eaten roast duck?"

Tā chīguo kǎoyā méiyou?

"Has she ever eaten roast duck?"

Nǐmen yǒu méiyou zhàoguguo xiǎo háizi?
"Have you ever taken care of little kids?"

Nǐmen zhàoguguo xiǎo háizi méiyou?
"Have you ever taken care of little kids?"

Tāmen yǒu méiyou hēzuìguo?
"Have they ever gotten drunk?"

Tāmen hēzuìguo méiyou?
"Have they ever gotten drunk?"

Xiǎo Wáng, nǐ yǒu méiyou kǎoguo jīròu?
"Little Wang, have you ever roasted chicken before?"

Xiǎo Wáng, nǐ kǎoguo jīròu méiyou?
"Little Wang, have you ever roasted chicken before?"

Nǐmen yǒu méiyou zuòguo huǒchē?
"Have you ever ridden in a train before?"

Nǐmen zuòguo huǒchē méiyou?
"Have you ever ridden in a train before?"

4. Transform the sentences spoken by the woman from Beijing, which contain the Northern Chinese–style pattern VERB + **-guo** + **méiyou**, to the Southern Chinese–style pattern **yǒu méiyou** + VERB + **-guo**.

Nǐ qíguo mótuōchē méiyou?
"Have you ever ridden on a motorcycle before?"

Nǐ yǒu méiyou qíguo mótuōchē?
"Have you ever ridden on a motorcycle before?"

Tā líguo hūn méiyou?
"Has he ever gotten divorced before?"

Tā yǒu méiyou líguo hūn?
"Has he ever gotten divorced before?"

Nǐ chídàoguo méiyou?
"Have you ever been late?"

Nǐ yǒu méiyou chídàoguo?
"Have you ever been late?"

Nǐmen táoguo kè méiyou?
"Have you ever skipped class?"

Nǐmen yǒu méiyou táoguo kè?
"Have you ever skipped class?"

Xiǎo Zhāng, nǐ bānguo jiā méiyou?
"Little Zhang, have you ever moved before?"

Xiǎo Zhāng, nǐ yǒu méiyou bānguo jiā?
"Little Zhang, have you ever moved before?"

Lǎo Lín, nǐ jiāguo yóu méiyou?
"Old Lin, have you ever bought gas before?"

Lǎo Lín, nǐ yǒu méiyou jiāguo yóu?
"Old Lin, have you ever bought gas before?"

. . . .

Unit 15, Part 3: Transformation and Response Drills

1. The speaker will ask you to do something. Confirm her request with the phrase **Nǐ shì bu shi yào wǒ...** "Is it the case that you want me to..." followed by the **bǎ** construction.

Fàn qǐng nǐ chīwán.

"Please eat up the food."

Nǐ shì bu shi yào wǒ bǎ fàn chīwán?

"You want me to eat up the food?"

Dōngxi qǐng nǐ fàngzai zhèli.

"Please put the stuff here."

Nǐ shì bu shi yào wǒ bǎ dōngxi fàngzai zhèli?

"You want me to put the stuff here?"

Diànnǎo qǐng nǐ bāndao nàr qù.

"Please move the computer over there."

Nǐ shì bu shi yào wǒ bǎ diànnǎo bāndao nàr qù?

"You want me to move the computer over there?"

Zhèige lǐwù qǐng nǐ sònggei tā.

"Please give this present to her."

Nǐ shì bu shi yào wǒ bǎ zhèige lǐwù sònggei tā?

"You want me to give her this present?"

Xíngli qǐng nǐ bānshang chēzi.

"Please put the luggage in the car."

Nǐ shì bu shi yào wǒ bǎ xíngli bānshang chēzi?

"You want me to put the luggage in the car?"

Chēzi qǐng nǐ jiāmǎn yóu.

"Please fill up the gas in the car."

Nǐ shì bu shi yào wǒ bǎ chēzi jiāmǎn yóu?

"You want me to fill up the gas in the car?"

Zhèizhāng báobǐng qǐng nǐ juǎnqilai.

"Please roll up this pancake."

Nǐ shì bu shi yào wǒ bǎ zhèizhāng báobǐng juǎnqilai?

"You want me to roll up this pancake?"

Zhèizhī yuánzhūbǐ qǐng nǐ nágei Xiǎo Wáng.

"Please give this ball-point pen to Little Wang."

Nǐ shì bu shi yào wǒ bǎ zhèizhī yuánzhūbǐ nágei Xiǎo Wáng?

"You want me to give this ball-point pen to Little Wang?"

Unit 15, Part 4: Transformation and Response Drills

1. Combine the two shorter sentences you hear into one longer sentence containing the pattern **chúle... zhīwài**.

Wǒ zhǐ yǒu nǐ zhèige péngyou. Wǒ méiyǒu biéde péngyǒu.

"I only have you as a friend. I don't have any other friends."

Wǒ chúle nǐ zhīwài, méiyǒu biéde péngyǒu.

"Except for you, I don't have any other friends."

Wǒ xǐhuan kǎoyā. Wǒ yě xǐhuan jiǎozi.

"I like roast duck. I also like dumplings."

Wǒ chúle kǎoyā zhīwài, yě xǐhuan jiǎozi.

"Besides roast duck, I also like dumplings."

Tā ài tāde xiānsheng. Tā yě ài tāde nánpéngyou.

"She loves her husband. She also loves her boyfriend."

Tā chúle ài tāde xiānsheng zhīwài, yě ài tāde nánpéngyou.

"Besides loving her husband, she also loves her boyfriend."

Tā zhǐ chīdeguàn Táiwān cài. Qítāde cài tā chībuguàn.

"He's only used to eating Taiwanese food. He's not used to eating any other food."

Tā chúle Táiwān cài zhīwài, qítāde cài dōu chībuguàn.

"Aside from Taiwanese food, he's not used to eating any other food."

Nǐ tiāntiān shuìjiào. Nǐ hái huì zuò shémme shì?

"You sleep every day. What else can you do?"

Nǐ tiāntiān chúle shuìjiào zhīwài, hái huì zuò shémme shì?

"Aside from sleeping every day, what else can you do?"

Xiǎo Zhāng zhōumò hē jiǔ. Tā qítā shíhou dōu bù hē jiǔ.

"Little Zhang drinks on weekends. The rest of the time he doesn't drink."

Xiǎo Zhāng chúle zhōumò hē jiǔ zhīwài, qítā shíhou tā dōu bù hē jiǔ.

"Except for drinking on weekends, Little Zhang doesn't drink the rest of the time."

2. Combine the two shorter sentences you hear into a longer sentence containing the pattern **chúle... yǐwài**.

Táiwān hěn rè. Táiwān yě hěn cháoshī.

"Taiwan is very hot. Taiwan is also very humid."

Táiwān chúle hěn rè yǐwài, yě hěn cháoshī.

"Besides being very hot, Taiwan is also very humid."

Lǎo Lín hěn bèn. Lǎo Lín yě hěn lǎn.

"Old Lin is very stupid. Old Lin is also very lazy."

Lǎo Lín chúle hěn bèn yǐwài, yě hěn lǎn.

"Aside from being very stupid, Old Lin is also very lazy."

Wǒ děi zhàogu wǒ fùmǔ. Wǒ yě děi zhàogu wǒ dìdi.

"I have to take care of my parents. I also have to take care of my younger brother."

Wǒ chúle děi zhàogu wǒ fùmǔ yǐwài, yě děi zhàogu wǒ dìdi.

"Besides having to take care of my parents, I also have to take care of my younger brother."

Zàizuòde yǒu wǒde tóngshì. Zàizuòde yě yǒu wǒde péngyou.

"Those present include my colleagues. Those present also include my friends."

Zàizuòde chúle yǒu wǒde tóngshì yǐwài, yě yǒu wǒde péngyou.

"Besides my colleagues, those present also include my friends."

Zhèitàng huǒchē dào Táizhōng. Zhèitàng huǒchē yě dào Táinán.

"This train goes to Taizhong. This train also goes to Tainan."

Zhèitàng huǒchē chúle dào Táizhōng yǐwài, yě dào Táinán.

"Besides going to Taizhong, this train also goes to Tainan."

Zhèizhāng báobǐng lǐmiàn kéyi fàng kǎoyā. Zhèizhāng báobǐng lǐmiàn yě kéyi fàng cōng gēn tiánmiànjiàng shemmede.

"You can put roast duck in this pancake. You can also put scallions, sweet flour sauce, and so on in this pancake."

Zhèizhāng báobǐng lǐmiàn chúle kéyi fàng kǎoyā yǐwài, yě kéyi fàng cōng gēn tiánmiànjiàng shemmede.

"Aside from putting roast duck in this pancake, you can also put in scallions, sweet flour sauce, and so on."

3. Transform the two separate clauses that you hear into a longer sentence that uses **-de** to indicate extent.

Wǒ nèmme máng, wǒ méi shíjiān chīfàn.

"I'm that busy, I don't have time to eat."

Wǒ mángde méi shíjiān chīfàn.

"I'm so busy I don't have time to eat."

Wǒ nèmme lèi, wǒ bù xiǎng dòng.

"I'm that tired, I don't want to move."

Wǒ lèide bù xiǎng dòng.

"I'm so tired I don't want to move."

Tā nèmme jǐnzhāng, tā shuōbuchū huà lái.

"He's that nervous, he can't speak."

Tā jǐnzhāngde shuōbuchū huà lái.

"He's so nervous he can't speak."

Xiǎo Lín nèmme gāoxìng, tā shuìbuzháo jiào.

"Little Lin is that happy, he can't fall asleep."

Xiǎo Lín gāoxìngde shuìbuzháo jiào.

"Little Lin is so happy he can't fall asleep."

Zhèijiàn xíngli nèmme zhòng, méiyou rén néng bāndedòng.

"This piece of luggage is that heavy, no one is able to move it."

Zhèijiàn xíngli zhòngde méiyou rén néng bāndedòng.

"This piece of luggage is so heavy no one is able to move it."

Nǐ nèmme cōngming, nǐ shémme dōu xuédehuì.

"You're that smart, you can learn anything."

Nǐ cōngmingde shémme dōu xuédehuì.

"You're so smart you can learn anything."

For the remaining pages of Transformation and Response Drills (**Unit 16, Part 1** through **Unit 24, Part 4**), please refer to the disc.

4. Role Play Exercises

Unit 11, Part 1: Role Play Exercises

Practice these role plays in Chinese to improve your spoken fluency.

1. A: To the Beijing Zoo.

    B: O.K. *(after a while)* Your Chinese is pretty good. Where did you learn it?

    A: I studied it in America at ___ College/University.

    B: So how long have you been in Beijing?

    A: I've been here for a little over a month.

    (switch to another pair of students)

    A: You're driving too fast, this is terrifying! Please drive a little slower, O.K.?

    B: No problem, relax! *(after a while)* Beijing Zoo is up front there.

    A: How much is it?

    B: 29 RMB.

    A: Here's 30 RMB. You don't need to make change.

2. A: To the Hilton (**Xī'ěrdūn**) Hotel.

    B: O.K. *(after a while)* You speak Mandarin pretty well! Where did you learn it?

    A: My Mandarin isn't very good. I studied it in America, mainland China, and Taiwan. Do you speak English?

    B: I only know a little. So how long have you been in Taipei?

    A: I've been here for a little over a week.

    (switch to another pair of students)

    A: Could you please drive a little faster? I definitely have to get to the Hilton Hotel before 5:00, but I'm afraid I won't make it on time.

    B: No problem, relax! *(after a while)* It's up ahead.

    A: *(cab arrives at the Hilton Hotel)* How much is it?

    B: 131 NT.

    A: Here's 135 NT. You don't need to make change.

3. A: To the Summer Palace.

    B: O.K. *(after a while)* You speak Mandarin quite well. Where did you learn it?

    A: I studied it both in America, Taiwan, and in mainland China.

    B: So how long have you been in Beijing?

    A: I've been here for a little over a year.

    (switch to another pair of students)

    A: *(after a while)* You're driving too fast, this is scary! Please drive a little slower, O.K.?

    B: No problem, relax! *(after a while)* O.K., this is the Summer Palace!

    A: How much is it?

    B: 48.50 RMB.

    A: Here's 50 RMB, you don't need to make change.

. . . .

Unit 11, Part 2: Role Play Exercises

Practice these role plays in Chinese to improve your spoken fluency.

1. A: Excuse me, how do you get to the Bank of Taiwan?

    B: Oh dear, I haven't gone for a long time, I'm also not very clear.

    A: Can one take the bus?

    B: Of course you can take the bus. Otherwise, you can also take the MRT. Go to the 7-Eleven across the street and ask.

    (switch to another pair of students)

    A: Excuse me, I want to take the bus to Bank of Taiwan. I should take what number?

    B: 235 or 556 both can be taken.

    A: About how often is there a bus?

    B: 556 takes longer. For 235, it seems every ten minutes there is a run, very quick.

    (switch to another pair of students)

    A: Thank you. Then while I'm at it, I'll buy a 500 dollar stored-value ticket.

    B: Oh, it's embarrassing. The 500 dollar ones are sold out. Only 100-dollar ones are left.

    A: In that case, I'll buy five 100-dollar ones.

    B: All right. In all that's 500 dollars. Thanks. Goodbye.

2. A: To the Bank of America.

    B: O.K. *(after a while)* Your Mandarin is pretty good. I haven't heard a foreigner speak such good Chinese for a long time! Where did you learn your Mandarin?

    A: I don't speak it well. I studied it on the mainland for half a year.

    B: So how long have you been in Taiwan?

    (switch to another pair of students)

    A: I've been here for a little over two weeks. *(after a while)* Yikes, you're driving way too fast! Slow down a little, all right?

    B: No problem, relax! *(after a while)* O.K., Bank of Taiwan has arrived.

    A: How much is it?

    B: 285 NT.

    A: I'm embarrassed, I only have a 1,000 NT bill.

    B: Sorry, I have no way to make change for you. Ask at that company across the street.

    A: O.K. Please wait.

3. A: Excuse me, to get to Muzha, what number bus does one take?

    B: I'm embarrassed, I haven't taken a bus for 2 or 3 years, I don't know either. Go to that company across the street and ask.

    A: O.K., thank you.

    B: You're welcome.

4. A: I'll buy two big ones and four small ones.

    B: Oh, I'm embarrassed, the big ones are all sold out. Only small ones are left.

    A: Never mind, then I'll buy six small ones. How much is that in all?

    B: 120 dollars.

    A: O.K., here's 120 dollars.

Unit 11, Part 3: Role Play Exercises

Practice these role plays in Chinese to improve your spoken fluency.

1. A: *(on the telephone)* Hello?

    B: Hello? Old (other student's last name), I'm Little (your own last name). I tell you,
    I've been driving ("turning") all over the place, and no matter how hard I look, I can't find your home.

    A: Where are you now?

    B: I'm at the entrance to the Bank of China, calling you on a public telephone.

    (switch to another pair of students)

    A: O.K., I tell you, you continue going toward the left.

    B: You say continue going toward the right?

    A: No, continue going toward the left. About a hundred meters and you will see a furniture store.

    B: You say about a hundred meters, I'll see a…what?

    A: A furniture store! The store is not too big, pay attention. In back of that furniture store, the second
    building on the 5th floor, that's my home.

    B: O.K., I know now. Thanks! See you in a little while.

    A: See you in a little while...

2. A: *(on the telephone)* Hello?

    B: Hello? Little (use other student's last name), I'm Old (use your own last name). I tell you, I've been
    looking all over the place, and no matter how hard I look, I can't find your home.

    A: Where are you now?

    B: I'm at the entrance to the post office, calling you on a public telephone.

    (switch to another pair of students)

    A: O.K., I tell you, across from the post office is a public toilet. Did you see it?

    B: Yes, I saw it. Little (use other student's last name), your home is next to the public toilet?

    A: Of course it isn't! But to the right of the public toilet is a 7-Eleven, right? In back of the 7-Eleven is a
    lane. Turning in from that lane, the third building on the left-hand side, 2nd floor, is our home.

    B: O.K., I get it. Thanks! See you soon.

3. A: *(on the telephone)* Hello?

    B: Hello? Old (use other student's last name), I'm Little (use your own last name). I tell you, I've been
    walking back and forth, and no matter how hard I search, I just can't find that bank you were talking
    about. Where is it?

    A: O.K., relax, I'll tell you. You know where Beijing Zoo is, right? Keep walking toward the zoo. About
    150 meters and you'll see a furniture store. The furniture store isn't very large, pay a little attention,
    don't miss it. Across from the furniture store is a post office. Behind the post office is the bank. Now
    you're clear, I suppose?

    B: Now I'm clear, too clear. Thank you. See you tomorrow!

    A: See you tomorrow...

Unit 11, Part 4: Role Play Exercises

Practice these role plays in Chinese to improve your spoken fluency.

1. A: Welcome (to our establishment)! Excuse me, what kind of gas do you want to add?

   B: 95. Thirty liters—uh, I think on reflection it might still be better to just fill it up.

   A: O.K., no problem. Please take a look, it's now starting from zero, right? All right, in all that's 625 dollars.

   B: This is 1,000 dollars.

   (switch to another pair of students)

   A: Excuse me, your unified serial number is...

   B: It's not necessary.

   A: Not necessary?

   B: Yes, it's not necessary.

   (switch to another pair of students)

   A: O.K. I'll give you back 375 dollars in change. Thank you!

   B: Thank you! Oh, yes, I've heard that the price of gas is going to go up again?

   A: Yeah. Starting next Monday, the price of gas is going to be adjusted again, so the number of cars tanking up today is especially many. Look, they've formed a huge line!

   B: Darn it! What is one to do?

2. A: Welcome (to our establishment)! Excuse me, what kind of gas do you want to add?

   B: 98. Ten—uh, I think on reflection it might still be better to just fill it up.

   A: You want to fill it up? O.K., no problem. Please take a look, it's now starting from zero. All right, in all that's 435 dollars.

   B: This is 500 dollars.

   A: Thank you.

   (switch to another pair of students)

   A: Excuse me, your unified serial number is...

   B: 23235599.

   A: O.K. I'll give you back 65 dollars in change. Thank you!

   B: Thank you. It seems starting from tomorrow, the price of gas is going to go up again?

   A: Actually, the price of gas was already adjusted this morning.

   B: Dang it! What is one to do?

3. A: I heard that the price of gas is going to increase again?

   B: Yeah, that's right.

   A: Right now one liter is how much?

   B: Right now one liter is 31 dollars. Starting March 1, one liter is 32 dollars.

   A: Rats! What is one to do?

4. A: Teacher Zhang, the class time for First-year Chinese must be adjusted!

   B: School Director, you say the class time for First-year Chinese will be adjusted again?

   A: Yes, from the 1st of next month, First-year Chinese will start every day at 7:00 A.M.

   B: I'm afraid...I'm afraid the students aren't going to like it.

   A: I think you're the one who doesn't like it!

Unit 12, Part 1: Role Play Exercises

Practice these role plays in Chinese to improve your spoken fluency.

1. A: Ice pops, ice pops! A dollar each.

   B: I'll buy two.

   A: Red bean or cream?

   B: One of each.

   A: That'll be two dollars in all.

   B: O.K., here's ten dollars.

   A: And here's eight dollars in change. Hold on tight!

2. A: Ice pops, ice pops! Three dollars each.

   B: I'll buy five.

   A: Cream or red bean?

   B: Two cream ones, and three red bean ones.

   A: That'll be fifteen dollars in all.

   B: O.K., here's twenty dollars.

   A: And here's five dollars in change. Hold it well!

3. A: Book bags, book bags! Thirty dollars each.

   B: I'll buy two.

   A: Blue or green?

   B: One blue one and one green one.

   A: That'll be sixty dollars in all.

   B: O.K., here's a hundred dollars.

   A: And here's forty dollars in change. Hold on tight!

4. A: What's your major?

   B: My major is Chinese. What's your major?

   A: My major is economics. (**jīngjì**)

5. A: What's your major?

   B: My major is Japanese. What's your major?

   A: My major is biology. (**shēngwù**)

6. A: What's your major?

   B: My major is English. What's your major?

   A: I haven't yet decided my major.

7. A: What's your major?

   B: I haven't yet decided my major. How about you?

   A: I also haven't yet decided my major.

8. A: I'm studying in the Economics Department. What department are you studying in?

   B: I'm studying in the Biology Department. I like biology very much!

. . . .

Unit 12, Part 2: Role Play Exercises

Practice these role plays in Chinese to improve your spoken fluency.

1. A: This American friend wants to try out that kind of ball-point pen. Is that O.K.?

    B: Sure. Does she want a black one, a blue one, or a green one?

    A: I'll ask her. *(after a few seconds)* She wants a black one. How much are they each?

    B: Ten dollars each.

    A: Are there cheaper ones?

    B: There are. This kind is eight dollars each, and that kind is five dollars each.

    A: O.K., I'll tell her. *(after a few seconds)* She says she wants to buy three of them.

2. A: I want to buy a map of Xi'an. Do you have any?

    B: Yes, we do. How is this kind?

    A: Do you have any bigger ones?

    B: We do. How is that kind?

    (switch to another pair of students)

    A: That kind is fine. How much are those maps each?

    B: 25 dollars each. How many do you want?

    A: Two. My friend also wants one.

    B: Would you like something else?

    A: I also want to buy a good Chinese-English dictionary and a newspaper.

    B: Sorry, we don't sell these things here. You can go to the bookstore next door to buy them.

3. A: I'd like to buy a newspaper, two notebooks, and an English-Chinese dictionary.

    B: Notebooks, we have blue, red, and green ones. What color do you want?

    A: I'd like to buy a red-colored notebook. How much are notebooks each?

    B: 12 dollars each. O.K., in all that's 96 dollars.

    A: Here's 100 dollars.

    B: And here's 4 dollars in change. Hold on to it well.

    A: Thank you. Goodbye!

4. A: I want to buy a good ball-point pen. Do you have any?

    B: I'm sorry, we don't sell ball-point pens.

    A: Oh, you don't sell ball-point pens? Well, then, do you sell writing brushes?

    B: Yes, we do sell writing brushes. Do you want big ones or small ones?

    A: Small ones.

    (switch to another pair of students)

    B: How is this kind of writing brush?

    A: That kind looks pretty good. Could I try it?

    B: Of course you can.

    A: How much are these writing brushes each?

    B: 20 dollars each, or three for 50 dollars.

    A: Then I'll buy three.

    B: All right, in all that's 50 dollars.

    A: Here's the money.

Unit 12, Part 3: Role Play Exercises

Practice these role plays in Chinese to improve your spoken fluency.

1. A: Sir, how much are the green peppers?

    B: 55 dollars per catty. Look, they're both big and crisp!

    A: How come they're so expensive?

    B: They're imported from Japan and better than those from Taiwan.

    A: Are they fresh?

    B: I guarantee that they're very fresh.

    (switch to another pair of students)

    A: I'll take three catties of green peppers.

    B: Would you like something else?

    A: Not today. I'll just buy the green peppers.

    B: All right. In all that's 165 dollars.

    A: Here's 200 dollars.

    B: And here's 35 dollars in change. Thanks! Come again.

2. A: How much is the cabbage?

    B: 20 dollars for half a catty. Look, it's both big and fresh!

    A: How come it's so expensive?

    B: It only arrived yesterday. It's imported from America and bigger than that from China.

    A: Is it really fresh?

    B: I guarantee that it's very fresh.

    (switch to another pair of students)

    A: O.K., I'll take two catties of cabbage.

    B: Would you like something else? Today tomatoes are also pretty good.

    A: Not today. I'll just buy the cabbage.

    B: That's 40 dollars.

    A: Here's 100 dollars.

    B: And here's 60 dollars in change. Thank you! Come again.

3. A: How much is the celery?

    B: 65 dollars per catty. Look, it's both big and crisp!

    A: How come it's so expensive?

    B: It only arrived this morning. This celery is imported from South Korea and it tastes better than that from Taiwan.

    A: O.K., I'll take two catties.

    B: All right. Would you like something else?

    (switch to another pair of students)

    A: What other green vegetables do you have?

    B: We have green peppers, cabbage, lettuce, and tomatoes. What would you like?

    A: How much are the tomatoes per catty?

    B: 90 dollars per catty. They're both big and fresh.

    A: I think...I think today I'll just buy the celery. Here's 200 dollars.

    B: And here's 70 dollars in change. Thanks! Come again.

. . . .

Unit 12, Part 4: Role Play Exercises

Practice these role plays in Chinese to improve your spoken fluency.

1. A: Please weigh out for me a catty of bananas. Pick out fresher ones.

    B: Do you want the ¥ 2.00 per catty ones or the ¥ 3.00 per catty ones?

    A: I want the ¥ 3.00 per catty ones.

    B: The ¥ 3.00 ones are much bigger than the ¥ 2.00 ones. Do you want anything else? How about buying some Ya pears?

    (switch to another pair of students)

    A: How much are the Ya pears per catty?

    B: They're ¥ 5.00 per catty.

    A: Why don't you give me two catties. How much is that in all?

    B: In all it's ¥ 13.00.

    A: This is ¥ 20.00. The bananas and the Ya pears, please wrap them up for me.

    B: O.K., no problem. I'll give you ¥ 7.00 in change. Please count it.

2. A: Please weigh out for me a catty of apples. Pick out fresher ones.

    B: Do you want the ¥ 4.00 per catty ones or the ¥ 6.00 per catty ones?

    A: I want the ¥ 6.00 per catty ones.

    B: The ¥ 6.00 ones taste much better than the ¥ 4.00 ones. Do you want anything else?

    (switch to another pair of students)

    A: What other fruit is there?

    B: There are oranges, peaches, and grapes.

    A: How much are the grapes per catty?

    B: They're ¥ 20.00 per catty.

    A: How come they're so expensive?

    B: They just arrived today. They're imported from Japan, and both look nice and taste good.

    (switch to another pair of students)

    A: Why don't you give me one catty. How much is that in all?

    B: In all it's ¥ 26.00.

    A: This is ¥ 30.00. The apples and the grapes, please wrap them up for me.

    B: O.K., no problem. I'll give you ¥ 4.00 in change. Please count it.

    A: All right, thank you. Goodbye.

3. A: Hey, I heard that when Mrs. Zhang was young, she was very poor.

    B: I heard that also. But about 10 years ago, she opened a factory, and now she's very rich.

4. A: Those people, can you see them?

    B: What people? It's too far, I can't see them.

5. A: Little Chen, can you hear?

    B: What? What? I can't hear!

6. A: I want you to go out! Did you hear?

    B: I heard. All right, I'll go out, I'll go out. Don't get angry, don't get angry!

Unit 13, Part 1: Role Play Exercises

Practice these role plays in Chinese to improve your spoken fluency.

1. A: Please weigh out ¥20 worth of mutton for me.

    B: Uh-huh.

    A: That mutton over there is leaner, why don't you cut that over there for me.

    B: Actually, it's all about the same. Do you want anything else?

    (switch to another pair of students)

    A: No, I don't. Just this, I guess. I'll give you ¥50.

    B: And I'll give you ¥30 in change.

    A: Oh, excuse me, here in the vicinity is there a grocery store?

    B: There is. In the vicinity there's a grocery store and a bakery.

    (switch to another pair of students)

    A: Is the grocery store far away?

    B: It's extremely close, not far away at all. It's right in the next alley.

    A: Thank you.

    B: You're welcome.

2. A: Please weigh out ¥50 worth of beef for me.

    B: Uh-huh.

    A: That beef over there is too fat. This beef is leaner, cut this over here for me.

    B: Actually, it's all about the same. Do you want anything else?

    (switch to another pair of students)

    A: Do you have chicken meat or duck meat?

    B: Chicken meat and duck meat, we here don't sell.

    A: O.K., never mind. I'll give you the money. This is ¥100.

    B: I'll give you ¥50 in change.

    A: Thank you, goodbye.

3. A: Do you like to eat pork or beef?

    B: I don't eat meat; I'm a vegetarian.

    A: Meat, you don't even eat a little?

    B: I don't even eat a little. I've been a vegetarian since I was 16 years old.

4. A: Have some more of this food!

    B: I'm sorry, I can't eat fish and shrimp, I can't eat even a little.

    A: Sorry, I didn't know!

5. A: Is there a post office in the vicinity?

    B: There is. It's extremely close, not at all far away.

6. A: Are there gas stations or banks in the vicinity?

    B: There is a gas station in the vicinity. It's extremely close, not at all far away. But there is no bank in the vicinity.

. . . .

Unit 13, Part 2: Role Play Exercises

Practice these role plays in Chinese to improve your spoken fluency.

1. A: I'm going to the supermarket to buy some things. Do you want to go together with me?

   B: O.K. I also was just thinking of buying some meat, vegetables, fruit, and so on.

   A: Let's do this: In order to save time, you buy your stuff, I'll buy my stuff, and in 10 minutes, we'll see each other at the counter by the exit. How would that be?

   B: Good idea! See you in a little while!

2. A: I'm going to the supermarket to buy some things. Do you want to go together with me?

   B: All right. I also was just thinking of buying some bread, fruit, coffee and so on.

   A: Let's do this: In order to save time, you buy your stuff, I'll buy my stuff, and in 15 minutes, we'll meet at the counter by the exit. How would that be?

   B: Good idea! See you in a little while.

   A: See you in a little while.

3. A: I'm going to the supermarket to buy some things. Do you want to go together with me?

   B: O.K. I also was just thinking of buying some beef, shrimp, apples, oranges and so on.

   A: Let's do this: In order to save time, you buy your stuff, I'll buy my stuff, and in half an hour, we'll meet each other at the counter by the exit, how would that be?

   B: Or how would this be: When I have finished buying, I'll go looking for you, O.K.?

   A: That also would be O.K.

   B: Let's go!

4. A: How do you feel gas stations in China compare with those in America?

   B: They're all about the same. The Chinese ones are probably a bit smaller than the American ones, and they're not so widespread as in America.

   A: It's possible that it must come slowly. I think in the future they're likely to be more widespread each year.

   B: Right. It is like this.

5. A: How do you feel Little Li's English compares with Old Wang's?

   B: Old Wang's English is probably a bit better than Little Li's, but they're both about the same.

   A: Little Li is very diligent. I think in the future her English will become better every day.

6. A: How do you feel your English compares with my Chinese?

   B: Your Chinese is a lot better than my English!

   A: Actually, I think they're both about the same.

   B: But you're so diligent, I think in the future your Chinese will become better every day.

   A: Not at all! You're more diligent than I am. Your English is getting better day by day. In the future your English will be a lot better than my Chinese!

Unit 13, Part 3: Role Play Exercises

Practice these role plays in Chinese to improve your spoken fluency.

1. A: I want to buy a pair of shoes.

    B: What size do you wear?

    A: In America I wear size 11. I wonder if your sizes are the same as or different from American sizes?

    B: The sizes are different, but I can help you try some on and see. How is the size of this pair?

    (switch to another pair of students)

    A: They seem too big. Do you have any that are one size smaller?

    B: This pair is one size smaller, try it on.

    A: This pair is just right. How much does this pair sell for?

    B: ¥ 200.

    (switch to another pair of students)

    A: Hmm, they do look nice, but ¥ 200 is too expensive. Could you reduce the price a little?

    B: Sorry, they just came on the market, nothing I can do.

    A: Then I'll look around some more.

    B: O.K. If you need anything, you're welcome to come again.

    A: All right, thank you. Goodbye!

2. A: I want to buy a pair of white shoes.

    B: What size do you wear?

    A: In America I wear size 7. I wonder if your sizes are the same as or different from American sizes?

    B: The sizes are different, but I can help you try some on and see. How is the size of this pair?

    (switch to another pair of students)

    A: They seem too small. Do you have any that are one size bigger?

    B: This pair is one size bigger, size 8. Try it on.

    A: This pair is just right. How much does this pair sell for?

    B: 3,000 NT.

    A: Hmm, they do look nice, but 3,000 NT is too expensive. Could you reduce the price a little?

    B: They just came on the market, nothing I can do.

    A: Never mind, then I'll look around some more.

    (switch to another pair of students)

    B: Please wait a minute. I'll go ask the manager. *(after a short while)* The manager says because you're a friend from America, 2,500 NT and it'll be fine.

    A: Good, 2,500 NT, that's O.K. Oh, that's right, I also need 3 pairs of socks. Do you have black socks?

    B: Yes, we have black socks. One pair is 100 NT, 3 pairs are 250 NT. So in all 2,750 NT.

    A: All right, I'll give you the money.

    B: Thank you. I'll wrap it up for you. O.K., I'll give you the shoes and socks. Goodbye!

. . . .

Unit 13, Part 4: Role Play Exercises

Practice these role plays in Chinese to improve your spoken fluency.

1. A: Store proprietor, do you have long pants that little girls wear?

    B: Yes, please come over and take a look. How old is the child?

    A: She's nine, almost ten.

    B: Size eight should be no problem. Take a look at this pair.

    (switch to another pair of students)

    A: The color is fine, but I wonder if they're going to be too big or too small?

    B: It doesn't matter. If they don't fit, you can bring them here within 10 days for exchange.

    A: How much are they?

    B: These pants originally were ￥100 per pair. This week they just happen to be 20% off, only ￥80 per pair.

    (switch to another pair of students)

    A: All right, I'll buy this pair. Can I use a credit card?

    B: Of course you may use a credit card.

    A: All right, here's my credit card.

    B: Just a minute, please. All right, the receipt is inside. Thank you! Please come again.

    A: Thank you. Goodbye.

2. A: Sir, do you sell short pants that little boys wear?

    B: Yes, please come over and take a look. How old is the child?

    A: He's eleven, almost twelve.

    B: Size ten should be no problem. What color would you like?

    (switch to another pair of students)

    A: Do you have blue-colored short pants?

    B: Yes, we do. This pair is blue-colored. This is size ten. Take a look at this pair and see how it is.

    A: The color is fine, but I wonder if they're going to be too big or too small?

    B: Never mind. If they don't fit, you can bring them here within a month for exchange.

    (switch to another pair of students)

    A: How much is this pair of short pants?

    B: These short pants originally were 300 NT per pair. Today they just happen to be 30% off, only 210 NT.

    A: All right, I'll buy two pairs. Oh, that's right, do you have shirts that children wear?

    B: Ordinarily we do but it just happens that we sold out yesterday.

    A: O.K., never mind, then I'll just buy the pants. Can I use a credit card?

    B: I'm sorry, we don't accept credit cards.

    (switch to another pair of students)

    A: O.K., then I'll give you cash. This is 1,000 NT.

    B: All right, just a minute, please. O.K., here's 400 NT in change.

    A: Didn't you say 210 NT per pair? Two pairs ought to be 420 NT, right?

    B: Oh, I'm embarrassed, I got it wrong. What you say is correct. Two pairs are 420 NT in all. I'll give you 580 NT in change. The receipt is inside. Thank you! Please come again.

Unit 14, Part 1: Role Play Exercises

Practice these role plays in Chinese to improve your spoken fluency.

1. A: Little (surname of B), which restaurant do you think we should eat at?

   B: As you like, any one is fine.

   A: This one has few people, why don't we eat here.

   B: O.K., no problem. Let's go in...

   (switch to another pair of students)

   A: Little (surname of B), you look at the menu first; see what you'd like to eat.

   B: Anything's fine. Why don't you order.

   C: What would the two of you like to eat?

   A: One Pockmarked Old Woman's Tofu and one Ants Climb Trees.

   C: Anything else?

   B: Can we order a bowl of rice?

   A: One bowl of rice is not enough. Bring two bowls of rice. That's about it.

   C: O.K., please wait just a little while.

2. A: Old (surname of B), which restaurant do you think we should eat at?

   B: As you like, any restaurant is fine.

   A: That one has many people, the food is definitely good. Why don't we eat there.

   B: O.K., no problem. You go in first...

   (switch to another pair of students)

   B: I'd like to use the bathroom. Where is the bathroom?

   C: You speak Chinese great! The bathroom is in the back.

   A: (after B returns) You look at the menu first; see what you'd like to eat.

   B: Anything's fine. Why don't you order.

   C: What dishes would the two of you like to order?

   A: One Fish Fragrant Meat Shreds and one Pockmarked Old Woman's Tofu. That's about it. And bring two bowls of egg soup.

   (switch to another pair of students)

   C: All right, one Fish Fragrant Meat Shreds, one Pockmarked Old Woman's Tofu, and two bowls of beef soup.

   A: It's not beef soup, it's egg soup.

   C: Oh, sorry, I got it wrong. Two bowls of egg soup.

   B: And also bring two bowls of rice. I really like to eat rice!

   A: Right, right, right. Two bowls of rice.

   B: *(after the food is brought out)* Little (surname of A), look, there's an ant in my soup!

3. A: Little (surname of B), do you know how to use chopsticks?

   B: Of course I can use chopsticks!

   A: *(after a while)* How come you're not eating?

   B: Do you think that...they here would have knife, fork, and spoon?

   A: I'm afraid this kind of restaurant doesn't have knife, fork, and spoon. Come, I'll teach you how to eat with chopsticks...

   B: It's embarrassing...

. . . .

Unit 14, Part 2: Role Play Exercises

Practice these role plays in Chinese to improve your spoken fluency.

1. A: For the Pockmarked Old Woman's Tofu don't put in too many hot peppers, I'm afraid my American friend wouldn't be able to stand it.

   B: It's O.K. if you put in a lot, I can eat hot spicy foods.

   C: All right. What do you want for your main food? Rice or steamed buns?

   A: Eight ounces of rice.

   B: I especially like to eat steamed buns.

   A: All right, then also bring four steamed buns.

   C: O.K., eight ounces of rice and four steamed buns. What would you like to drink?

   (switch to another pair of students)

   A: Do you have beer here?

   C: Yes. There's Chinese beer, and there's imported beer.

   A: Then why don't you first bring us one bottle of Chinese beer, **Qīngdǎo** beer.

   C: O.K., no problem. One bottle of **Qīngdǎo** beer.

   A: That's all, I guess. We're in a great hurry, so please bring the food as fast as you can.

   C: O.K., no problem. You all wait just a little while.

   B: In the U.S., only when you've reached the age of 21 can you drink alcohol!

   A: I know. But here is China, it isn't the U.S.!

2. A: For the Pockmarked Old Woman's Tofu don't put in too many hot peppers, I'm afraid my American friend wouldn't be able to stand it.

   C: O.K., don't put in too many hot peppers. No problem.

   B: Actually, I can eat hot foods. Sour things, sweet things, bitter things, spicy things, and salty things, I can eat them all. But excuse me, does the Pockmarked Old Woman's Tofu have meat? I don't eat meat; I'm a vegetarian.

   C: I'm afraid it has meat in it, but it only has a little meat, not much.

   B: Then never mind, I can eat it.

   A: Also bring one order of Fish Fragrant Meat Shreds and one order of Ants Climb Trees. And also bring a large bowl of egg soup.

   C: All right. What do you want for your main food? Rice or steamed buns?

   A: Six steamed buns.

   (switch to another pair of students)

   B: I like to eat rice! Could we also eat some rice?

   A: O.K., then also bring eight ounces of rice.

   C: All right, six steamed buns and eight ounces of rice. What would you like to drink?

   A: Little (surname of B), can you drink beer? I've heard that in the U.S., only when you've reached the age of 21 can you drink alcohol.

   B: In May of this year I already became 21 years old.

   A: O.K., then why don't you first bring us one bottle of beer.

   B: Two bottles, O.K.?

   C: O.K., two bottles of beer, no problem.

   A: That's all, I guess. We're in a great hurry, so please bring the food as fast as you can.

   C: O.K., it'll be ready in 10 minutes.

Unit 14, Part 3: Role Play Exercises

Practice these role plays in Chinese to improve your spoken fluency.

1. A: Excuse me, I'd like to make a reservation for a banquet.

   B: When? For how many people?

   A: The fifth, Sunday, at 5:30 P.M. I reckon there will be about a dozen people attending.

   B: I think dividing into two tables would be best, what do you think?

   A: Actually, that's not necessary. One table can seat 12 people, so one table is enough.

   B: Oh, O.K., then one table.

   A: What price level do you plan to book? There are 50 yuan and 80 yuan per person ones. A little higher class, there are also 100 yuan and 150 yuan per person ones.

   B: Oh, I guess one at 50 yuan for each person.

2. A: Excuse me, I'd like to make a reservation for a banquet.

   B: When? For how many people?

   A: The 20th, Friday, at 6:30 P.M. I reckon there will be about thirty people attending.

   B: I think dividing into three tables would be best, what do you think?

   A: O.K., we'll divide into three tables.

   (switch to another pair of students)

   A: How much is one table?

   B: What price level do you plan to book? There are 100 yuan and 120 yuan per person ones. A little higher class, there are also 150 yuan and 200 yuan per person ones.

   A: Oh, I guess the best one, the one at 200 yuan per person.

   B: O.K., no problem. Thirty people. Friday, April 20, 6:30 P.M. What is your name and phone number?

   A: My last name is Zhang. My phone number is 2393-9439.

   B: All right, thank you Mr./Ms. Zhang. See you April 20!

3. A: Oh, Old (surname of B), do you know how to cook?

   B: Of course I know how to cook!

   A: Where did you learn?

   B: My mother taught me. Do you know how to cook?

   A: I can cook Western-style food, but I don't know how to cook Chinese-style food.

   B: Then I'll teach you how to cook Chinese food.

   A: And I can teach you how to cook Western-style food.

   B: Fantastic!

4. A: Little (surname of B), do you know how to cook Chinese food?

   B: Chinese food, Western food, I know how to cook both of them!

   A: That's great! Can you cook for me this evening?

   B: Of course I can. Do you feel like eating Chinese food or Western food?

   A: Tonight make Chinese food for me. Tomorrow night make Western food for me, O.K.?

   B: All right, tonight I'll make Chinese food for you. But I think tomorrow night you should cook!

Unit 14, Part 4: Role Play Exercises

Practice these role plays in Chinese to improve your spoken fluency.

1. A: Will you order the dishes yourself, or should they be arranged by us?

   B: I'm not very familiar with your Sichuan cuisine; it might be better if you arranged it for us.

   A: All right. Two cold dishes, six hot dishes, two soups, and a dessert. Will that do?

   B: That sounds very good, thank you.

   A: Please leave your name, address, and phone number, so that we can contact you, all right?

   B: All right, this is my name card. My name, address, and phone number are all on it. Much obliged!

   A: You're welcome.

2. A: Excuse me, will you order the dishes yourself, or should they be arranged by us?

   B: To tell the truth, I'm a foreigner, so I don't very much know how to order Chinese dishes. I'm also not very familiar with your Beijing cuisine, so it might be better if you arranged it for us.

   A: No problem. One cold dish, ten hot dishes, a soup, and a dessert. Will that do?

   B: I think one cold dish is too few; two cold dishes, all right?

   A: Of course that is fine. Please leave your name, address, and phone number, so that we can contact you.

   B: All right, this is my name card. Much obliged!

3. A: So will you order the dishes yourself, or should they be arranged by us?

   B: Actually, I'm not very familiar with your Guangdong cuisine; it might be better if you arranged it for us.

   A: All right. Ten cold dishes, twelve hot dishes, two soups, and two desserts. Will that do?

   B: I suppose that is too much! I think half of that would be about right.

   A: All right, then five cold dishes, six hot dishes, one soup, and one dessert, O.K.?

   B: Like that is very good, thank you.

   A: Please leave your name, address, and phone number, so that we can contact you.

   B: All right, this is my name card. My name, address, and phone number are all on it. Much obliged!

4. A: Do you know how to cook Chinese food?

   B: Of course I know how to cook Chinese food!

   A: What can you cook?

   B: I know how to make...fried rice. My fried rice is delicious!

   A: Fried rice? Anybody can make fried rice. You don't know how to make other things?

   B: Of course I know how to make other things.

   A: Well, then, what else can you make? Can you make Pockmarked Old Woman's Tofu, or Ants Climb Trees, or Fish Fragrant Meat Shreds?

   B: No, I can't. But I know how to make...fried noodles!

Unit 15, Part 1: Role Play Exercises

Practice these role plays in Chinese to improve your spoken fluency.

1. A: I'll first simply say a few words. Today all of us have gathered here for a meal to welcome Mr. and Mrs. Chen to our company to work. We wish them that their work here go smoothly and that their life be happy! Now let's show our respect and toast the two of them with a glass of wine!

   B: Thank you, everyone. We're very pleased to have the chance to come to China. At the same time, we also very much appreciate the help and care you've given us the past few weeks. I'm afraid in the future we'll still need to call on you frequently.

2. A: I'll first simply say a few words. Today all of us have gathered here for a meal to welcome Ms. Zhang to our company to work. We wish her that her work here go smoothly and that her life be happy! Now let's show our respect and toast her with a glass of wine!

   B: Thank you, everyone. I'm very pleased to have the chance to come to China. At the same time, I also very much appreciate the help and care you've given me the past few weeks. I'm afraid in the future I'll still need to call on you frequently.

3. A: I'll first simply say a few words. Today all of us have gathered here for a meal to welcome Mr. Bai to our company. We wish him that his work here go smoothly and that his life be happy! Now let's show our respect and toast him with a glass of wine!

   B: Thank you, everyone. I'm very pleased to have the chance to come to China. At the same time, I also very much appreciate the help and care you've given me the past few weeks. I'm afraid in the future I'll still need to call on you frequently.

4. A: Little Wang, I hear today is your birthday. I wish you birthday happiness!

   B: Actually, my birthday was yesterday, it's not today.

   A: Oh, sorry, I got it wrong!

   B: I still thank you.

5. A: Now I will toast you with a glass of wine!

   B: Thank you, but my health ("body") is not good, so I can't drink wine.

   A: Oh, sorry, I didn't know!

   B: It's O.K.

6. A: Can you cook Chinese food?

   B: I can make several simple dishes, like fried rice or fried noodles. And you?

   A: I can only make spaghetti. (**Yìdàlì miàn** "Italian noodles")

   B: That's also pretty good!

7. A: Excuse me, Teacher Li, what does this sentence mean?

   B: The meaning of this sentence is that any problem can be solved.

   A: Any problem can be solved? Oh, now I understand. Thank you!

   B: You're welcome!

Unit 15, Part 2: Role Play Exercises

Practice these role plays in Chinese to improve your spoken fluency.

1. A: I propose a toast to the health of the host and everyone here.

    B: Professor Smith, try this dish.

    A: Thank you, I'll help myself. Mmm, it tastes really good.

    B: Professor Smith, Mrs. Smith, let me drink a toast to the two of you. So how do you like eating Chinese food?

    (switch to another pair of students)

    A: We like to eat it very much. Come, let's also drink a toast to you!

    B: This is duck gizzard and liver. Do you like it?

    A: It's good. The more I eat, the better it tastes.

    B: Hey, the duck is here! Professor Smith, have you ever eaten roast duck before?

    A: Roast duck? I heard of it long ago, but have never eaten it before. This roast duck is really good...

2. A: I propose a toast to the health of the host and everyone here.

    B: Professor Mo, try this dish.

    A: Thank you, I'll help myself. Mmm, it tastes really good.

    B: Professor Mo, Mrs. Mo, let me drink a toast to the two of you. So how do you like eating American food?

    (switch to another pair of students)

    A: We like to eat it very much. Come, let's also drink a toast to you!

    B: This is French onion soup (**Fǎshì yángcōng tāng**). Do you like it?

    A: It's extremely good! The more I eat, the better it tastes.

    B: Hey, the steak (**niúpái**) is here! Professor Mo, have you ever eaten steak before?

    A: I heard of it long ago, but have never eaten it before. Mmm, it's very good!

3. A: I propose a toast to the health of the host and everyone here!

    B: General Manager, try this dish.

    A: Thank you, I'll help myself. Mmm, it tastes really good.

    B: General Manager, let me drink a toast to you. So do you like eating American food?

    (switch to another pair of students)

    A: I like to eat it very much. Come, I'll also drink a toast to you!

    B: This is vegetable soup. Do you like it?

    A: It's not bad. The more I eat, the better it tastes.

    B: Hey, the lobster (**lóngxiā**) is here! General Manager, have you ever eaten lobster before?

    A: I heard of it long ago, but have never eaten it before. Mmm, lobster is really very good!

4. A: Old (surname of B), cheers!

    B: Old (surname of A), cheers!

    A: Old (surname of B), look, I think the host and guests are all drunk.

    B: Old (surname of A), I think we're drunk too!

    A: I suppose you must be drunk. I'm not drunk.

Unit 15, Part 3: Role Play Exercises

Practice these role plays in Chinese to improve your spoken fluency.

1. A: Professor Vargas, you have to first take a pancake and spread the sweet flour sauce onto the pancake, then put on scallions, and after that put the duck meat in the middle.

   B: After that, you must roll up the pancake and then you can eat it.

   C: All right, let me try. Mmm, it's delicious!

   B: Professor Vargas, you're not eating enough. Have a little more of this dish!

   C: I've already had a lot. Don't only serve me food. You yourself eat, too!

   A: Professor Vargas, how come you're not eating anymore? Have some more!

   B: I've eaten too much, I really can't eat any more. There was so much food today! Very special thanks to our hosts and to everyone here.

2. A: General Manager, cheers!

   B: General Manager, cheers!

   C: General Manager, cheers!

   A: General Manager, you have to first take a pancake and spread the sweet flour sauce onto the pancake, then put on scallions, and after that put the duck meat in the middle. Roll up the pancake and you can eat it.

   (switch to another group of students)

   D: All right, let me try. Mmm, it's delicious!

   B: General Manager, you're not eating enough. Have a little more of this dish!

   D: I've already had a lot. Don't only serve me food. You yourself eat, too!

   C: General Manager, how come you're not eating anymore? Have some more!

   D: I've eaten too much, I really can't eat any more. There was so much food today! Very special thanks to our hosts and to everyone here.

3. A: I propose a toast to the health of the School President and everyone here.

   B: School President, cheers!

   C: School President, cheers!

   D: So, let me ask, what is the name of this dish?

   A: This dish is called "Beijing Roast Duck."

   B: School President, you have to first take a pancake and spread the sweet flour sauce onto the pancake, then put on scallions, and after that put the duck meat in the middle.

   C: And after that, you have to roll up the pancake and then you can eat it!

   (switch to another group of students)

   D: All right, let me try. Mmm, it's delicious!

   A: School President, you're not eating enough. Have a little more of this dish!

   D: I've already had a lot. Don't only serve me food. You yourself eat, too!

   C: School President, how come you're not eating anymore? Have some more!

   D: I've eaten too much, I really can't eat any more. There was so much food today! Very special thanks to our hosts and to everyone here.

4. A: It's winter now. This piece of clothing is too thin, that one is thicker. Wear that one.

   B: Relax! I'm not accustomed to wearing thick clothes. I like wearing thinner clothing.

Unit 15, Part 4: Role Play Exercises

Practice these role plays in Chinese to improve your spoken fluency.

1. A: Would you like to go to my place this weekend to eat dumplings?

   B: Of course I would. *(later)* These are the dumplings you mentioned? They're beautiful!

   A: This is the dumpling filling.

   B: What all is in it?

   A: It's mainly meat and cabbage. Besides these, there are also some condiments: scallions, ginger, soy sauce, salt and sesame oil.

   (switch to another pair of students)

   B: It smells real good! Could you boil a few dumplings first and let me taste them?

   A: Of course I can. I'll go boil them right now. *(later)* The dumplings are ready (**hǎole** "ready"). Please eat some, don't be polite.

   B: Wow, they're incredibly delicious!

   A: If they're good, have some more!

2. A: Would you like to go to our home tomorrow night to wrap dumplings?

   B: Of course I'd like to! *(later)* These are the dumplings you talked about? They're beautiful! What's this?

   A: This is the dumpling filling.

   B: What all is in it?

   A: It's mainly pork and cabbage. Besides the pork and cabbage, there are also some condiments: scallions, ginger, soy sauce, salt and sesame oil.

   (switch to another pair of students)

   B: It smells so good, I'm hungry. Could you boil a few first and let me taste them?

   A: Of course I can. I'll go boil them right now. *(later)* The dumplings are ready now. Please eat some, don't be polite.

   B: Wow, these dumplings are incredibly delicious!

   A: If they're good, have some more.

3. A: Would you like to go to my home tomorrow night to make dumplings?

   B: Of course I'd like to! *(later)* These are the dumplings you talked about? What's this?

   A: This is the dumpling filling.

   B: What all is in it?

   A: It's mainly beef and cabbage. Besides the beef and cabbage, there are also some condiments: scallions, ginger, soy sauce, salt and sesame oil.

   (switch to another pair of students)

   B: It smells real good! It smells so good, I'm hungry. Could you boil a few dumplings first and let me taste them?

   A: Of course I can. I'll go boil them right now. *(later)* The dumplings are ready now. Please eat some, don't be polite.

   B: Wow, these dumplings are incredibly delicious!

   A: If they're good, have some more. Oh, I'm embarrassed, I forgot to ask you. What would you like to drink? How about beer?

   B: O.K., beer will be fine. Thank you.

Unit 16, Part 1: Role Play Exercises

Practice these role plays in Chinese to improve your spoken fluency.

1. A: Hi, Tom! Have you eaten yet?

    B: Not yet. I just made up a class at my cram school. And you?

    A: I haven't eaten yet either. I'm very hungry. How about it? Do you want to go eat together?

    B: Sure!

    (switch to another group of students)

    C: Welcome! How many?

    A: Two. ... How's the beef? Is it good?

    B: It's quite tasty, it's just that it's a little tough. How do you feel the fish is?

    A: The fish is quite tender. ... The check, please.

    C: O.K., please wait a minute.

    (switch to another pair of students)

    B: How much is it? I'll pay.

    A: No, today I'm treating.

    B: Come on, let me pay.

    A: Oh, don't be polite. It's only a simple meal.

    B: How embarrassing to let you go to such expense. Next time I'll be the host!

2. A: What did you do just now?

    B: I just made up a class.

    A: Which class was it?

    B: French. How about you? What did you just do?

    A: I had a meal.

    B: How was the food?

    A: Not too bad. I ate fish, it was quite tender, it's just that there were too many bones. But the server was really handsome...

    B: I only asked you how the food was.

    A: I'm joking around with you!

3. A: Today I'm treating!

    B: That's embarrassing. Last time you already treated.

    A: It doesn't matter. How do you feel the chicken is?

    B: The chicken is very tough, and it's a little too spicy hot.

    A: Really? How about the fish?

    B: I'm afraid this fish is also not very good to eat.

    (switch to another group of students)

    A: Really? The fish is also not very good to eat? Why?

    B: This fish has too many fish bones. Excuse me, I'm going to the bathroom for a minute...

    A: Some other day I'll invite you to my house for a meal. The dishes my mother makes are all too delicious. Server, the bill!

    C: This (lady/gentleman) has already paid.

    A: What? You've already paid? Oh, that's embarrassing, that's embarrassing!

. . . .

Unit 16, Part 2: Role Play Exercises

Practice these role plays in Chinese to improve your spoken fluency.

1. A: Today we're having a welcome dinner for Old Wang. Welcome back to America! Those present are all old friends. Come, let's toast Old Wang!

   B: Thank you, I really don't dare accept this honor.

   C: Old Wang, come, here's to you! Bottoms up, O.K.?

   B: I'm not much of a drinker. You drink bottoms up, I'll just have a little.

   C: Hey, your capacity for drinking is limitless. Come on, bottoms up!

   B: It's better to obey than to show respect. So I'll drink bottoms up first to show my respect!

   A: Wow, Old Wang, your capacity really is limitless!

2. A: This evening we're having a welcome dinner for Teacher Smith. Welcome back to China! Those present are all old friends. Come, let's toast Teacher Smith!

   B: Thank you, I really don't dare accept this honor.

   C: Teacher Smith, come, here's to you! Bottoms up, O.K.?

   B: I'm not much of a drinker. You drink bottoms up, I'll just have a little.

   C: Hey, your capacity is limitless. Come on, bottoms up!

   B: It's better to obey than to show respect. So I'll drink bottoms up first to show my respect!

   A: Wow, Teacher Smith, your capacity really is limitless!

3. A: This is Little Li, his alcohol drinking capacity is limitless.

   B: Yes, I have a limitless capacity. Here, bottoms up!

   A: To show respect is not as good as following orders. So I'll drink bottoms up, too.

   B. Drink one more glass!

   A: O.K., no problem. Bottoms up!

   B: You've already had more than 10 glasses. You have a limitless capacity too!

   A: Yes, when I was in college, I was very good at drinking, but now I haven't drunk liquor for a long time...

4. A: I can't see. Is that the ocean?

   B: It's not the ocean, it's a lake.

   A: Is it a lake or a river?

   B: No, it's not a river, it's a lake. It really is a lake.

   A: You say it's a lake?

   (switch to another pair of students)

   A: Well, then, is the water in this lake very deep?

   B: No, the water in the lake is not very deep, the water in the lake is very shallow.

   A: Is the rainfall in this place very great?

   B: Whether the rainfall is great or not, that I'm not clear about.

   A: Look! It's already started raining, and pretty heavily, too!

   B: Then I suppose the rainfall here must be great!

Unit 16, Part 3: Role Play Exercises

Practice these role plays in Chinese to improve your spoken fluency.

1. A: Come, Older Brother, let me toast you, too. Bottoms up!

    B: How about half a glass?

    A: Older Brother, Older Sister, today you prepared so many dishes!

    C: The food is nothing special, really very simple. Don't be polite! Here, this is Sweet and Sour Pork, I remember this was your favorite.

    (switch to another group of students)

    A: Mmm, the aroma smells really great! I really haven't had it for 5 or 6 years now.

    C: I remember too that you love to eat hot spicy food. This dish is hot and spicy, I especially made it for you. I guess you can't reach it? Let me serve you some.

    A: I can reach it, I'll help myself.

    D: Teacher Smith, Older Brother, Older Sister, excuse us, we have something we have to do, we must leave early. We would like to toast everyone. Enjoy your meal!

2. A: This aroma, I haven't smelled it in 2 or 3 years! What is it?

    B: It is the Sweet and Sour Pork that I made especially for you.

    A: You remembered that this is my favorite dish!

    B: Of course I remember!

    (switch to another pair of students)

    A: Thanks so much! I really haven't eaten it in 2 or 3 years. I'm really happy today.

    B: Good, then have some more, and invite your husband/wife to eat some, too.

    A: My husband/wife doesn't eat pork.

    B: Oh, I'm sorry, I'm embarrassed.

    A: Never mind. There are so many other delicious things to eat...

3. A: Here, here's to you! Welcome back to Hong Kong!

    B: Thank you!

    C: I remember these dishes are you favorite. Today you should eat a lot and drink a lot!

    B: These dishes, I really haven't had them in 7 or 8 years. Thank you, Older Sister!

    C: You're welcome. Actually, today there isn't any food to speak of.

    A: Come, let me drink to everyone! Bottoms up, bottoms up!

    (switch to another group of students)

    A: Older Sister especially prepared these dishes for you. Don't be polite, have more to eat.

    C: I suppose you can't reach; let me serve you some.

    B: Thank you, but I can reach it, I'll help myself. ... Mmm, it's delicious!

    C: If it's delicious, then eat some more!

    A: Come, let's drink a little wine. Here's to you! Bottoms up!

4. A: Excuse us, we have something we have to do, we must leave early. We'd like to toast everyone. Mr. and Mrs. Li, thank you. Everyone enjoy your meal!

    B: O.K., take it easy. Next Saturday I'm treating again. You definitely must come!

    A: No problem, if you invite me, I definitely will come.

    B: Then see you next Saturday. Goodbye!

Unit 16, Part 4: Role Play Exercises

Practice these role plays in Chinese to improve your spoken fluency.

1. A: Teacher Smith, come on, have some more liquor. To you!

   B: I've already had too much to drink. I really can't drink any more. I'll substitute cola for liquor. Older Sister, the food you cook really is perfect in color, aroma, and taste. Not even a restaurant could compare!

   C: Thank you. It's just a little home-style cooking. But though the food is nothing special, you do have to get enough to eat, you know!

   B: I've already eaten so much, I'm going to burst. It was really delicious. Such a sumptuous meal, Older Sister worked very hard today. Let me toast the two of you! And I made all of you go to the trouble of coming here from far away. Here's to all of you! Let's just consider this a last "bottoms up!"

   A: O.K. now, all of you please go to the living room and have a seat. Drink some tea and eat some fruit!

2. A: General Manager Li, come on, have some more liquor. To you!

   B: I've already had too much to drink. I really can't drink any more. I'll substitute soda for liquor. Older Brother, the food you cook really is perfect in color, aroma, and taste. Not even a restaurant could compare!

   C: Thank you. It's just a little home-style cooking. But though the food is nothing special, you do have to get enough to eat, you know!

   B: I've already eaten so much, I'm going to burst. It was really delicious. Such a sumptuous meal, Older Brother and Older Sister worked very hard today. Let me toast the two of you! And I made all of you go to the trouble of coming here from far away. Here's to all of you! Let's just consider this a last "bottoms up!"

   A: All right, now everyone please come in the living room and have a seat. Drink some tea and eat some fruit!

3. A: This Sweet and Sour Pork, although it can't compare to the restaurants back in Taiwan, it's still very good to eat. I haven't had it for 2 or 3 years.

   B: Mmm, it really is quite good. It's complete in color, aroma, and taste, and the meat is very tender.

   A: Everything is very good, it's just that the meat is a little spicy hot. I can't eat hot things!

   B: You think it's spicy hot? I feel it isn't the least bit hot. Come, drink some beer!

   A: O.K., bottoms up!

4. A: These dishes are really good to eat! I'm already so full I'm bursting.

   B: This restaurant is good. Such a sumptuous meal, I'm sure you couldn't eat it in the U.S.

   A: Yes, in America you can't eat such good Chinese food. However, San Francisco and New York City do have a few good Chinese restaurants.

   B: Yes, Los Angeles (**Luòshānjī**) and Washington (**Huáshèngdùn**) also have a few pretty good Chinese restaurants. Come, let me drink to you! Let me substitute tea for liquor. Bottoms up!

   A: O.K., bottoms up, bottoms up!

Unit 17, Part 1: Role Play Exercises

Practice these role plays in Chinese to improve your spoken fluency.

1. A: Hello? Who would you like to speak with?

    B: Is Chen Liyuan in?

    A: Speaking. Excuse me, who is this?

    B: I'm Lesley Smith. How are you, Liyuan?

    (switch to another pair of students)

    A: Oh, don't mention it! The last few days I've been incredibly busy. How about you?

    B: I've also been incredibly busy.

    A: Is something up?

    B: Liyuan, listen. This Sunday evening the Shanghai Club is having a concert. I wonder if you'd be free?

    A: Sure. What time on Sunday?

    B: The concert is at eight o'clock. We'll meet 20 minutes beforehand at the entrance to the club, O.K.?

    (switch to another pair of students)

    A: O.K., agreed. Oh, yes, could you get a few more tickets? My older sister and her boyfriend are also quite interested in music.

    B: I think there should be no big problem with that.

    A: O.K., then that's how it will be. See you when the time comes!

    B: Then it's settled like this. Bye!

2. A: Hello? Who would you like to speak with?

    B: Is Jimmy in?

    A: Jimmy who?

    B: Jimmy Hu. He's a Chinese-American guy, a college classmate of mine. He told me he works at your company.

    A: Oh, yes. Hu Zhijie. Yes, he's in, just wait a sec.

    (switch to another pair of students)

    C: Hello, this is Jimmy Hu. You are...?

    B: Rigoberto. Remember me? How are you, Jimmy?

    C: Oh, Rigoberto. I...the last few days I've been incredibly busy. Something up?

    B: Jimmy, listen. This Friday evening the Italian Club is having an Italian music concert. I wonder if you'd be free?

    C: The Italian Club is having an Italian music concert? Um, sure. What time on Friday?

    (switch to another pair of students)

    B: The concert is at nine o'clock. We'll meet 25 minutes beforehand at the entrance to the club, O.K.?

    C: O.K., agreed. Oh, yes, could you get a few more tickets? My parents are also quite interested in Italian music. You know, my maternal grandparents are Italian.

    B: I'm really sorry, but I'm afraid that all the tickets are sold out.

    C: O.K., never mind. Then that's how it will be. See you when the time comes!

    B: Then it's settled like this. Bye!

Unit 17, Part 2: Role Play Exercises

Practice these role plays in Chinese to improve your spoken fluency.

1. A: Hello? Please transfer me to 865.

    B: I'm sorry, extension 865 is busy. Will you wait a while or call back later?

    A: I'll wait.

    B: Hello? You can speak with extension 865 now.

    (switch to another pair of students)

    C: Hello? Who do you want?

    A: My name is Zaparelli, with Sino-American Trading Company. Could you please find Zhang Jianbang for me?

    C: Zhang Jianbang? O.K., please wait a minute, I'll go find him for you. Don't hang up.

    (switch to another pair of students)

    C: Hello? Mr. Zhang is in a meeting right now. Do you want to leave him a message?

    A: When he's finished with his meeting, please have him give me a call.

    C: Could you say your name again, please?

    A: My last name is Zaparelli, from Sino-American Trading Company. As soon as you mention my name, he'll know.

    C: O.K., I've written it down. As soon as he's finished with his meeting, I'll tell him.

    A: Much obliged.

2. A: Hello? Please transfer me to 2113.

    B: I'm sorry, extension 2113 is busy. Will you wait a while or call back later?

    A: I'll wait.

    B: It's possible that you might have to wait a long time.

    A: That's O.K.

    B: All right. (after a few minutes) Hello? You can speak with extension 2113 now.

    (switch to another pair of students)

    C: Hello? Who do you want?

    A: My name is Wang Lixian, with China Travel Agency. Could you please find Ms. Anne Toumanian?

    C: Anne Toumanian? O.K., please wait a minute, I'll go find her for you. Don't hang up.

    (switch to another pair of students)

    C: Hello? Ms. Toumanian is in a meeting right now. Do you want to leave her a message?

    A: When she's finished with her meeting, please have her give me a call.

    C: Could you say your name again, please?

    A: My name is Li, from China Travel Agency. Once you mention my name, she'll know.

    C: O.K., I've written it down. As soon as she's finished with her meeting, I'll tell her.

    A: Much obliged.

3. A: This fax, could you please take it up?

    B: I already took it up.

    A: Oh, O.K., thank you!

    B: You're welcome!

Unit 17, Part 3 : Role Play Exercises

Practice these role plays in Chinese to improve your spoken fluency.

1. A: Hello? In today's newspaper I saw your advertisement—

   B: Sorry, there's too much static on your line, I can't hear clearly. Speak a little louder.

   A: Hello? I said that I saw your advertisement in the newspaper (Yeah.), you have an apartment to rent out (Yes.). I wonder if it has been rented out or not?

   (switch to another pair of students)

   B: The apartment hasn't been rented out yet, but this afternoon an American university professor and her husband came to look at it, and they seem to be quite interested (Oh.). If you want to come look at it, you'd better come soon.

   A: Excuse me, how big is the apartment?

   B: It's about 22 ping. It has a living room, dining room, 2 bedrooms, a bathroom, and a kitchen.

   A: Oh... 22 ping is a little small. We need 3 or 4 bedrooms. Never mind. Thank you!

2. A: Hello?

   B: Hello? In yesterday's newspaper I saw your advertisement—

   A: I'm sorry, there's too much static on your line, I can't hear clearly. Please speak a little louder.

   B: Hello? I said that I saw your advertisement in the newspaper (Yeah.), you have an apartment to rent out (Yes.). I wonder if it has been rented out or not?

   (switch to another pair of students)

   A: Not yet, but this afternoon two foreign students came to look at it, and they seem to be quite interested (Oh.). If you want to come look at it, you'd better come soon.

   B: Excuse me, how big is the apartment?

   A: It's about 110 square meters. It has a living room, dining room, 4 bedrooms, 2 bathrooms, and a kitchen. Every room has big windows. The apartment has air conditioning, and it's quiet.

   B: O.K., I'll come immediately, please wait for me, my name is Smith.

   A: All right, Mr./Ms. Smith, see you in a little while.

3. A: Hello? I saw your ad in the paper that you have a computer for sale.

   B: Sorry, there's too much static on the line. Please speak up!

   A: O.K. Can you hear clearly now?

   B: Now it's too loud. Please speak a little quieter.

   (switch to another pair of students)

   A: I said, I saw your ad in the paper that you have a computer for sale.

   B: Sorry, the computer has already been sold.

   A: The computer has already been sold?

   B: Yeah, it was already sold this morning.

   A: Do you have any other computers you want to sell?

   B: We're not a computer company. We only had that one computer to sell. Now it has already been sold.

   A: Never mind. Thank you. Goodbye.

Unit 17, Part 4: Role Play Exercises

Practice these role plays in Chinese to improve your spoken fluency.

1. A: Hello? I saw your advertisement in the newspaper, you have an apartment to rent out. I wonder if it has been rented out or not?

   B: The apartment hasn't been rented out yet, but a lot of people have already come to look at it, so if you're interested you'd better come soon.

   A: Excuse me, how big is the apartment?

   B: It's about 85 square meters. It has a living room, dining room, 3 bedrooms, a bathroom, and a kitchen.

   (switch to another pair of students)

   A: Does the apartment have furniture?

   B: It has some simple furniture like sofa, dining table, desk, bed, closet, and so on.

   A: About how much would the rent per month be?

   B: 2,500 RMB per month, with water and electricity not included.

   A: Do you want a deposit?

   B: Yes, we do. The deposit is one month's rent.

   (switch to another pair of students)

   A: So when would it be convenient for me to come take a look at it?

   B: You could come right now, I'm in the apartment right now. Or this afternoon would also work. Any later and I'm afraid somebody else might already want to sign a lease.

   A: If I arrived this afternoon around 3:30, would that be convenient?

   B: No problem. What's your last name?

   A: My last name is Zhu, Zhu Dan.

   B: All right, Mr./Ms. Zhu, see you at four o'clock.

2. A: Little Wang, I found a great apartment. Would you be interested in living with us?

   B: Where is the apartment?

   A: Close to Peking University and Qinghua University. Transportation is really convenient. Buying things is also convenient. Do you want to take a look at it this evening?

   B: How big is the apartment?

   (switch to another pair of students)

   A: It has 4 bedrooms, 2 bathrooms, a living room, a dining room, and a huge kitchen.

   B: How much is the rent?

   A: In all it's 4,000 RMB per month, so each person would pay 1,000 RMB.

   B: Does the rent include utilities?

   (switch to another pair of students)

   A: No, it doesn't include utilities.

   B: Is there furniture?

   A: No, you'd have to buy your own furniture.

   B: Who all is going to live there besides you?

   A: There's me, Little He, and Little Zheng. The fourth person hasn't yet been decided.

   B: I'm interested. I'll go to your dorm at 7:00 tonight and maybe then we can go to take a look at the apartment, O.K.?

   A: No problem. Then let's decide to do that.

Unit 18, Part 1: Role Play Exercises

Practice these role plays in Chinese to improve your spoken fluency.

1. A: Hello, Mrs. Li! Is Little Wang home?

    B: Yes, he is. Little Chen, come in and sit down. He'll be right here. Have some tea.

    C: Little Wang, I'm sorry, I'm just in the midst of shaving. I'll be finished in a second.

    A: Little Wang, you've grown a moustache!

    C: No, no, I haven't grown a moustache, I'm just shaving. I'll be right there!

    A: O.K., Little Wang, you take your time, don't rush.

    C: All right, see you in a little while.

    D: Grandma!

    B: Little Chen, have you met my grandson Haohao before?

    A: Yes, I have.

    B: Haohao, say hello to Uncle Chen.

    D: Hello, Uncle Chen!

    A: Hi, Haohao! The more you grow, the taller you get. This is a little present for you!

    D: Thank you, Uncle!

    B: You're too polite! Haohao, now go outside and play with your little friends. Kids do find it hard to stay indoors...

2. A: Xiaoping, your American friend Ben is here to see you.

    B: Mom, could you tell him I'm shaving and that I'll be finished right away?

    A: O.K., I'll tell him. You be busy with your things. Ben is outside playing with Pengpeng.

    B: Yes, Ben loves kids and kids love him.

    (switch to another pair of students)

    A: Ben seems like a fine young man. I invited him for dinner tonight and he accepted.

    B: Really? Great! Mom, what are you cooking for dinner?

    A: Sweet and Sour Pork and some other things.

    B: Sweet and Sour Pork?

    A: Is anything the matter? Isn't Sweet and Sour Pork one of your favorite dishes?

    B: It's possible there is a small problem. Ben is Jewish (**Yóutài rén**) and he can't eat pork...

3. A: Hello, Mrs. Zhang, is Zhenjie in?

    B: Hi, Bill! Yes, Zhenjie is in. He's shaving right now. Sit down, have some tea!

    A: Thank you, thank you. Mmm, it smells really good! You're cooking right now, aren't you? What are you preparing?

    B: Oh, I'm cooking Sweet and Sour Pork. That's my granddaughter Jiajia's favorite dish. Bill, why don't you have dinner with us tonight!

    (switch to another pair of students)

    A: Wouldn't it be too much trouble?

    B: No trouble at all! So it's decided, you'll have dinner here with us.

    A: Well, thank you very much. Please keep it simple. Is there anything I can do to help?

    B: That's not necessary, thank you. Why don't you go out and play with Jiajia. When Zhenjie is finished, I'll call you.

    A: O.K., then I'll go out and play with Jiajia. Come, Jiajia, let's go out and play!

Unit 18, Part 2: Role Play Exercises

Practice these role plays in Chinese to improve your spoken fluency.

1. A: I'm coming, I'm coming! Little Sun, sorry to keep you waiting so long.

    B: Don't worry about it.

    C: Little Sun, have lunch here!

    B: It isn't necessary. In a little while when I finish talking with Little Wang, I'll go home.

    C: No, Little Sun, why don't you just have lunch here. You guys can talk while you eat.

    B: Well, all right. But keep it simple, don't go to too much trouble!

    C: Oh, it's no trouble, it'll be ready in no time.

    (switch to another pair of students)

    B: Little Wang, it's getting late, I should be going now.

    A: Why don't you sit a while longer?

    B: No, I still have to go out on the street to take care of some stuff.

    A: O.K. Since you still have things to do, I won't make you stay. Come again when you're free.

    B: Mrs. Wang, I'll be leaving. Thank you for inviting me for lunch. Little Wang, see you at the company tomorrow!

    A: See you tomorrow. I won't see you out, take care!

2. A: I'm coming, I'm coming! Little Zheng, sorry to keep you waiting so long.

    B: Don't worry about it. I can wait.

    C: Little Zheng, have dumplings with us!

    B: It isn't necessary. In a little while when I finish talking with Little Chen, I'll go home.

    C: No, Little Zheng, why don't you just eat with us. You guys can talk while you eat dumplings.

    B: Well, all right. But keep it simple, don't go to too much trouble!

    C: Oh, it's no trouble, the dumplings will be ready in no time.

    (switch to another pair of students)

    B: Little Chen, it's getting late, I should be going now.

    A: Why don't you sit a while longer?

    B: No, I still have to go out on the street to buy some things for my mother.

    A: O.K. Since you still have stuff to do, I won't make you stay. Come again when you're free.

    B: Mrs. Chen, the dumplings were delicious! I have to be leaving now. Little Chen, see you at the company tomorrow!

    A: Little Zheng, see you tomorrow. I won't see you out, take care!

3. A: Little Zhu, have breakfast with us!

    B: It isn't necessary. In a little while when I finish talking with Little Shi, I'll go home.

    A: No, Little Zhu, why don't you just eat breakfast with us. You guys can talk while you eat breakfast.

    B: Well, all right. But keep it simple, don't go to too much trouble.

    A: Oh, it's no trouble at all, breakfast will be ready in no time.

    B: All right, then thanks in advance. Little Shi, hurry up! I have something important to talk to you about...

Unit 18, Part 3: Role Play Exercises

Practice these role plays in Chinese to improve your spoken fluency.

1. A: Mr./Ms. Zhang, welcome, welcome!

   B: I'm sorry, I'm late because something came up at the last minute.

   A: That's O.K. No need to take off your shoes.

   B: I'll take them off anyway, it's more comfortable. I also like this custom. Uh, Mr./Ms. Xie, this is a little something for you.

   A: Oh! You're too polite. Please have a seat, I'll go make some tea.

   (switch to another pair of students)

   A: Please have a cigarette.

   B: Oh, I don't smoke, thanks.

   A: Mr./Ms. Zhang, you said on the phone this morning you wanted to see me about some matter.

   B: Yes, sorry to bother you with this. There's a little matter I'd like to ask for your help with.

   (switch to another pair of students)

   A: Please have some tea.

   B: Thank you. You're too polite.

   A: Not at all. All right, you said there's a matter you'd like to ask for my help with.

   B: All right. Uh, well, uh, well, uh, the matter is like this...

2. A: Mr./Ms. He, welcome, welcome!

   B: I'm sorry, I'm late because something came up at the last minute.

   A: That's O.K. No need to take off your shoes.

   B: I'll take them off anyway, it's more comfortable. I also like this custom. Uh, Mr./Ms. Bai, this is a little something for you.

   A: Oh! You're too polite. Please have a seat. Please drink a little coffee.

   (switch to another pair of students)

   A: Please have a cigarette.

   B: Oh, I don't smoke, thanks.

   A: You said on the phone last Friday you wanted to see me about some matter.

   B: Yes, sorry to bother you. There's a little matter I need to ask for your help with.

   A: Don't be polite, please be frank. What kind of matter is it?

   B: All right. Uh, well, uh, well, uh, the matter is like this...

3. A: Could I ask you, what's the relationship between those two people?

   B: Those two people? Well, uh, I'm not very clear about that myself, but it's possible that it's a relationship of boyfriend and girlfriend.

4. A: Welcome to our restaurant! How many in your party?

   B: We're five in all. Do you divide it into a smoking section and a non-smoking section?

   A: Correct, there's a smoking section and a non-smoking section.

   B: We would like to sit in the non-smoking section. Thank you.

   A: All right, no problem. The non-smoking section is over there. Please follow me.

Unit 18, Part 4: Role Play Exercises

Practice these role plays in Chinese to improve your spoken fluency.

1. A: Mr./Ms. Ouyang, I'll do my best to help you find out about this matter. At the latest I'll give you an answer by next Monday, all right?

   B: I'm really putting you to too much trouble. But if it's not easy to find out, don't try too hard.

   A: I know. I'll just do my best.

   B: Mr./Ms. Guo, it's getting late, so I won't disturb you any more. I'll be on my way.

   A: Why the rush? Sit a bit longer.

   B: No, uh, I'll come again to visit some other day.

   (switch to another pair of students)

   A: Oh, that's right, I just thought of something. Next Monday I'm going to go to Shanghai to see a friend, and I won't be in Beijing. So you could also call me on Sunday.

   B: All right.

   A: Let me see you downstairs.

   B: That's not necessary, please stay inside.

   A: Well, all right. Take care. Goodbye!

   B: Goodbye!

2. A: Why the rush? Sit a bit longer.

   B: Sorry, I need to go home. My boyfriend/girlfriend prepared dinner for me.

   A: All right, since there's something you need to do, I won't keep you.

   B: I'll visit you again some other day.

   A: I'll see you downstairs.

   B: It's not necessary.

   A: Give me a call if there is anything you need help with.

   B: O.K. Thank you, goodbye!

3. A: Hello, may I please speak to Mr./Ms. Hu.

   B: Mr./Ms. Hu? My last name is Hu.

   A: Mr./Ms. Hu, my name is Li Dan. I have a little matter to talk about with you.

   B: Oh, Mr./Ms. Li! I remember you. Don't be polite, tell me frankly.

   (switch to another pair of students)

   A: You said last time you wanted to sell your house. Would you be willing to sell it to me?

   B: This is a little too sudden. Can you give me some time to think about it?

   A: Of course I can. Do you know when you can give me an answer?

   B: Um, I'll let you know next Monday, all right?

   A: All right, then we'll talk again next week. I won't disturb you anymore. Goodbye.

   B: Bye.

4. A: Do you want to go upstairs or do you want to go downstairs?

   B: I have to first go upstairs and then go downstairs.

   A: You have to first go upstairs and then go downstairs? Why?

   B: Because my mom is waiting for me upstairs, but my dad is waiting for me downstairs!

Unit 19, Part 1: Role Play Exercises

Practice these role plays in Chinese to improve your spoken fluency.

1. A: Hello, Mrs. Xie!

   B: Come in. Jiaxi is lying in bed in the bedroom.

   A: Jiaxi, I heard you were sick. Are you better now?

   C: I'm already a lot better. Actually, it isn't anything serious. Thanks for coming over to see me.

   A: Ordinarily, I should have come to see you a long time ago, it's just that the last few days I was always busy and never had time, that's why I didn't come until today. Oh, that's right, I brought you some tea.

   C: Thanks! So, what have you been busy with the last few days?

   A: I've been busy with final exams, what else? I've been taking tests every day; soon I'm going to get dizzy from all this testing!

2. A: Hello, Mrs. Jin!

   B: Come in. Nianping is lying down in the bedroom.

   A: Nianping, I heard you were sick. Are you better now?

   C: I'm a lot better. Actually, it isn't anything serious. Thanks for coming to see me!

   A: Ordinarily, I should have come to see you a long time ago, it's just that the last few weeks I was always busy and never had time, that's why I didn't come until today. Oh, that's right, I brought you some bread imported from Germany.

   C: Thanks! So, what have you been busy with the last few weeks?

   A: I've been busy with mid-term exams, and some other things, too. I've been taking tests every day; soon I'm going to get dizzy from all this testing!

3. A: I've heard you're sick. How are you now? A little better, I suppose?

   B: A lot better. Thanks for coming to visit!

   A: I should have come long ago. Here, this is a little something for you.

   B: You really are too polite!

4. A: I go running every morning at 7:00. Do you want to go running with me tomorrow?

   B: O.K. Agreed with one word! See you tomorrow morning at 7:00 AM outside the dorm.

   A: See you tomorrow morning!

5. A: What's the matter with you? Are you sick?

   B: It's nothing. I'd just like to sit down for a while, I'm a little dizzy.

   A: Here's a chair. Why don't you sit down. Rest well. I'll go get a cup of water.

   B: Thank you.

6. A: Do you know Mr. and Mrs. Li?

   B: I know them. What about them?

   A: They're very interesting. Mrs. Li is busy earning money, Mr. Li is busy spending money!

Unit 19, Part 2: Role Play Exercises

Practice these role plays in Chinese to improve your spoken fluency.

1. A: How did you do on your final exams?

   B: So-so, I guess. The grades aren't out yet. Jiaxi, you rest real well. I'll be going on my way. In a few days, I'll come visit you again.

   A: Why don't you have dinner with us before you leave?

   B: No, thanks, I must be going now. Jiaxi, you watch your health. Don't tire yourself out. If there should be anything, give us a call, everybody can help you.

   A: Thanks so much. If there is anything, I'll be sure to let you know.

   B: Mrs. Xie, I'll be going now.

   C: Thanks for coming to see Jiaxi. Come again to visit some other day!

   B: O.K., I'll definitely come. Bye!

2. A: How did you do on your mid-term exams?

   B: So-so, I guess. The grades aren't out yet. Nianping, you rest real well. I'll be going on my way. In a few days, I'll come visit you again.

   A: Why don't you have lunch with us before you leave?

   B: No, thanks, I must be going now. Nianping, you watch your health. Don't tire yourself out. If there should be anything, give us a call, everybody can help you.

   A: Thanks so much. If there is anything, I'll be sure to let you know.

   B: Mrs. Jin, I'll be going now. This is a little something my Mom wanted me to give you.

   C: Oh, it's not necessary. You're so polite!

   B: It's nothing. Goodbye!

   C: Goodbye! Thanks for coming to see Nianping. Come again to visit some other day!

3. A: How many courses did you choose this term?

   B: This term I chose four courses. And you?

   A: This term I also chose four courses, but next semester I'm going to take five courses!

4. A: How many credits did you take last term?

   B: Last term I took 16 credits. And you?

   A: Same as you, 16 credits. I heard Little Wang took 21 credits.

   B: I really don't understand why Little Wang is taking so many credits each semester!

5. A: This semester I'm writing two term papers.

   B: What are your term papers about?

   A: The first term paper is about Chinese-American commerce. The second term paper is about Taiwanese beer.

   B: Taiwanese beer? You must be kidding me!

   A: No, really. In the researching of it, it's very interesting.

   B: Next semester I'm going to write an honors thesis.

   A: What's your honors thesis about?

   B: I haven't decided yet, but probably it will be about Chinese culture. This afternoon I'm going to go talk with Professor Gu.

Unit 19, Part 3: Role Play Exercises

Practice these role plays in Chinese to improve your spoken fluency.

1. A: Excuse me, is this Professor Shi's home?

    B: Yes, please come in. Old Shi, you have a guest.

    C: Who is it? Oh, it's you! Come in, sit down.

    A: Professor, I'm returning to the States. I've come to bid you farewell.

    C: When are you leaving?

    A: Next Monday.

    C: Gosh, time really passes quickly! In the blink of an eye six months have passed. I remember when you had just come, you couldn't say even a simple phrase in Chinese. Now you can already converse quite fluently.

    A: It's all thanks to your help. This past half year I've really put you to too much trouble.

2. A: I've come to bid you farewell!

    B: When are you leaving?

    A: This Friday. I have a lot of things I want to tell you, but I don't know how to say them.

    B: Things in the past, let's not mention them. When you return to the U.S., please be sure to take good care of your health.

    A: I will. And you make sure you get more rest! O.K., the time isn't early anymore, I should be leaving now.

    B: Goodbye!

3. A: Gosh, time passes really quickly.

    B: Yes it does.

    A: I remember you couldn't even cook rice when I first met you, but now you even know how to make Sweet and Sour Pork!

    B: It's all thanks to your excellent teaching.

    A: Not at all.

    (switch to another pair of students)

    A: I hope you'll continue to cook Chinese dishes when you return to the U.S.

    B: I will for sure. My parents will be so happy to know that I learned not only Chinese language but also Chinese cooking during my study abroad in China. Goodbye!

    A: Goodbye! Be sure to call us when you get to the U.S.

    B: I'll be sure to do that.

4. A: That student's pronunciation is quite good.

    B: Yes, but her grammar is not clean, and she doesn't have enough vocabulary.

5. A: You speak Mandarin both correctly and fluently.

    B: Not at all! I still have a long ways to go...

6. A: General Manager, what does your factory produce?

    B: We produce shoes. Lots of shoes. Every month we produce over 20,000 pairs of shoes. Almost all of them are exported overseas.

Unit 19, Part 4: Role Play Exercises

Practice these role plays in Chinese to improve your spoken fluency.

1. A: Professor, to tell the truth, if it hadn't been for your excellent teaching, I wouldn't have been able to progress so quickly.

   B: Not at all. This is what a teacher is supposed to do! Actually, this is mostly the result of your own hard work.

   A: Professor, it's getting late, I should be going home now.

   B: Why don't you stay a bit longer?

   A: Thank you, but I have something else I have to do.

   B: O.K., then I won't keep you. When you get back to America, please give my best to your parents. Don't forget to send us a letter when you have time.

   A: Goodbye, Professor!

   B: Goodbye!

2. A: Professor Zhang, I'm returning to the States. I've come to bid you farewell. I brought you some apples imported from America.

   B: Thank you, you're too polite. So when are you leaving?

   A: This Saturday.

   B: Gosh, time really passes quickly! In the blink of an eye a year has passed. I remember when you had just come, you couldn't say even a simple phrase in Chinese. Now you can already converse quite fluently.

   (switch to another pair of students)

   A: It's all thanks to your help. To tell the truth, if it hadn't been for your excellent teaching, I wouldn't have been able to progress so quickly.

   B: Not at all. This is what a teacher is supposed to do. Actually, this is mostly the result of your own hard work.

   A: Professor, it's getting late, I should be going home now. Goodbye!

   B: O.K., then I won't keep you. When you get back to America, please give my best to your teacher Professor Chen. We've known each other for many years. And don't forget to send us a letter when you have time.

   A: I definitely will. All right. Goodbye, Professor!

   B: Goodbye!

3. A: Who are you going to send such a big parcel?

   B: I have a classmate who's studying abroad in England. It's her birthday.

   A: Oh, now I understand. Shall I help you carry it?

   B: Thanks, but no problem.

4. A: Excuse me, if I send this postcard by airmail, how much do I have to put on it?

   B: Where do you want to send it?

   A: I want to send it to America.

   B: You need to put ¥ 4.5 on it.

   A: All right, this is ¥ 5.

   B: And here is ¥ .50 in change.

Unit 20, Part 1: Role Play Exercises

Practice these role plays in Chinese to improve your spoken fluency.

1. A: Old Li, do you have any hobbies?

    B: Painting, especially Chinese painting.

    A: Besides painting, do you have any other hobbies?

    B: I also like to play chess. How about you? What are your hobbies?

    (switch to another pair of students)

    A: I like music. From the time I was little, I've been studying piano. Recently I also started learning how to play the violin.

    B: No wonder I often see you humming a tune while you walk! Besides music, do you have any other hobbies?

    A: I like singing and I enjoy reading novels. Actually, I like reading any kind of book.

    B: It seems like you have lots of hobbies!

2. A: Little Chen, do you have any hobbies?

    B: I like music. From the time I was little, I've been studying piano. Sometimes I play five or six hours a day of piano.

    A: No wonder I often see you singing while you walk.

    B: Really? I sing while I walk? I didn't know at all. Sorry!

    (switch to another pair of students)

    A: It's fine. I like it; it's pretty! Besides music, do you have any other hobbies?

    B: I also like to read novels, or visit museums, or go to the zoo to see the animals. And you? What are your hobbies?

    A: Painting, especially Chinese painting, also playing Chinese chess. Go, Chinese chess, Chinese checkers, I play them all.

    B: I like playing chess, too. I haven't played chess for a long time! Do you have time now? Would you like to play chess with me?

    A: O.K.! No problem at all. Then we'll play chess right now!

3. A: What are your hobbies?

    B: I like to read and I like to play chess. How about you? What are your hobbies?

    A: I especially like visiting museums. I've liked visiting museums since I was little.

    B: Do you like to cook?

    A: No, but my mom's hobby is cooking, so at home we have good food all the time.

4. A: Do you like to sing?

    B: Yes, I very much like to sing.

    A: The songs you sing are really pretty!

    B: Actually, I don't sing very well, but I like to sing.

5. A: Excuse me, could I ask you to take a picture for us?

    B: Of course, no problem. Say "eggplant." (**qiézi** "eggplant")

    A: "Eggplant." Thank you very much!

    B: You're welcome.

. . . .

Unit 20, Part 2: Role Play Exercises

Practice these role plays in Chinese to improve your spoken fluency.

1. A: Do you have any hobbies?

    B: I like to watch Peking opera.

    A: You're interested in Peking opera?

    B: Though I don't understand it very well, I do love to watch it.

    (switch to another pair of students)

    A: This Friday evening I'm going to People's Theater with my parents to see "Chronicle of the White Snake." I just happen to have two extra tickets. Would you and your sister like to go together with me?

    B: Great! What time does it begin?

    A: At 9:00. I'll come to your house looking for you Friday night at 8:30.

    B: O.K., thanks so much!

    A: No need to thank me. See you Friday!

2. A: Rigoberto, the Italian music concert last night, can you tell me about how many students from our class went?

    B: Oh, I think about three-fourths of the students in our class went.

    A: And that is to say, about one-fourth of the students didn't go, right?

    B: Correct. But why do you ask me this?

    A: Don't concern yourself with that. All right, thank you. I'll go tell Principal Wang.

3. A: Little He, did you know that only about 9% of American college students study foreign languages?

    B: Only 9%? That's really too few. In China, everybody must learn English, and many students learn a second foreign language.

    A: I know. I hope in the future there are even more Americans who study Chinese!

    B: I also hope this. (**zhèiyang xīwàng** "in this way hope")

4. A: Excuse me, is Fragrant Hills far from here?

    B: Fragrant Hills, is that it? I have a map, let me take a look. Fragrant Hills is about 3.3 or 3.4 kilometers from here.

    A: O.K., now I'm clear about it. Thanks!

    B: Don't mention it.

5. A: I'm afraid learning Chinese characters is of no use...

    B: How can you say that? Learning Chinese characters is very useful! If you can read Chinese characters, you can read Chinese books, newspapers, and magazines.

    A: But learning Chinese characters is too hard!

    B: Do it slow and easy. Learn 5 or 6 characters each day. That way it's not too hard.

6. A: How is everyone? I'm so happy to be here in Taiwan, People's Republic of China!

    B: "People's Republic of China" is mainland China. Taiwan is called Republic of China.

    A: Oh, sorry about that. I mean, I'm so happy to be here in Taiwan, Republic of China!

Unit 20, Part 3: Role Play Exercises

Practice these role plays in Chinese to improve your spoken fluency.

1. A: Come in.

    B: Hi!

    A: Hey, Li Jing!

    B: What are you up to?

    A: Studying.

    B: Really? Uh, are you free this evening? Would you like to go see a movie?

    A: Sure. Are there any good films?

    B: Recently there's a new film that just began playing. It's the story of a famous musician in China in the 1940s; it's titled "The Pianist." I've heard it's pretty good.

2. A: Come in.

    B: Hi, Little Zheng!

    A: Hey, Little Lin!

    B: What are you up to?

    A: Reading.

    B: Really? What are you reading? Oh, you're reading that kind of book! Uh, Little Zheng, are you free tomorrow evening? Would you like to go see a movie with me?

    (switch to another pair of students)

    A: Sure. Are there any good films?

    B: Recently there's a new film that just began playing. It's the story of a famous novelist in France in the 1950s. I've heard it's very good. You like to read novels; you should go!

    A: All right, agreed! Where and what time do you want to meet?

    B: Main entrance to the university, tomorrow evening, 6:45.

    A: O.K., see you tomorrow. Goodbye. Sorry, I want to continue reading...

3. A: Excuse me, is there a movie theater in the vicinity?

    B: Yes, it's not very far from here. Go straight and turn right at the second intersection.

4. A: Old Wang, you're good at storytelling. Tell us a story, all right?

    B: O.K., I'll tell you a story. Once upon a time, there was an old man...

5. A: What are your plans for the future?

    B: In the future I want to be a painter. How about you? What are your plans?

    A: In the future I want to be a pianist.

6. A: What are your plans for the future?

    B: In the future I want to serve as a doctor. And you? What are your future plans?

    A: In the future I want to be a banker.

7. A: What are your plans for the future?

    B: I don't have any plans yet. I am interested in many things, but I haven't yet decided what I want to be in the future.

Unit 20, Part 4: Role Play Exercises

Practice these role plays in Chinese to improve your spoken fluency.

1. A: I've never before seen that kind of film. Where's it showing? What time does it start?

   B: At "New China Movie Theater" at 8:30 P.M.

   A: I'll come looking for you at 8:15, O.K.?

   B: O.K.

   A: All right, bye.

   (switch to another pair of students)

   B: Which row are we sitting in?

   A: The seats are pretty good. Downstairs, row 12, numbers 8 and 10. Let's go in. What do you think of this movie?

   B: It was fantastic! Very touching.

   A: Could you understand everything they said?

   B: I understood most of it. In some places they spoke too fast and I couldn't understand very well. But I was able to understand the gist of the film.

2. A: I've never before seen that kind of film. Where's it showing? When does it start?

   B: At "New Shanghai Movie Theater" at 9:15 P.M.

   A: I'll come looking for you at 8:50, O.K.?

   B: O.K.

   A: All right, see you in a little while.

   B: Bye.

   (switch to another pair of students)

   B: Which row are we sitting in?

   A: The seats are pretty good. Upstairs, row 6, seat numbers 14 and 16. Let's go in. So what do you think of this movie?

   B: It was fantastic! Very touching. The director and the actors were all very good.

   A: Could you understand everything they said?

   B: I was able to understand the gist of the film. But in some places they spoke too fast and I couldn't understand very well. Did you think they spoke very fast?

   A: No, they spoke neither fast nor slow. But if you had me watch an American movie, I'm sure I wouldn't understand a lot of it either!

3. A: What kind of films do you like?

   B: I don't know exactly. What kind of films are playing?

   A: Do you like comedies?

   B: Comedies? Not so much.

   A: Detective films?

   B: Detective films? Not very much.

   A: Horror films?

   B: Horror films? Oh, no, I don't like horror movies at all.

   A: Then tell me, what do you like?

   B: I like romantic films!

Unit 21, Part 1: Role Play Exercises

Practice these role plays in Chinese to improve your spoken fluency.

1. A: Which sports do you like?

   B: I like to play baseball and Ping-Pong. Before, when I was in China, I also often jogged in the morning. And you?

   A: I like tennis and swimming, and occasionally I also play badminton. Hey, you're so tall, you ought to be pretty good at basketball!

   B: Actually, in the past when I was in high school, I was on the school basketball team. But now I haven't played for a long time.

   A: Wow! So, having been in China so long, did you learn any different sports, for example, Chinese martial arts, kung fu, and so forth?

   B: Yes, when I was in China I would get up every morning at 5:00 and go to a nearby park to learn how to shadow box.

2. A: Which sports do you like?

   B: I like to play basketball and baseball. I also like to play tennis and go swimming. How about you? What sports do you like?

   A: I also like to play basketball. And I like to play badminton and occasionally I play Ping-Pong. On the weekend I often go jogging in the morning. Hey, do you want to play basketball with me some time?

   B: Actually, when I was in high school, I was on the school basketball team. However, I haven't played for a long, long time. O.K., we can find a time to play basketball together.

   A: How about this Saturday at 10:00 AM?

   B: Deal!

   A: I'll come to your dorm looking for you at 10:00. See you when the time comes!

3. A: Every Sunday I learn shadow boxing.

   B: Wow, is that some sort of Korean martial arts?

   A: No, it's a kind of Chinese martial arts that many old people practice.

   B: But you're not old!

   A: Of course young people can practice it, too. Shadow boxing is good for the health!

   B: Can you teach me?

   A: Sure. Since you know so many sports, you definitely can learn it very quickly.

4. A: You have succeeded, I'm really happy for you!

   B: If I have succeeded, it's all because of your help. Thank you!

   A: You're really too polite.

5. A: You better be careful. In that place there's lots of crime.

   B: What do you mean?

   A: For example, recently there have often been robberies.

   B: Oh, I'm not worried.

   A: You're not worried? Why not?

   B: I've learned Chinese martial arts!

Unit 21, Part 2: Role Play Exercises

Practice these role plays in Chinese to improve your spoken fluency.

1. A: My roommate is learning shadow boxing. He/she says the people learning with her/him are mostly middle-aged or older people. Don't tell me that Chinese young people all dislike practicing shadow boxing?

   B: Chinese young people prefer going dancing in the evening, or going walking in the countryside on weekends. To shadow box you have to go out at 5:00 or 5:30 A.M. As far as they're concerned, that's too early. They can't get up!

   A: So that's how it is.

   B: The other day (**Nèitiān**) you said you like jogging. Actually, every morning from 7:00 to 7:30, I jog for half an hour. How about it? Would you be interested in running with me tomorrow?

   A: Sure! I haven't run for a long time. Where shall we meet?

   B: Tomorrow at 7:00 sharp I'll wait for you in front of the Peking University gym, O.K.?

   A: All right, agreed.

   B: See you tomorrow!

2. A: Which is your favorite − spring, summer, or winter break?

   B: I like summer vacation the best.

   A: Why?

   B: You ask me why? Because I don't need to be in school for three months!

   A: What do you do in those three months?

   B: Eat. Sleep. I also play basketball, baseball, tennis, badminton, go swimming and so on.

3. A: How long is summer vacation at universities in America?

   B: About three months, more or less.

   A: How long is winter vacation?

   B: Winter vacation is two to six weeks. Each university is different.

   A: Do American universities have a spring break?

   B: Yes, they do. Most have a one-week spring break, but a few have a two-week break.

4. A: In my freshman year, I joined seven clubs.

   B: That's way too many! I only joined two clubs. What clubs are you joining next year?

   A: I haven't yet decided which clubs to join next year.

   B: What do you plan to do doing during summer vacation this year?

   A: I'm working as an intern at a bank in New York. You? (**shíxí** "work as an intern")

   B: I'm doing an internship at a trading company in Hong Kong.

5. A: Is General Manager Dong in? (**Dǒng** [SN])

   B: She took several days of vacation and won't be back until Monday.

6. A: Professor, my parents want me to return home for a few days, there's something I have to take care of at home. I'd like to ask you for three days of leave.

   B: All right, no problem.

Unit 21, Part 3: Role Play Exercises

Practice these role plays in Chinese to improve your spoken fluency.

1. A: What good programs are on now?

    B: Let me see. On channel 3 there is a soap opera and on channel 5 there is a soccer match. Which one do you want to see?

    A: Let's watch the soccer. Which team is playing against which team?

    B: Korea vs. Spain.

    (switch to another group of students)

    A: So hurry up and turn on the TV. Oh, no, the game has already begun!

    B: At least it only just started. Wow! It's already 4 to 3.

    A: Oh, good ball, fantastic! Who do you think will win?

    B: Hard to say. These two teams are both world-famous strong teams. Whoever is lucky will win.

2. A: What good programs are on now?

    B: On channel 1 is news, on channel 4 there is a variety show, and on channel 7 is the World Cup Soccer match. Which program do you want to see?

    A: Which one do you want to see?

    B: It makes no difference. You decide.

    A: All right, let's watch the soccer. Hurry up and turn on the TV.

    B: Oh, no, the game has already begun! I don't understand soccer. So which team is playing against which team?

    A: Germany vs. Italy. At least it only just started.

    (switch to another group of students)

    B: What's the score now?

    A: 3 to 2. Oh, good ball, fantastic! Now it's tied, 3 to 3.

    B: So who do you think will win?

    A: Hard to say. Germany is a world-famous strong team, and Italy isn't weak either. Whoever is lucky will win.

    B: You mean, whoever is unlucky will lose.

    A: You could also say it that way. Let's watch the match...

3. A: Hey, which team do you think will win?

    B: I don't know which team will win, they both look strong.

    A: Which team do you think will lose?

    B: I don't know which team will lose, they both look strong.

    A: Which team has better luck?

    B: I don't know, they're both not weak. Don't ask so many questions, watch the match!

4. A: Do you like to watch TV?

    B: I'm too busy, I seldom watch. Occasionally I watch the news. How about you?

    A: I love watching TV. I watch several hours a day.

    B: What kind of TV programs do you like to watch?

    A: Soap operas, comedies, news, variety shows, sports competitions, I like them all!

· ·

Unit 21, Part 4: Role Play Exercises

Practice these role plays in Chinese to improve your spoken fluency.

1. A: Look, I've finally climbed onto the Great Wall!

    B: Yes. Chinese people often say: "If you don't go to the Great Wall, you're not a brave man." Now you, too, can be regarded as a brave man!

    A: Wow, it really lives up to its reputation. How long really is the Great Wall?

    B: I think it's almost 4,000 miles long.

    (switch to another group of students)

    A: When was the Great Wall built?

    B: They began building it during the Warring States Period, over 2,000 years ago. Later in successive dynasties it kept being expanded. But this section here was built during the Ming Dynasty.

    A: It must have really been quite difficult to build it at that time!

    B: That's for sure. The material all had to be transported by hand. No one knows how many people died...

2. A: We've climbed onto the Great Wall. It's not only long, it's also wide!

    B: Yes. Are you happy? Do you know how long the Great Wall is?

    A: I've heard it's about 6,000 kilometers long.

    B: How many miles is that?

    A: How many miles? Who knows how many miles. We're now in China, not in the U.S. Chinese people use kilometers, they don't use miles.

    (switch to another group of students)

    A: Actually, of all the countries in the world, only the U.S. still uses miles. I really don't understand why the U.S. doesn't use kilometers.

    B: O.K., O.K., from now on we'll all use kilometers. Let me ask you, do you know when this section of the Great Wall was built?

    A: It says here it was built in the Ming Dynasty.

    B: At that time to build it, it must have been really hard.

    A: Yeah, I don't know how many people died. They had to move all these materials by hand. I really don't know how they did it...

3. A: In that war, very many people died.

    B: That's for sure. I really don't know why there are wars.

    A: What we need is world peace.

    B: Yes, world peace. Why can't everyone just play soccer. Use soccer to compete, not war.

    A: Good idea.

    (switch to another group of students)

    A: Did you know that the Great Wall of China was started in the Warring States Period?

    B: I've heard that. I've been to the Great Wall. At that time it must have been really hard to build. They had to move all the materials by hand. I don't know how many people died.

    A: Yes, I'm sure it was very difficult. But why are we talking about the Great Wall? On TV there is a soccer match, England vs. Brazil. It just started.

    B: A soccer match? So hurry up and turn on the TV!

Unit 22, Part 1: Role Play Exercises

Practice these role plays in Chinese to improve your spoken fluency.

1. A: Strange, I don't feel very good.

    B: Where does it hurt? Are you sick? Do you want to go to a hospital to see a doctor?

    A: My head hurts, I'm nauseous, and I feel like throwing up. I'm weak all over and I think I have a fever.

    B: Did you catch a cold?

    A: It's possible, I don't know.

    (switch to another group of students)

    B: There's now a huge change in temperatures from morning to evening. If you're not careful, it's easy to catch cold.

    A: If I rest a day or two, I should be all right.

    B: I think you better go to a hospital to see a doctor.

    A: Go to a hospital?

    B: If you don't get better, it could turn into pneumonia! I'll take you there. Comrade, this friend of mine is ill. He/she can't speak Chinese. Is there a doctor who knows English?

    C: Wait just a moment. That doctor is busy right now. He/she'll be here in a moment.

2. A: Are you not feeling well?

    B: No, I don't feel very well. I think I'm sick...

    A: Where does it hurt?

    B: I'm nauseous and I feel like throwing up.

    A: Do you have a headache?

    B: Yes, my head hurts and I feel weak all over.

    A: Do you want to go to the hospital and have them take a look?

    B: I don't think I need to. I just need to rest for a day or two.

    A: Really? Well, all right. Let me take you home. My car is parked right outside.

3. A: Are you O.K.? You don't look too good.

    B: I don't know. I think maybe I ate something wrong for dinner last night.

    A: What did you have?

    B: Sweet and Sour Pork. I think maybe I ate too much, or maybe it was bad.

    A: Does your belly hurt?

    B: Yes, my belly hurts. I have a fever and I'm nauseous and I've been having diarrhea.

    A: Let me take you to the hospital, it's not very far from here.

    B: Thank you very much. I'm really sorry to bother you. Before we leave, I better go the bathroom one more time...

4. A: If you don't feel well, it's best to go see a doctor as soon as you can.

    B: I think I just need to rest for a few more days...

    A: You've rested a few days already. I think you need to go to the hospital right now! Don't worry, I'll find you an English-speaking doctor.

    B: But what about papers and final exams?

    A: One's health comes first. Everything else is unimportant.

Unit 22, Part 2: Role Play Exercises

Practice these role plays in Chinese to improve your spoken fluency.

1. A: Thief! Somebody stole my purse!

   B: What? What happened?

   A: It's that woman! Hurry up and catch her, don't let her run away. Is there a policeman nearby?

   B: I'll go call a policeman.

   (switch to another pair of students)

   A: I'm Japanese, I'm studying at the Peking University Chinese Language Training Center. My purse, passport, and all kinds of IDs were stolen. I don't know where that woman ran to. What should I do now? I've got to get those things of mine back!

   C: Don't worry. We'll definitely do our best to help you find them. Please first go to the police station with me.

   A: All right. Thank you.

2. A: Thief! Somebody stole my wallet!

   B: What? What happened?

   A: That guy! Hurry up, catch him, don't let him run away. Is there a policeman around?

   B: I'll go call a policeman. Wait just a minute, don't leave.

   (switch to another group of students)

   A: I'm Korean. I'm studying Chinese at the National Taiwan Normal University Mandarin Training Center. About 10 minutes ago, my wallet, passport, and all kinds of IDs were stolen. I don't know where that man ran to. What should I do now? I've got to get those things of mine back!

   C: Don't worry. We'll definitely do our best to help you find them. Please first go to the police station with me.

   A: Well, O.K.

3. A: What happened?

   B: My purse/wallet was stolen!

   A: This morning my purse/wallet was also stolen. We better go find a policeman.

4. A: How come your little brother is crying? (**kū** "cry")

   B: He was scolded by his teacher.

5. A: How come you're so sad?

   B: I was scolded by my parents.

6. A: How come my money is all gone?

   B: You were tricked by them! You don't know yet?

7. A: There's no furniture in the room anymore. Where is all the furniture?

   B: The furniture was all moved away by Little Li. (**bānzǒu** "move away")

   A: I truly don't understand why Little Li would move away the furniture...

Unit 22, Part 3: Role Play Exercises

Practice these role plays in Chinese to improve your spoken fluency.

1. A: Sir, I lost a bag this afternoon. I wonder if anybody picked it up?

   B: Does your bag have any special characteristics?

   A: It's red in color, probably three times as big as this bag of mine. It has "Yankee" written on it. Inside, in addition to over two thousand NT, there are also my passport, student ID, and library card.

   B: What country are you from? What's your name?

   A: I'm American, my name is ___.

   (switch to another pair of students)

   B: Take a look, is this your bag?

   A: No, it's not mine. But wait, that bag over there, that's mine!

   B: O.K. Please examine it to see if everything is there.

   A: Let me see. My money, my passport, student ID, library card, everything is there. Thanks so much!

   B: You're welcome, that's my job. In the future, be more careful! Please sign your name here.

2. A: Miss, I lost my purse/wallet last night. I wonder if anybody picked it up?

   B: Does your purse/wallet have any special characteristics?

   A: It's green in color, probably twice as big as this one. It has "Daytona" written on it. Inside, in addition to over five thousand RMB, there are also my passport, student ID, and library card.

   B: What country are you from? What's your name?

   A: I'm Canadian, my name is ___.

   (switch to another pair of students)

   B: Take a look, is this your purse/wallet?

   A: That's right, that's mine!

   B: Please examine it to see if everything is there.

   A: Let me see *(checks the purse/wallet)*, the passport, student ID, library card, they're all there *(searches some more)*, but the money is gone!

   B: The money is gone? How much did you say was in there?

   A: Five thousand RMB. It's all gone!

   B: I'm afraid there's nothing one can do about that. In the future, please be more careful! Please sign your name here.

   A: O.K.

3. A: Help! Help! Fire!

   B: Fire? Where?

   A: At my home. Come quick!

4. A: These things of mine, when you're finished using them, give them back to me.

   B: Of course! I can give them back to you in about half an hour. Is that O.K.?

   A: No problem.

· ·

Unit 22, Part 4: Role Play Exercises

Practice these role plays in Chinese to improve your spoken fluency.

1. A: Miss/Sir, I'm sorry. Are you O.K.? Did you get hurt?

    B: I'm pretty much all right, I guess. But take a look, a big hole got torn in my shirt, and what has become of my motorcycle? If I hadn't dodged quickly, who knows how dangerous it could have been!

    A: Sorry, sorry, I really am sorry. But to tell the truth, this isn't entirely my fault either. I tried to dodge someone who was crossing the street, and that's how I hit you.

    B: So this is how it was. Now what are we going to do?

    (switch to another pair of students)

    C: What's going on here? What happened?

    B: That foreigner hit me! Take a look, a big hole got torn in my shirt, and what has become of my motorcycle? If I hadn't dodged quickly, who knows how dangerous it could have been!

    A: To tell the truth, this isn't entirely my fault either. I tried to dodge someone who was crossing the street, and that's how I hit her/him. Shall we go look for a traffic policeman?

    C: Look for a traffic policeman? Why not just settle privately. You compensate her/him for a shirt, plus give her/him a little for the costs of repairing her/his motorcycle. If you call the cops, you'll end up wasting a lot of time. It's just not worth it.

    (switch to another pair of students)

    B: All right, forget about the shirt. Just give me 100 RMB to repair my motorcycle.

    A: Do you feel 100 RMB is reasonable? (**hélǐ** "be reasonable")

    C: Yeah, that's reasonable, 100 RMB is reasonable.

    A: I'm really sorry. Here's 100 RMB. Today I guess both of us are out of luck. Thanks.

    C: Don't mention it. If nobody got hurt, then it's O.K.

2. A: How are you? Are you O.K.? Did you get hurt?

    B: My hand got injured and my head hurts. Look, a big hole got torn in my pants. And what has happened to my bicycle! What were you doing? Don't you know how to drive?

    A: I'm really sorry. To tell the truth, this isn't entirely my fault either. I tried to avoid someone who was crossing the street, and it was as a result that I hit you. I didn't see you at all! Let me take you to the hospital. Or should we call the traffic police?

    B: I don't need to go to the hospital. And let's not call the police. Why don't we just settle this privately? You compensate me with some money and that will be the end of it. If you call the police, we'll have to waste a lot of time, it's just not worth it.

    A: So how much do you want me to compensate you?

    B: I want you to compensate me 5,000 RMB.

    A: 5,000 RMB? Uh, I think it would be better after all to call the traffic police...

3. A: Up ahead a vehicular accident has occurred.

    B: Did anyone get hurt?

    A: Yes, two or three people got hurt, I'm not exactly sure. I didn't bring my cell phone. Could you please call the police?

    B: Sure, I'll call the police right now.

· ·

Unit 23, Part 1: Role Play Exercises

Practice these role plays in Chinese to improve your spoken fluency.

1. A: Since this is your first time in Hong Kong, I'd be happy to volunteer to be your guide and take you around to see things.

   B: That's awesome! I truly can't thank you enough. Could you give me a simple introduction to Hong Kong?

   A: Of course. Hong Kong is composed of Hong Kong Island, the Kowloon Peninsula, the New Territories, and more than 200 islands. Hong Kong's total area is more than 1,100 square kilometers, which is 30 times that of Macao and twice that of Singapore.

   B: I didn't know that Hong Kong is bigger than Singapore!

   A: Yes, it's twice as big as Singapore.

   (switch to another pair of students)

   B: What about the population of Hong Kong?

   A: It's over 7 million, including almost 600,000 foreigners, among which Filipinos and Indians predominate. There are also large numbers of British, Americans, and Koreans.

   B: That's very interesting. I didn't realize that Hong Kong was so large. Could you briefly tell me about the history of Hong Kong?

   (switch to another pair of students)

   A: Of course, no problem. You probably know that in the 19th century, after the Opium War, the British occupied Hong Kong. At that time, Hong Kong only had some small fishing villages. Later, China and Britain signed the Treaty of Nanking and Hong Kong became a British colony. Not until 1997 did Hong Kong revert to China, becoming the Hong Kong Special Administrative Region of the People's Republic of China and implementing "One Country, Two Systems," meaning that except for foreign affairs and national defense, Hong Kong may for 50 years enjoy a high degree of autonomy, without changing its capitalist economic system.

   B: But how will it be after the year 2047?

   A: After the year 2047? Oh, that's hard to say. No matter what one says, I think by that time mainland China, Hong Kong, Macao, and Taiwan will all be very different from now...

2. A: Since this is your first time in Taipei, I'd be happy to volunteer to be your guide and take you around to see things.

   B: That's awesome! Because I can't understand Chinese, I'm a little afraid of traveling alone. I truly can't thank you enough. Could you give me a simple introduction to Taipei and tell me a little about the history and culture of Taiwan?

   A: No problem! All right, then let me get started. Including several offshore islands, Taiwan's total area is about 14,000 square miles, which is about one-fourth the area of the state of Florida (**Fóluólǐdá zhōu**). So Taiwan's area is actually not very big. However, Taiwan's population is not small ("not few"), over 23 million people, including about 500,000 aboriginal peoples. (**yuánzhùmín** "native or aboriginal people")

   B: That's very interesting. Thank you.

3. A: Since this is your first time in Finland, I'd be happy to volunteer to act as your guide and take you around to see things. (**Fēnlán** "Finland")

   B: That's not necessary. My custom is to travel alone. However, I still thank you!

· ·

Unit 23, Part 2: Role Play Exercises

Practice these role plays in Chinese to improve your spoken fluency.

1. A: I've heard that in Hong Kong the economy trumps everything else. Is that true?

    B: Yes, you could say that. Hong Kong is one of the important financial and trade centers in the world, with banking being particularly well developed. I'm sure you've heard of the Hong Kong Stock Exchange? Did you know it's ranked number five in the world?

    A: I didn't know. And what is Hong Kong like in the area of culture?

    B: Well, one distinctive feature of Hong Kong is that it's a place where the East and West really intersect and merge. Although Hong Kong used to be a British colony, it has preserved a lot of traditional Chinese culture. For example, feng shui is very important to Hong Kong people.

    (switch to another pair of students)

    A: Wow! Look, so many cameras, cell phones, TVs, computers, and other electronic products!

    B: Yes, Hong Kong is a shopper's paradise. It's a free port. That means it doesn't levy customs duties on ordinary imported goods.

    A: Can you haggle when you buy stuff here?

    B: At department stores and larger shops generally you can't haggle. But at smaller shops or open-air markets you often can. But before you buy, it's best to go to several different stores to compare prices. And you know, some places in Hong Kong sell pirated or fake goods, so you have to be careful lest you get cheated!

    (switch to another pair of students)

    B: Have you been to this kind of place before? Hong Kong people like to come to Cantonese-style restaurants to have tea and dim sum.

    A: What exactly does **yǐnchá** mean?

    B: **Yǐnchá** is Mandarin. In Cantonese **yǐnchá** is called **yámchàh**; it means "drink tea."

    A: You mean we've come here just to drink tea? I'm starving! Could we eat something?

    B: Sure, relax! I've ordered some of Hong Kong's most famous dim sum: steamed white flour buns with barbecued pork filling, shrimp dumplings, and small steamed dumplings with pork.

    A: Mmm, yummy! They're so good. Now I finally understand why everybody calls Hong Kong "food heaven"!

    B: If it's good, then have some more.

2. A: Wow! Look, so many cameras, cell phones, computers, and other electronic products!

    B: Yes, Singapore is a shopper's paradise. You know, it's a free port; that means it doesn't levy customs duties on ordinary imported goods.

    A: Can you haggle when you buy things here?

    B: At department stores and larger shops generally you can't haggle. At smaller shops you can try, but it's not as easy as in mainland China or Hong Kong. Before you buy, it's best to go to several different stores to compare prices. It's much better than China, but there are still some places that sell pirated or fake goods. You do have to be careful so you don't get cheated.

3. A: I've heard that in Tokyo the economy trumps everything else.

    B: Yes, Tokyo is one of the most important financial and trade centers in the world, banking being particularly well developed. The Tokyo Stock Exchange is ranked number two in the world.

Unit 23, Part 3: Role Play Exercises

Practice these role plays in Chinese to improve your spoken fluency.

1. A: What's the official language of Hong Kong?

    B: Hong Kong has two official languages: Chinese and English. However, over 95% of the people ordinarily speak a Chinese dialect, Cantonese.

    A: If I speak Mandarin with Hong Kong people, will they understand?

    B: It has to do with their level of education. If they are university students or business people, then in general they'll be able to understand and speak it, though they may have a Cantonese accent. But if it's older people and the less educated, then it's quite possible they won't understand.

    (switch to another pair of students)

    A: Do public schools in Hong Kong teach Mandarin?

    B: Hong Kong practices a policy of native language education, that is, in elementary schools and middle schools they basically use the students' native language, Cantonese, for instruction. But since Hong Kong's return to China in 1997, most schools have several hours per week of Mandarin class.

    A: I have one more question. Does Hong Kong use traditional or simplified characters?

    B: In schools they teach traditional characters. Books and periodicals are in general also printed in traditional characters. However, in the last few years, because there are so many people from mainland China coming to Hong Kong on tourism, one sees simplified characters a lot more than before, for example, in advertisements for mainlanders.

    (switch to another pair of students)

    A: I'm interested in Chinese dialects. Could you teach me a few phrases in Cantonese?

    B: Sure! All right, repeat after me: **Yāt, yih, sāam.**

    A: **Yāt, yih, sāam.** What does that mean?

    B: "One, two, three." Very good, your pronunciation is quite accurate. All right, the next phrase is **Néih hóu!** Repeat after me: **Néih hóu!**

    A: **Néih hóu!**

    B: Excellent! That means "How are you?" And the last phrase is: **Joigin.**

    A: **Joigin.** What does **joigin** mean?

    B: **Joigin** means "goodbye."

    A: Cantonese seems like a lot of fun! I want to learn some more when I get a chance.

2. A: Is Chinese widely spoken in America?

    B: Not very widely, except for places where there are lots of Chinese people. Actually, in America less than 1% of the people have studied Chinese.

    A: That's not very many.

    B: I know.

    A: In China more than 30% of the people have studied English.

    B: I guess we Americans are going to have to try harder! (**jiāyóu** "add gas; work harder")

3. A: Oh, it's so cold here! I really can't stand it.

    B: Yes, in winter the weather here often gets cold to where it's below zero degrees.

    A: You don't say?

• •

Unit 23, Part 4: Role Play Exercises

Practice these role plays in Chinese to improve your spoken fluency.

1. A: Excuse me, are you Jesse?

    B: Yes. And you must be Mr./Ms. Wong?

    A: Yes. I'm Wong Kam Fat, your mother's friend. Welcome to Macao! Is this your first time in Macao?

    A: Yes, it's my first time here. I've heard that Macao has a long history, and what's more that Portuguese-Macanese food is delicious. I've long wanted to come visit. I really can hardly wait! Could you give me a little introduction to Macao? Whether it's geography, history, economy, trade, or culture, I want to know about all of it!

    (switch to another student)

    B: Of course. No problem! We'll talk about it while we tour. All right, let's go! Well, we'll first talk about the geography. Macao is located at the mouth of the Pearl River. Macao is made up of the Macao Peninsula and the two offshore islands of Taipa and Coloane. Macao is about 40 miles from Hong Kong. It has a population of over 500,000 and a population density that is possibly the highest in the world, though the population density of Singapore, Taiwan, and the Netherlands (**Hélán**) is also very high.

    (switch to another student)

    B: In the 16th century the Portuguese first came to Macao, and in the latter half of the 19th century Macao formally became a Portuguese colony. The interesting thing is that Macao was the European colonialists' first colony in Asia, and it was also the last one!

    (switch to another student)

    B: On Dec. 20, 1999, Macao followed Hong Kong in reverting to the People's Republic of China. Like Hong Kong, it became another special administrative region of China. Under the policy of "One Country, Two Systems," except for foreign relations and national defense, everything can maintain the status quo, not changing for 50 years.

    (switch to another pair of students)

    B: Let's go in this little side alley and try some of Macao's famous egg tarts.

    A: Great idea. Mmm, the egg tarts taste so good! What other famous dishes does Macao have that are worth sampling? What are the characteristics of Macanese cuisine?

    B: Macanese cuisine was uniquely created by mixing together Chinese and Portuguese food, which has a saltier flavor, and then adding spices such as curry, coconut juice, and cinnamon, which come from Africa, India, and Southeast Asia. Famous dishes include African Chicken and large Chili Shrimp. Macanese food is a perfect combination of color, flavor, and taste. When you eat it, it makes you savor the aftertaste for a long time.

    (switch to another pair of students)

    A: I've heard that gambling is legal in Macao?

    B: That's right. Tourism in Macao is very developed, and about 50% of the government's sources of income come from gambling. Macao's casinos are the most profitable in the world. But there are age limits; foreigners must be over 18 and residents of Macao have to be 21 to be admitted. The funny thing is, Macao is also one of the areas whose residents have the longest average life expectancies in the world.

    A: That's interesting! Highest population density, but also longest average life expectancy. And gambling is legal. I think I'm going to really like Macao!

. . . .

Unit 24, Part 1: Role Play Exercises

Practice these role plays in Chinese to improve your spoken fluency.

1. A: Hi, Amanda/Felix, long time no see! Wow, these tropical flowers and trees are really very pretty! This is my first time at Singapore Botanic Gardens. Could you tell me a little about the history of Singapore Botanic Gardens?

   B: No problem. So far as I know, this botanic garden already has a history of nearly 200 years. It was founded by the Englishman Sir Stamford Raffles in 1822. This botanic garden has made a big contribution to Singapore. For example, the rubber tree, which is extremely important to the Southeast Asian economy, was cultivated here.

   A: Thank you, you explained very clearly. I have another question I want to ask you. I've heard most of the people in Singapore are Chinese? Is that correct?

   B: Well, about three-fourths of the population is Chinese; the remainder are mainly Malays and Indians, plus some people from other countries all over the globe.

   (switch to another pair of students)

   A :So do Singaporeans speak mostly Chinese?

   B: Not necessarily. Singapore has four official languages: Chinese, Malay, Tamil, and English. Then there are also many Chinese dialects in use: Hokkien (**Fújiàn huà**), Cantonese, Hakka (**Kèjiā huà**), Hainanese (**Hǎinán huà**), and so forth. Most people can use at least two languages, and not a few people can speak three or four languages or dialects. But almost all people use English as their formal working language.

   (switch to another pair of students)

   A: Excuse me, I still have one more question. What is the difference between your **Huáyǔ** and mainland China's **Pǔtōnghuà** and Taiwan's **Guóyǔ**?

   B: Singapore's **Huáyǔ** may carry the intonation of local dialects, and there's a part of the vocabulary that has been influenced by the local languages. But actually Singapore's **Huáyǔ** can basically be said to be largely the same as **Pǔtōnghuà** and **Guóyǔ**.

2. A: Cassandra/Merlin, these tropical flowers and trees are so beautiful! Thank you so much for bringing me to Singapore Botanic Gardens!

   B: You don't need to thank me. I'm also happy to have a chance to come. You know, this botanic garden has a history of nearly 200 years. It was founded by Sir Stamford Raffles and has made a big contribution to Singapore. For example, the rubber tree, which is extremely important to the Southeast Asian economy, was cultivated here.

   A: I have a question. Are most people in Singapore Chinese?

   B: 74% of the people are Chinese, 13% are Malays, and about 9% Indians. The other 4% of the population is from many other countries all over the globe.

   (switch to another pair of students)

   A: You're very clear about everything. Can I ask you what languages Singaporeans use?

   B: Of course you can. Singapore has 4 official languages: Chinese, Malay, Tamil, and English. Most people can speak at least 2 languages, and some people can speak 3 or 4.

   A: I've heard that Singaporean English is sometimes called "Singlish"?

   B: Yes, English in Singapore has been influenced by local languages and dialects. For example, in Singlish many sentences have a "lah" at the end, as in "O.K. lah".

   A: That's interesting!

. . . .

Unit 24, Part 2: Role Play Exercises

Practice these role plays in Chinese to improve your spoken fluency.

1. A: Gladys/Lincoln, is that a tiger?

   B: It's not a tiger, it's a lion. And the lion is the symbol of Singapore.

   A: Oh. Look at that monkey! It's so cute! I've liked monkeys since I was a kid.

   B: That's not a monkey; it's an orangutan. They're highly intelligent. They used to be very common in Malaysia and Indonesia. Unfortunately, due to the constant destruction of their natural environment, orangutans have now reached the point where they're facing extinction.

   (switch to another pair of students)

   A: That's really a shame. We ought to protect nature! Sometimes I feel that locking these cute animals up in zoo cages is a little cruel.

   B: That's right! However, if zoos are managed well, they can also have a pretty big educational function, don't you think?

   A: That's for sure. I love giant pandas. I saw several pandas at the Beijing Zoo last year. Does Singapore Zoo have any giant pandas?

   B: Giant pandas? Currently we don't have any. But I read in the paper that the Singapore government recently signed an agreement with the Chinese government that the Chinese government would give Singapore a pair of giant pandas. But it seems one of them hasn't been weaned yet, so it won't arrive here until next year. We have no choice but to wait another year!

2. A: Mindy/Raymond, is that a tiger or a lion?

   B: It's a tiger, not a lion. The tiger is the symbol of Malaysia. The lion is the symbol of Singapore.

   A: And over there is a kangaroo. The kangaroo is the symbol of Australia. Oh, and look at that little chimpanzee. It's so cute! I've liked chimps since I was little.

   B: That's not a chimpanzee; it's a gorilla. Everybody is afraid of gorillas, but actually they are highly intelligent animals. Gorillas used to be very common in Africa but unfortunately, due to the constant destruction of their natural environment, gorillas have now reached the point where soon they'll be facing extinction.

   (switch to another pair of students)

   A: That's really a shame. We ought to protect nature!

   B: Yes, protecting nature is extremely important.

   A: Sometimes I also feel that locking these animals up in zoo cages is a little cruel. Maybe it's we people who should be locked up in cages!

   B: You want to lock me up in a cage?!

   (switch to another pair of students)

   A: Except for chimpanzees, my favorite animal is the giraffe. Does this zoo have giraffes?

   B: Currently there aren't any. But I read in the newspaper a few days ago that the government signed an agreement with South Africa (**Nánfēi**) that the South African government would give a giraffe to Singapore. But it won't arrive until December.

   A: Will Singapore give any animals to South Africa?

   B: I've heard we're going to give them an orangutan.

. . . .

Unit 24, Part 3: Role Play Exercises

Practice these role plays in Chinese to improve your spoken fluency.

1. A: Excuse me, is this school public or private? (**sīlì** "private")

   B: We're a private middle school mainly supported by the Chinese community.

   A: What classes do you have every day, and what languages are they taught in?

   B: We study mainly Chinese language and literature; of course, we also study English, math, geography, history and so forth. Our primary language of instruction is Chinese. Of course, English class is taught in English.

   (switch to another pair of students)

   A: Your school accepts only female students and doesn't accept male students, right? Aren't there classmates of yours who feel that such a school is too dry and uninteresting and lacking in variety?

   B: Yes, some of my classmates feel that way. Although it's probably not as much fun as coeducation would be, I do believe that discipline at girls' schools is better.

   A: Penang is a very interesting place! Could you tell me a little about its history and distinctive culture?

   B: Penang was a British colony from 1786 until 1957. The great majority of the inhabitants here are immigrants who came from southern China and India, and there are also the island's native Malay peoples, so Penang's culture is really quite diverse and multi-ethnic.

2. A: Little Bai, I still don't really understand. So is this school of yours public, private, or independent?

   B: We're an independent middle school mainly supported by the Chinese community.

   A: What classes do you have every day? What languages are they taught in?

   B: Mainly language and literature; of course, also math, geography, history and so forth. Our language of instruction is Chinese.

   (switch to another pair of students)

   A: Your school accepts only male students and doesn't accept female students; aren't there classmates of yours who feel that it's too dry and uninteresting and lacking in variety?

   B: Well, even though it's not as much fun as coeducation would be, I do think that discipline is much better than at a school where boys and girls both go.

   A: I really like Penang. I'd really like to understand more about its history and culture. Could you briefly introduce its history and distinctive cultural features for me?

   B: Sure. Until about 50 years ago, Penang used to be a British colony. The great majority of its inhabitants are immigrants who came from southern China and India, plus the island's Malay native peoples. So Penang's culture is truly very diverse and multi-ethnic.

3. A: Mr./Ms. He, could I ask you, did you graduate from a public high school or from a private high school?

   B: I graduated from a private high school.

   A: I graduated from a public high school. So do you think public schools are better, or do you think private schools are better?

   B: They're all different. For example, the high school that I attended was private and it was very good. But the high school that my daughter attends is public, and it's also quite good.

Unit 24, Part 4: Role Play Exercises

Practice these role plays in Chinese to improve your spoken fluency.

1. A: Hello, sir! I'd like to buy the newest model of laptop computer. What models do you have?

    B: What's it going to be used for?

    A: It'll be used for traveling. What features does this one have?

    B: This computer's multimedia entertainment functions are very powerful, and it can connect to the Internet via Wi-Fi.

    A: Has Chinese and English language software already been installed?

    B: Yes, an English language operating system and some applications have already been installed.

    (switch to another pair of students)

    A: Where was this laptop manufactured?

    B: In Singapore.

    A: And how much does it sell for?

    B: 1,999 Ringgit.

    A: Is there a warranty?

    B: Yes, the warranty is for one year.

    A: Can you pay by installments?

    B: Right now we don't have that yet.

    A: O.K., never mind. I'll just buy this one.

2. A: Hello, miss! I'd like to buy the newest model of laptop computer. What models do you have?

    B: What's it going to be used for?

    A: It'll be used mainly for business, you know, I have to write reports and so forth. My children might also use it for entertainment. So what features does this laptop have?

    B: This computer's multimedia entertainment functions are very powerful, and it can connect to the Internet via Wi-Fi.

    (switch to another pair of students)

    A: Has an operating system already been installed?

    B: Yes, an English language operating system as well as English and Chinese software have already been installed.

    A: Where was this laptop manufactured?

    B: This laptop was manufactured in Taiwan, it's the newest model.

    (switch to another pair of students)

    A: Is there a warranty for it?

    B: Yes, there is. The warranty is for three years.

    A: That's quite long! Can one pay in installments?

    B: Of course you can. 150 Ringgit per month for 36 months.

    (switch to another pair of students)

    A: And if you pay cash, what's the total price?

    B: 3,999 Ringgit.

    A: 3,999 Ringgit? How could it be so expensive? In that case, I'd rather order online. If you order online, it's several hundred Ringgit cheaper.

    B: Wait a minute, don't leave yet. Let me ask the manager if I can make it a little cheaper...

5. Listening Comprehension Exercises

Unit 11, Part 1: Listening Comprehension Exercises

NAME_____ COURSE_____ DATE_____

Based on the recorded passages, circle the best response to each of the questions that follow. You may listen to each passage as many times as needed.

EXERCISE ONE: QUESTIONS

1. **What is the woman doing right now?**
   (A) Buying things
   (B) Conversing with a Chinese student
   (C) Taking a taxi

2. **How long has the woman been learning Chinese?**
   (A) Five years
   (B) Six years
   (C) Seven years

3. **How long has the woman been in Beijing?**
   (A) One month
   (B) Two months
   (C) Three months

4. **What is the woman doing in Beijing?**
   (A) Studying at a college
   (B) Working at a bank
   (C) Working at an embassy

EXERCISE TWO: QUESTIONS

1. **Why is the one speaker hesitant about taking a taxi to the Summer Palace?**
   (A) It could be unsafe.
   (B) It would be expensive.
   (C) It might not be so convenient.

2. **Why is the other speaker hesitant about driving there themselves?**
   (A) It could be unsafe.
   (B) Parking might be a problem.
   (C) He isn't sure about how to get there.

3. **About how much does it cost to go to the Summer Palace by taxi?**
   (A) 50 RMB
   (B) 70 RMB
   (C) 90 RMB

4. **Where are the two speakers going to meet tomorrow?**
   (A) In the dorm
   (B) At the entrance to the school
   (C) At the front gate of the Summer Palace

. . . .

Unit 11, Part 2: Listening Comprehension Exercises

NAME_____ COURSE _____ DATE _____

Based on the recorded passages, circle the best response to each of the questions that follow. You may listen to each passage as many times as needed.

EXERCISE ONE: QUESTIONS

1. **Where does the woman want to go?**

    (A) Downtown

    (B) College campus

    (C) Zoo

2. **How much does it cost to go to Muzha?**

    (A) 20 NT

    (B) 25 NT

    (C) 30 NT

3. **How much did the female speaker spend on stored-value tickets?**

    (A) 300 NT

    (B) 500 NT

    (C) 600 NT

EXERCISE TWO: QUESTIONS

1. **In which city does this conversation take place?**

    (A) Beijing

    (B) Guangzhou

    (C) Shanghai

2. **How often does Bus 103 arrive?**

    (A) About every 5 minutes

    (B) About every 10 minutes

    (C) About every 15 minutes

3. **At which bus stop should the man get off?**

    (A) Huayuancun

    (B) Kejiguan

    (C) Nanmen

Unit 11, Part 3: Listening Comprehension Exercises

NAME _____ COURSE _____ DATE _____

Based on the recorded passages, circle the best response to each of the questions that follow. You may listen to each passage as many times as needed.

EXERCISE ONE: QUESTIONS

1. **Where was the woman when this conversation took place?**

    (A) In an alley

    (B) At a bus station

    (C) Next to a bank

2. **In which direction is the speaker told to proceed?**

    (A) Toward the south

    (B) Toward the east

    (C) Toward the west

3. **How many more minutes will it take for the woman to reach her destination?**

    (A) About 3 minutes

    (B) About 5 minutes

    (C) About 8 minutes

EXERCISE TWO: QUESTIONS

1. **What is the basic problem?**

    (A) Someone is late.

    (B) The male speaker made a mistake.

    (C) The female speaker misread a map.

2. **Who is the guilty party?**

    (A) Little Zhang

    (B) The male speaker

    (C) The female speaker

3. **Besides the public restroom, what other landmark is mentioned?**

    (A) Bank

    (B) Post office

    (C) Store

4. **In the end, it turns out that after passing the public restroom, Little Zhang is supposed to go in what direction?**

    (A) Right

    (B) Left

    (C) Straight ahead

Unit 11, Part 4: Listening Comprehension Exercises

NAME _____ COURSE _____ DATE _____

Based on the recorded passages, circle the best response to each of the questions that follow. You may listen to each passage as many times as needed.

EXERCISE ONE: QUESTIONS

1. **Starting when will the price of gasoline increase?**
   (A) Later today
   (B) Tomorrow
   (C) The day after tomorrow

2. **How much is 93-octane gasoline per liter?**
   (A) 4.65 RMB
   (B) 4.96 RMB
   (C) 4.97 RMB

3. **How many liters of gas does the man want?**
   (A) 20
   (B) 25
   (C) 30

EXERCISE TWO: QUESTIONS

1. **How much did the price of 93-octane gas increase per liter?**
   (A) 0.31RMB
   (B) 0.40 RMB
   (C) 0.41 RMB

2. **What kind of vehicle does the male speaker drive?**
   (A) Small car
   (B) Large car
   (C) Motorcycle

3. **Which kind of gasoline does the male speaker use?**
   (A) 93-octane gas
   (B) 95-octane gas
   (C) 97-octane gas

Unit 12, Part 1: Listening Comprehension Exercises

NAME _____ COURSE _____ DATE _____

Based on the recorded passages, circle the best response to each of the questions that follow. You may listen to each passage as many times as needed.

EXERCISE ONE: QUESTIONS

1. **How much are backpacks?**
    (A) 65 RMB each
    (B) 70 RMB each
    (C) 130 RMB each

2. **In what color are backpacks NOT available?**
    (A) Black
    (B) Blue
    (C) Yellow

3. **How much money did the customer hand the salesman?**
    (A) 130 RMB
    (B) 150 RMB
    (C) 200 RMB

4. **With how many backpacks did the customer walk home?**
    (A) One
    (B) Two
    (C) Three

EXERCISE TWO: QUESTIONS

1. **What does the one speaker's daughter do?**
    (A) Have fun
    (B) Study
    (C) Work

2. **What does the other speaker's son do?**
    (A) Have fun
    (B) Study
    (C) Work

3. **Which college major is mentioned?**
    (A) Chinese
    (B) English
    (C) Japanese

Unit 12, Part 2: Listening Comprehension Exercises

NAME _____ COURSE _____ DATE _____

Based on the recorded passages, circle the best response to each of the questions that follow. You may listen to each passage as many times as needed.

EXERCISE ONE: QUESTIONS

1. **What did the customer want to buy?**

   (A) Ballpoint pens

   (B) Notebooks

   (C) Pencils

2. **How much does the customer have to pay in all?**

   (A) 6 RMB

   (B) 9.5 RMB

   (C) 12 RMB

3. **What color did the customer choose?**

   (A) Black

   (B) Blue

   (C) Red

EXERCISE TWO: QUESTIONS

1. **Where did the male speaker go?**

   (A) Bookstore

   (B) Newspaper kiosk

   (C) Post office

2. **Where did the female speaker go?**

   (A) Bookstore

   (B) Newspaper kiosk

   (C) Post office

3. **What did the male speaker buy?**

   (A) Dictionary

   (B) Newspaper

   (C) None of the above

4. **What did the female speaker buy?**

   (A) Dictionary

   (B) Magazine

   (C) None of the above

Unit 12, Part 3: Listening Comprehension Exercises

NAME _____   COURSE _____   DATE _____

Based on the recorded passages, circle the best response to each of the questions that follow. You may listen to each passage as many times as needed.

EXERCISE ONE: QUESTIONS

1. **What is true about the celery?**
   (A) It's crisp and looks nice.
   (B) It costs 5.70 per catty.
   (C) It's imported from Japan.

2. **Name one item the woman bought yesterday.**
   (A) Cabbage
   (B) Celery
   (C) Tomatoes

3. **How much is the cabbage per catty?**
   (A) 2 RMB
   (B) 3 RMB
   (C) 7.50 RMB

4. **What is the total price the woman will pay for the cabbage?**
   (A) 2 RMB
   (B) 4 RMB
   (C) 6 RMB

EXERCISE TWO: QUESTIONS

1. **Which phrase would best describe the man?**
   (A) He's a good father.
   (B) He's slightly annoyed.
   (C) He knows how to bargain.

2. **What did the woman buy?**
   (A) Celery
   (B) Lettuce
   (C) Tomatoes

3. **When did this conversation take place?**
   (A) 1:30 PM
   (B) 2:10 PM
   (C) 2:30 PM

4. **What is the woman supposed to do in a little while?**
   (A) Buy groceries
   (B) Call her child
   (C) Wait for the man

Unit 12, Part 4: Listening Comprehension Exercises

NAME_____ COURSE_____ DATE_____

Based on the recorded passages, circle the best response to each of the questions that follow. You may listen to each passage as many times as needed.

EXERCISE ONE: QUESTIONS

1. **What do the two speakers decide to buy?**

    (A) Bananas

    (B) Grapes

    (C) Pears

2. **According to the passage, how do bananas and grapes compare?**

    (A) Bananas are cheaper than grapes.

    (B) Grapes are fresher than bananas.

    (C) The passage provides no information about this.

3. **According to the passage, how do bananas and pears compare?**

    (A) Bananas are cheaper than pears.

    (B) Pears are fresher than bananas.

    (C) The passage provides no information about this.

EXERCISE TWO: QUESTIONS

1. **What kind of fruit did the woman look at first?**

    (A) Apples

    (B) Peaches

    (C) Pears

2. **How much were they per catty?**

    (A) 2 RMB per catty

    (B) 2.5 RMB per catty

    (C) 4.5 RMB per catty

3. **What kind of fruit did the woman look at later?**

    (A) Apples

    (B) Peaches

    (C) Pears

4. **How much did she pay for the second kind of fruit she looked at?**

    (A) 2 RMB per catty

    (B) 2.5 RMB per catty

    (C) 4.5 RMB per catty

Unit 13, Part 1: Listening Comprehension Exercises

NAME _____ COURSE _____ DATE _____

Based on the recorded passages, circle the best response to each of the questions that follow. You may listen to each passage as many times as needed.

EXERCISE ONE: QUESTIONS

1. **What is the price of the apples the woman decided to buy?**
    (A) 2.5 RMB per catty
    (B) 4 RMB per catty
    (C) 10 RMB per catty

2. **What else did the female speaker want to buy?**
    (A) Bananas
    (B) Beef
    (C) Bread

3. **In what direction should the female speaker go in order to get to the grocery store?**
    (A) Turn right
    (B) Turn left
    (C) Go straight

EXERCISE TWO: QUESTIONS

1. **What does one of the speakers claim?**
    (A) In China men eat meat.
    (B) In China there are many vegetarians.
    (C) In China many women are vegetarians.

2. **What kind of meat is favored by the people from north China?**
    (A) Mutton
    (B) Chicken
    (C) Duck

3. **What can be inferred from the conversation?**
    (A) One of the speakers seldom eats meat.
    (B) One of the speakers doesn't eat poultry.
    (C) One of the speakers is from north China.

Unit 13, Part 2: Listening Comprehension Exercises

NAME _____ COURSE _____ DATE _____

Based on the recorded passages, circle the best response to each of the questions that follow. You may listen to each passage as many times as needed.

EXERCISE ONE: QUESTIONS

1. **Is there a Costco in Taipei?**

   (A) No, there isn't.

   (B) Yes, there is one.

   (C) Yes, there are several.

2. **What does the male speaker want to buy at Costco?**

   (A) Beef

   (B) Bread

   (C) Vegetables

3. **What does the female speaker want to buy at Costco?**

   (A) Beef

   (B) Bread

   (C) Vegetables

4. **When will the two speakers meet again?**

   (A) In about 15 minutes

   (B) In about 30 minutes

   (C) In about an hour

EXERCISE TWO: QUESTIONS

1. **At what age did the male speaker learn how to drive?**

   (A) 16

   (B) 17

   (C) 18

2. **According to the passage, how does the younger generation in China differ from the older generation?**

   (A) They're better educated.

   (B) They're more willing to spend money.

   (C) They're more influenced by Western culture.

3. **Which of the following statements is NOT true?**

   (A) Nowadays there are many cars in Beijing.

   (B) American cars are bigger than Chinese cars.

   (C) There are more buses in the U.S. than in China.

Unit 13, Part 3: Listening Comprehension Exercises

NAME _____ COURSE _____ DATE _____

Based on the recorded passages, circle the best response to each of the questions that follow. You may listen to each passage as many times as needed.

EXERCISE ONE: QUESTIONS

1. **What should the shoes the customer wants be like?**

    (A) They should be grey in color.

    (B) They should be high-heeled shoes.

    (C) They should be made of leather.

2. **What is the customer's Chinese shoe size?**

    (A) 7

    (B) 36

    (C) 37

3. **How much is the pair of shoes she looks at?**

    (A) 920 RMB

    (B) 1200 RMB

    (C) 2100 RMB

4. **In the end, why doesn't the customer buy the shoes?**

    (A) They don't fit right.

    (B) They're priced too high.

    (C) They're imported from America.

EXERCISE TWO: QUESTIONS

1. **About how long has Professor Li been in the U.S.?**

    (A) About five months

    (B) About ten months

    (C) About a year

2. **What does Professor Li like about the U.S.?**

    (A) America is clean.

    (B) America has many cars.

    (C) Transportation in America is convenient.

3. **What about the U.S. does Professor Li not like so much?**

    (A) Crime is rather high.

    (B) America has too many cars.

    (C) America has few buses.

· ·

Unit 13, Part 4: Listening Comprehension Exercises

NAME _____   COURSE _____   DATE _____

Based on the recorded passages, circle the best response to each of the questions that follow. You may listen to each passage as many times as needed.

EXERCISE ONE: QUESTIONS

1. **For whom is the skirt?**

   (A) For the female speaker

   (B) For the female speaker's daughter

   (C) For someone else

2. **How much of a discount is she offered?**

   (A) 30% off

   (B) 50% off

   (C) 70% off

3. **In the end, does the woman purchase the skirt?**

   (A) Yes, she pays for it with cash.

   (B) Yes, she pays for it with a credit card.

   (C) No, she doesn't, because it's too short.

EXERCISE TWO: QUESTIONS

1. **What did the male speaker buy?**

   (A) A shirt

   (B) A pair of pants

   (C) A pair of shoes

2. **What color did he end up deciding on?**

   (A) Black

   (B) Blue

   (C) Green

3. **What was the male speaker most concerned about?**

   (A) Whether there was a discount on the price

   (B) Whether his brother would like the color

   (C) Whether he could use a credit card for the purchase

4. **Does the store accept returns for exchange?**

   (A) Within one week

   (B) Within two weeks

   (C) Within a month

Unit 14, Part 1: Listening Comprehension Exercises

NAME _____ COURSE _____ DATE _____

Based on the recorded passages, circle the best response to each of the questions that follow. You may listen to each passage as many times as needed.

EXERCISE ONE: QUESTIONS

1. **Which meal of the day are the two speakers about to have?**
    (A) Breakfast
    (B) Lunch
    (C) Dinner

2. **What kind of restaurant does the man want to go to?**
    (A) Sichuan
    (B) Vegetarian
    (C) It doesn't matter.

3. **What kind of meat does the female speaker prefer?**
    (A) Chicken
    (B) Mutton
    (C) Pork

4. **How many dishes do they order?**
    (A) Two
    (B) Three
    (C) Four

EXERCISE TWO: QUESTIONS

1. **Not including the soup, how many dishes are the two speakers having?**
    (A) Two
    (B) Three
    (C) Four

2. **How many bowls of rice did they order in all?**
    (A) One
    (B) Two
    (C) Three

3. **Where is the restroom?**
    (A) At the end of the hallway
    (B) On the right-hand side of the hallway
    (C) On the left-hand side of the hallway

Unit 14, Part 2: Listening Comprehension Exercises

NAME _____   COURSE _____   DATE _____

Based on the recorded passages, circle the best response to each of the questions that follow. You may listen to each passage as many times as needed.

EXERCISE ONE: QUESTIONS

1. **What will the two men order as their staple food?**

   (A) Dumplings

   (B) Rice

   (C) Steamed buns

2. **What kind of foods can Li Tong not eat?**

   (A) Hot spicy foods

   (B) Salty foods

   (C) Foods containing meat

3. **Which of the following foods was NOT ordered?**

   (A) Tofu

   (B) Pork

   (C) Green vegetables

EXERCISE TWO: QUESTIONS

1. **Where is the male speaker from?**

   (A) Mainland China

   (B) Taiwan

   (C) Overseas

2. **Where is the foreigner who is mentioned from?**

   (A) England

   (B) Japan

   (C) U.S.

3. **The man requests that the food not be too what?**

   (A) Hot spicy

   (B) Salty

   (C) Sweet

4. **How many bottles of beer does the man order for himself and his friend?**

   (A) One

   (B) Two

   (C) Three

Unit 14, Part 3: Listening Comprehension Exercises

NAME_____ COURSE_____ DATE_____

Based on the recorded passages, circle the best response to each of the questions that follow. You may listen to each passage as many times as needed.

EXERCISE ONE: QUESTIONS

1. **On which date will the banquet be held?**
   (A) The 25th
   (B) The 27th
   (C) The 28th

2. **How many people will attend the banquet?**
   (A) About 50
   (B) About 80
   (C) About 100

3. **What price level did the male speaker book?**
   (A) 80 RMB per person
   (B) 100 RMB per person
   (C) 150 RMB per person

EXERCISE TWO: QUESTIONS

1. **For what time is the dinner reservation?**
   (A) 5:30 PM
   (B) 6:30 PM
   (C) 7:30 PM

2. **What type of cuisine will be served?**
   (A) Chinese
   (B) Japanese
   (C) Western

3. **About how many persons will be attending?**
   (A) Six people
   (B) Eight people
   (C) Ten people

. . . .

Unit 14, Part 4: Listening Comprehension Exercises

NAME _____ COURSE _____ DATE _____

Based on the recorded passages, circle the best response to each of the questions that follow. You may listen to each passage as many times as needed.

EXERCISE ONE: QUESTIONS

1. **Who is going to arrange the menu?**
   (A) Mr. Li
   (B) Mr. Li's secretary
   (C) The restaurant

2. **How many warm dishes will there be at the dinner?**
   (A) Two
   (B) Six
   (C) Eight

3. **What else will there be at the dinner?**
   (A) Cold dishes
   (B) Spicy hot dishes
   (C) Fruit

4. **What will be the overall flavor of the dishes?**
   (A) Salty
   (B) Spicy
   (C) Sweet

EXERCISE TWO: QUESTIONS

1. **Where does this conversation occur?**
   (A) In an office
   (B) On the telephone
   (C) In a person's home

2. **What is the surname of the person being sought?**
   (A) Zhān
   (B) Zhāng
   (C) Zhuāng

3. **When will this person be back?**
   (A) Around 2:30 PM
   (B) Around 3:00 PM
   (C) Around 4:00 PM

4. **What does the woman want?**
   (A) To ask questions
   (B) To sell products
   (C) To visit her old classmate

. . . .
Unit 15, Part 1: Listening Comprehension Exercises

NAME _____ COURSE _____ DATE _____

Based on the recorded passages, circle the best response to each of the questions that follow. You may listen to each passage as many times as needed.

EXERCISE ONE: QUESTIONS

1. **How long has the man been learning English?**

   (A) Two months

   (B) Two years

   (C) Five and one-half years

2. **How long has the woman been in China?**

   (A) Two months

   (B) Two years

   (C) Five and one-half years

3. **Why is the woman at first hesitant about speaking?**

   (A) She doesn't like to speak in public.

   (B) She lacks confidence in her Chinese.

   (C) She doesn't know what she should say.

4. **What was the main reason for this occasion?**

   (A) It was the woman's birthday.

   (B) The woman wanted to express her appreciation.

   (C) The man and the woman wanted to discuss language learning.

EXERCISE TWO: QUESTIONS

1. **How many times has Professor He been to China before?**

   (A) One time

   (B) Two times

   (C) Three times

2. **How long does Professor He plan to stay this time?**

   (A) Two months

   (B) Three months

   (C) Four months

3. **How long has Professor He been here already?**

   (A) Two months

   (B) Three months

   (C) Four months

4. **Where does this conversation most likely take place?**

   (A) Classroom

   (B) Office

   (C) Restaurant

Unit 15, Part 2: Listening Comprehension Exercises

NAME _____ COURSE _____ DATE _____

Based on the recorded passages, circle the best response to each of the questions that follow. You may listen to each passage as many times as needed.

EXERCISE ONE: QUESTIONS

1. **What is the Chinese man's surname?**

   (A) Zhāng

   (B) Zhōng

   (C) Zhèng

2. **What kind of meat are they eating?**

   (A) Duck

   (B) Mutton

   (C) Pork

3. **Where did Mr. Smith have this dish before?**

   (A) Beijing

   (B) New York City

   (C) Shanghai

4. **How many glasses of alcohol has Mr. Smith already had?**

   (A) One

   (B) Four

   (C) Seven

EXERCISE TWO: QUESTIONS

1. **How many bottles of beer has the male speaker drunk?**

   (A) Four

   (B) Five

   (C) Six

2. **How would the emotions of the female speaker be best described?**

   (A) Happy

   (B) Sad

   (C) Angry

For the remaining pages of Listening Comprehension Exercises (**Unit 15**, **Part 3** through **Unit 24**, **Part 4**) please refer to the disc.

6. Translation Exercises, Units 11–24: For Each Part (Lesson)

Unit 11, Part 1: Translation Exercise

NAME _____ COURSE _____ DATE _____

Translate the following sentences into Pinyin romanization with correct tone marks. If you have forgotten a word, consult the English-Chinese Glossary in the back of your textbook.

1. Relax, there is no problem.

2. Eat faster, we only have half an hour.

3. How long have you been in America?

4. That was terrifying! Drive more slowly, OK?

5. She has been working at the Bank of Taiwan for ten years.

. . . .

Unit 11, Part 2: Translation Exercise

NAME _____ COURSE _____ DATE _____

Translate the following sentences into Pinyin romanization with correct tone marks. If you have forgotten a word, consult the English-Chinese Glossary in the back of your textbook.

1. How often is there a bus?

2. There's a bus every fifteen minutes.

3. Strange, she hasn't come for two weeks.

4. I normally drive a car; I haven't taken the subway for a long time.

5. That's embarrassing; the $10 dollar ones are all sold out, only the $15 ones are left.

Unit 11, Part 3: Translation Exercise

NAME _____ COURSE _____ DATE _____

Translate the following sentences into Pinyin romanization with correct tone marks. If you have forgotten a word, consult the English-Chinese Glossary in the back of your textbook.

1. Pay a little attention, don't miss it!

2. I tell you, their house is on the left, not on the right.

3. I'm first going to the post office; see you in a little while!

4. I'm very tired, but no matter how hard I try, I can't fall asleep.

5. I've been searching all over the place; no matter how hard I try, I can't find it.

Unit 11, Part 4: Translation Exercise

NAME _____ COURSE _____ DATE _____

Translate the following sentences into Pinyin romanization with correct tone marks. If you have forgotten a word, consult the English-Chinese Glossary in the back of your textbook.

1. She rides a motorcycle; I like to walk.

2. I've heard the price of gas is going up again.

3. Next to the gas station there is a large parking lot.

4. Ten liters—uh, no, I think you might as well just fill it up.

5. Starting next Monday, we're going to begin learning Chinese characters.

Unit 12, Part 1: Translation Exercise

NAME_____ COURSE_____ DATE_____

Translate the following sentences into Pinyin romanization with correct tone marks. If you have forgotten a word, consult the English-Chinese Glossary in the back of your textbook.

1. What's your major?

2. Now ice pops are two dollars each.

3. They want to go to Hong Kong or Singapore.

4. Do you want to go to mainland China or Taiwan?

5. Little Li knows how to study but he doesn't know how to have fun.

Unit 12, Part 2: Translation Exercise

NAME _____ COURSE _____ DATE _____

Translate the following sentences into Pinyin romanization with correct tone marks. If you have forgotten a word, consult the English-Chinese Glossary in the back of your textbook.

1. Whose are those things?

2. Would you all like anything else?

3. I need an English-Chinese dictionary.

4. This kind of pencil is three dollars each.

5. I'd like to buy a newspaper, a notebook, and a map of Shanghai.

Unit 12, Part 3: Translation Exercise

NAME_____ COURSE_____ DATE_____

Translate the following sentences into Pinyin romanization with correct tone marks. If you have forgotten a word, consult the English-Chinese Glossary in the back of your textbook.

1. I only just arrived this morning.

2. Their celery is both fresh and crisp.

3. How come vegetables are so expensive?

4. A: How much is cabbage? B: 20 dollars per catty.

5. These green vegetables were all imported from abroad.

Unit 12, Part 4: Translation Exercise

NAME _____ COURSE _____ DATE _____

Translate the following sentences into Pinyin romanization with correct tone marks. If you have forgotten a word, consult the English-Chinese Glossary in the back of your textbook.

1. The fruit here is much prettier than the fruit there.

2. I'll give you $ 6.50 in change; please count your change!

3. The apples and the oranges, please wrap them up for me.

4. This kind of grape tastes much better than that kind of grape.

5. Please weigh me out three catties of peaches; pick out fresher ones.

Unit 13, Part 1: Translation Exercise

NAME_____ COURSE_____ DATE_____

Translate the following sentences into Pinyin romanization with correct tone marks. If you have forgotten a word, consult the English-Chinese Glossary in the back of your textbook.

1. This meat is not the least bit fat.

2. Is there a bakery in the vicinity?

3. The grocery store is extremely close.

4. She doesn't eat fish or shrimp; she's a vegetarian.

5. Please weigh me out ¥ 10.00 worth of chicken meat.

. . . .

Unit 13, Part 2: Translation Exercise

NAME _____ COURSE _____ DATE _____

Translate the following sentences into Pinyin romanization with correct tone marks. If you have forgotten a word, consult the English-Chinese Glossary in the back of your textbook.

1. I feel that Chinese is easier day by day.

2. She bought beef, mutton, fish, shrimp and so on.

3. China's bakeries are not as common as France's.

4. In order to save money, we decided not to eat lunch.

5. What are Shanghai's supermarkets like compared to America's?

Unit 13, Part 3: Translation Exercise

NAME _____ COURSE _____ DATE _____

Translate the following sentences into Pinyin romanization with correct tone marks. If you have forgotten a word, consult the English-Chinese Glossary in the back of your textbook.

1. I wear size 32; what size do you wear?

2. This kind and that kind are completely different.

3. I'm a student; could you reduce the price a little?

4. This pair of socks is one size bigger; that pair is one size smaller.

5. This pair of shoes is pretty, all right, but ¥ 400.00 is too expensive.

. . . .

Unit 13, Part 4: Translation Exercise

NAME _____ COURSE _____ DATE _____

Translate the following sentences into Pinyin romanization with correct tone marks. If you have forgotten a word, consult the English-Chinese Glossary in the back of your textbook.

1. If I have time, I'll definitely go.

2. Please come over and take a look.

3. It can be exchanged within 30 days.

4. This kind of pants today just happens to be 20% off.

5. A: Can one use a credit card here? B: Sorry, we don't accept credit cards.

Unit 14, Part 1: Translation Exercise

NAME _____   COURSE _____   DATE _____

Translate the following sentences into Pinyin romanization with correct tone marks. If you have forgotten a word, consult the English-Chinese Glossary in the back of your textbook.

1. Is ten dollars enough?

2. As you wish; any day will do.

3. Anything is fine; why don't you decide.

4. That child doesn't yet know how to eat with chopsticks.

5. One order of Pockmarked Old Woman's Tofu. And also bring a bowl of egg soup.

Unit 14, Part 2: Translation Exercise

NAME _____ COURSE _____ DATE _____

Translate the following sentences into Pinyin romanization with correct tone marks. If you have forgotten a word, consult the English-Chinese Glossary in the back of your textbook.

1. Eat more, drink more!

2. I have an urgent matter; please hurry up.

3. The books, now you can put them on the table.

4. Please don't put in too much meat. (="Please put in less meat.")

5. In Hong Kong, only when you've reached the age of 18 can you buy alcohol.

Unit 14, Part 3: Translation Exercise

NAME_____ COURSE_____ DATE_____

Translate the following sentences into Pinyin romanization with correct tone marks. If you have forgotten a word, consult the English-Chinese Glossary in the back of your textbook.

1. What price level do you all plan to book?

2. I don't know how to cook; can you teach me?

3. I think dividing into three tables would be good.

4. I reckon there will be about 50 people participating.

5. Do you prefer ("relatively like to eat") **Chinese-style food or Western-style food?**

. . . .

Unit 14, Part 4: Translation Exercise

NAME _____ COURSE _____ DATE _____

Translate the following sentences into Pinyin romanization with correct tone marks. If you have forgotten a word, consult the English-Chinese Glossary in the back of your textbook.

1. (We) welcome you to contact us.

2. We're not very familiar with your Taiwanese cuisine.

3. I myself know how to do it; you don't need to help me.

4. Please leave your phone number so we can contact you.

5. The dishes, is it that you yourselves will order them, or that they are arranged by us?

. . . .

Unit 15, Part 1: Translation Exercise

NAME _____ COURSE _____ DATE _____

Translate the following sentences into Pinyin romanization with correct tone marks. If you have forgotten a word, consult the English-Chinese Glossary in the back of your textbook.

1. All right, I'll simply say a few phrases.

2. Now I and my husband will toast you all.

3. Welcome everybody to come here to get together for a meal.

4. I wish you that your work goes smoothly and that your life is happy.

5. I very much thank everyone for the help and care you've given us these past few months.

Unit 15, Part 2: Translation Exercise

NAME _____ COURSE _____ DATE _____

Translate the following sentences into Pinyin romanization with correct tone marks. If you have forgotten a word, consult the English-Chinese Glossary in the back of your textbook.

1. A: Taste this dish! B: Thank you, I'll help myself.

2. The host is not drunk, but the guests are all drunk.

3. The roast duck, the more you eat it, the better it tastes.

4. This dish, I heard of it long ago, but I've never ever eaten it before.

5. Have you ever eaten Ants Climb Trees before? (use **-guo...méiyou**)

Unit 15, Part 3: Translation Exercise

NAME _____ COURSE _____ DATE _____

Translate the following sentences into Pinyin romanization with correct tone marks. If you have forgotten a word, consult the English-Chinese Glossary in the back of your textbook.

1. Take the pancake and roll it up.

2. Put the paper and pens on the table.

3. Chinese people first eat food and then drink soup.

4. First take a pancake and then put on scallions.

5. We've eaten too much; we really can't eat any more.

. . . .

Unit 15, Part 4: Translation Exercise

NAME _____   COURSE _____   DATE _____

Translate the following sentences into Pinyin romanization with correct tone marks. If you have forgotten a word, consult the English-Chinese Glossary in the back of your textbook.

1. I'm so busy I don't have time to sleep.

2. Besides soy sauce, there is also sesame oil.

3. The dumpling filling is mainly meat and cabbage.

4. Would you like to go to my place next weekend to eat dumplings?

5. You must be ("certainly are") **very thirsty; drink a little beer, how would that be?**

For the remaining pages of Translation Exercises for Each Part
(**Unit 16**, **Part 1** through **Unit 24**, **Part 4**)
please refer to the disc.

7. Translation Exercises, Units 11–24: For Each Complete Unit

....

Unit 11: Translation Exercise

NAME _____ COURSE _____ DATE _____

Translate the following sentences into Pinyin romanization with correct tone marks. If you have forgotten a word, consult the English-Chinese Glossary in the back of your textbook.

1. I haven't gone for half a year.

2. English, how long have you been studying it?

3. Mr. Zhou worked at that company for 2 years.

4. I've been working at this company for 3 months.

5. You're speaking too fast. Speak slower, all right?

6. A: How often is there a bus? B: There's one every 20 minutes.

7. I tell you, across the street there is a furniture store; you could go ask them.

8. They searched all over but no matter how hard they tried, they couldn't find it.

9. No matter how hard she tried, she just wasn't able to buy the book you mentioned.

10. Starting the day after tomorrow, the price of gasoline will rise again. What are we going to do?

Unit 12: Translation Exercise

NAME_____ COURSE_____ DATE_____

Translate the following sentences into Pinyin romanization with correct tone marks. If you have forgotten a word, consult the English-Chinese Glossary in the back of your textbook.

1. This kind of ball-point pen sells for ¥ 10.00 each.

2. I'd like to buy this magazine and 500 sheets of paper.

3. They won't graduate until June of the year after next.

4. How come the fruit and vegetables here are so cheap?

5. In the fall oranges are much more expensive than apples.

6. I'd like to take my friends to see the Great Wall or the Summer Palace.

7. Are you older than she or is she older than you? (use **dà** "big" for "old")

8. This kind of celery was imported from the U.S.; it both looks nice and is crisp.

9. The Ya pears Old Wang sells are a little fresher than the ones Old Zhang sells.

10. What I wanted was one Chinese-English dictionary, not two English-Chinese dictionaries!

Unit 13: Translation Exercise

NAME_____ COURSE _____ DATE _____

Translate the following sentences into Pinyin romanization with correct tone marks. If you have forgotten a word, consult the English-Chinese Glossary in the back of your textbook.

1. Chinese is hard, all right, but it's very interesting.

2. They want to go take a look at shirts, pants and so on.

3. If it doesn't fit, within one month you can bring it for exchange.

4. A: Is it expensive? B: It's extremely cheap, it's not at all expensive.

5. What do you think of American food as compared with Chinese food?

6. This pair of shoes is one size bigger, that pair of shoes is one size smaller.

7. In order to find the bread he liked to eat most, he went to many bakeries.

8. China's supermarkets are likely to become more widespread year by year.

9. This kind of watch was originally ¥ 400; this week they just happen to be 50% off.

10. A: Is Little He as tall as Little Zheng? B: No, Little Zheng is much taller than Little He.

Unit 14: Translation Exercise

NAME _____ COURSE _____ DATE _____

Translate the following sentences into Pinyin romanization with correct tone marks. If you have forgotten a word, consult the English-Chinese Glossary in the back of your textbook.

1. You're too fat; eat a little less!

2. If it tastes good, then eat more!

3. I'll definitely contact you next week.

4. Salty things, hot spicy things, I eat everything.

5. I'd like to use the bathroom; where is the bathroom?

6. Please leave your name card, so that we can contact you.

7. We're not very familiar with Spanish food; why don't you order.

8. We have something urgent; please bring the food to the table quickly.

9. A: What would you like to eat? B: As you like, anything would be fine.

10. In Japan, only when you've reached the age of 20 can you drink alcohol.

Unit 15: Translation Exercise

NAME _____ COURSE _____ DATE _____

Translate the following sentences into Pinyin romanization with correct tone marks. If you have forgotten a word, consult the English-Chinese Glossary in the back of your textbook.

1. The more he ate it, the more he liked it.

2. Please put the roast duck here, all right?

3. Ms. Xie, please introduce yourself simply.

4. We were so busy we didn't have time to eat.

5. The last few weeks I've been busy all the time.

6. I heard long ago that this university is extremely good.

7. Your daughter, the older she gets, the more beautiful she is!

8. Have you ever eaten pancakes before? (use **-guo...méiyou**)

9. The host first toasts the guests, and then the guests toast the host.

10. Besides meat and cabbage, the dumplings also have some seasonings.

Unit 16: Translation Exercise

NAME _____ COURSE _____ DATE _____

Translate the following sentences into Pinyin romanization with correct tone marks. If you have forgotten a word, consult the English-Chinese Glossary in the back of your textbook.

1. Besides the host, there were seven or eight guests.

2. A: Have you eaten yet? B: Yes, I have, thank you.

3. I ask you, what are you holding in your hand? (use -zhe)

4. Your teacher's English is not as good as yours. (use bù rú)

5. A: Can you reach? B: Thank you, I can reach it, I'll help myself.

6. The fish is quite tender, it's just that there a few too many fish bones.

7. We're leaving early; everyone enjoy your meal, sorry we have to leave.

8. The food today is nothing special, it's really very simple. (use -de hěn)

9. Although I'm already full, the food is so good I'm still going to eat a little more.

10. A: Bottoms up! B: I've already had too much too drink; I'll substitute soda for alcohol.

Unit 17: Translation Exercise

NAME _____ COURSE _____ DATE _____

Translate the following sentences into Pinyin romanization with correct tone marks. If you have forgotten a word, consult the English-Chinese Glossary in the back of your textbook.

1. I can't hear you; please speak a little louder.

2. As soon as you mention my name, she'll know.

3. I tell you, you had best not ask him that question.

4. How big is the house? How many rooms does it have?

5. There's too much static on your line; I can't hear clearly.

6. They're just eating right now; could you call again later?

7. The last few days we've really been incredibly busy. (use **bǎ**)

8. I'm very much interested in Chinese; what are you interested in?

9. I don't have free time today; it would be best if you came again tomorrow.

10. There is some simple furniture, like a dining room table, desk, bookcases, and so forth. (use **yìxiē**)

Unit 18: Translation Exercise

NAME_____ COURSE_____ DATE_____

Translate the following sentences into Pinyin romanization with correct tone marks. If you have forgotten a word, consult the English-Chinese Glossary in the back of your textbook.

1. It's getting late, I won't disturb you any more.

2. Mr. and Mrs. Li, this is a little something for you.

3. Since you're so smart, why don't you do it yourself!

4. He's very busy, so he often reads the newspaper while he eats.

5. A: I'll be there (come) right away! B: Take your time, don't rush.

6. She said that eating an ice pop while you're walking doesn't look nice.

7. Since you don't feel well today, why don't you just return home and rest.

8. I have a small matter where I'd like to request that you help. It's like this...

9. Oh, that's right, I just thought of something: I'm busy next week, so I can't go.

10. A: Let me see you downstairs. B: That's not necessary, please don't bother to see me out.

. . . .

Unit 19: Translation Exercise

NAME _____ COURSE _____ DATE _____

Translate the following sentences into Pinyin romanization with correct tone marks. If you have forgotten a word, consult the English-Chinese Glossary in the back of your textbook.

1. Don't get all excited; tell me slowly.

2. This college is expensive; study well!

3. I heard you were sick; are you better now?

4. She comes to class every day; everybody knows her.

5. This place is a little noisy; please speak a little louder.

6. He doesn't have even one friend; why do you think that is?

7. That character, even my teacher doesn't know how to write it!

8. After you return home, please send my regards to your colleagues.

9. Time passes really quickly; in the blink of an eye, three months have passed.

10. If you hadn't come to help me, I really don't know what I should have done.

Unit 20: Translation Exercise

NAME _____ COURSE _____ DATE _____

Translate the following sentences into Pinyin romanization with correct tone marks. If you have forgotten a word, consult the English-Chinese Glossary in the back of your textbook.

1. I've never before seen such a moving film.

2. Can you tell me what your plans for the future are?

3. She's a famous novelist; her older sister is a famous pianist.

4. Old Bai told me you're a famous painter; no wonder you paint so well!

5. Beijing Capital Airport is 15.4 miles from the Beijing Hotel. (yīnglǐ "mile")

6. One-fourth of the children in that school have never before visited a museum.

7. Peking opera, although I don't understand it very well, I do very much like to watch it.

8. The Chinese mainland is called "People's Republic of China"; Taiwan is called "Republic of China."

9. I think not even 1% of Americans know Ulan Bator (Wūlán Bātuō) is the capital of Mongolia (Měnggǔ).

10. That movie, most of it I understood, but some places they talked too fast and I couldn't understand very well.

Unit 21: Translation Exercise

NAME _____ COURSE _____ DATE _____

Translate the following sentences into Pinyin romanization with correct tone marks. If you have forgotten a word, consult the English-Chinese Glossary in the back of your textbook.

1. I'll eat whatever you eat, drink whatever you drink.

2. Those three teams are all world-famous strong teams.

3. I like baseball and swimming; which sports do you like?

4. I heard the Great Wall of China is over 4,000 miles long.

5. The dormmate who lives next to me goes jogging every morning.

6. Student life at this college really is quite intense. (use gòu...-de)

7. Tomorrow morning at six o'clock sharp I'll wait for you in front of the gym.

8. As far as I'm concerned, right now the most important thing is earning a little more money.

9. Such expensive cars, don't tell me that there really are people who would like to buy them?!

10. In high school I was on the school basketball team, but now I haven't played for a long time.

Unit 22: Translation Exercise

NAME_____ COURSE_____ DATE_____

Translate the following sentences into Pinyin romanization with correct tone marks. If you have forgotten a word, consult the English-Chinese Glossary in the back of your textbook.

1. I was tricked—I was tricked by my best friend!

2. I think you'd best go to a hospital to see a doctor.

3. What happened? How are they? Were they injured?

4. Could you find me a doctor who understands English?

5. I'm very embarrassed; could I borrow a little money from you?

6. I heard the population of mainland China is 58 times that of Taiwan.

7. You must apply for a new passport before January 1. (use fēi...bù kě)

8. A: What happened? B: My wallet was stolen. A: I'll go call a policeman.

9. Now there's a big change in temperatures between mornings and evenings.

10. That sofa is very uncomfortable; why don't you buy a new one. (use guài...-de)

Unit 23: Translation Exercise

NAME _____ COURSE _____ DATE _____

Translate the following sentences into Pinyin romanization with correct tone marks. If you have forgotten a word, consult the English-Chinese Glossary in the back of your textbook.

1. Macao's casinos are among the most profitable in the world.

2. Children ages 12 and below may not see that type of movie.

3. Shanghai is one of the most important financial and trade centers in the world.

4. No matter whether it's geography, history, or culture, we want to know everything.

5. Hong Kong's total area is twice that of Singapore and thirty times that of Macao.

6. Canada is composed of 10 provinces, its total area being 9,984,670 square kilometers.

7. Singapore's total population is 5,180,000, of which 1,400,000 are foreigners. (use **qízhōng**)

8. Singapore is like Hong Kong, everything taking the economy as being the most important thing.

9. If you go to open-air markets to purchase things, you definitely have to be careful, lest you get cheated.

10. Hong Kong's implementation of a native language education policy is related to its government's language policy.

Unit 24: Translation Exercise

NAME _____ COURSE _____ DATE _____

Translate the following sentences into Pinyin romanization with correct tone marks. If you have forgotten a word, consult the English-Chinese Glossary in the back of your textbook.

1. Penang's culture is diverse and multi-ethnic.

2. I'd rather order online than buy in the store.

3. That laptop computer was manufactured in Malaysia.

4. So far as I know, zoos can have a pretty big educational function.

5. Singapore Mandarin is basically largely the same as Mandarin in China.

6. They sell laptop computers, operating systems, software applications, etc.

7. I was influenced by my roommate, and only then decided to learn Chinese.

8. Recently the U.S. government signed an agreement with the Chinese government.

9. Over 70% of Singaporeans are Chinese, with the remainder being mainly Malays and Indians.

10. Due to destruction of the natural environment, pandas have reached the point where they're facing extinction.

Cornelius C. Kubler is Stanfield Professor of Asian Studies at Williams College, where he teaches Chinese and for many years chaired the Department of Asian Studies. He was formerly Chinese Language Training Supervisor and Chair of the Department of Asian and African Languages at the Foreign Service Institute, U.S. Department of State, where he trained American diplomats in Chinese and other languages, and he served for six years as Principal of the American Institute in Taiwan Chinese Language & Area Studies School. Kubler, who has directed intensive Chinese language training programs in the U.S., mainland China, and Taiwan, has been active in Chinese language test development and has authored or coauthored 20 books and over 50 articles on Chinese language pedagogy and linguistics. He has just completed a two-year tour as American Co-Director of the Johns Hopkins University–Nanjing University Center for Chinese & American Studies in Nanjing, China.

Yang Wang, native to Beijing, is Senior Lecturer in Chinese at Brown University, where she teaches all levels of modern Chinese language. Before joining the Brown faculty, she taught Chinese at The Ohio State University and Williams College. She also taught for several years at the Middlebury College Summer Chinese School. Wang is interested in the implications of pragmatics in Chinese pedagogical practice, teaching materials development, and the integration of technology into the curriculum.